# PRAISE FOR RELIGHTIN

"*Relighting the Cauldron* is an essential work at a pivotal point for humanity that encourages the reader to dig deeply and re-center nature in our practice. Van Allen draws upon her intimate knowledge and decades of experience as a practicing Wiccan, Lukumi priestess and minister, as well as her deep connections with people from other Earth-centered traditions, to show that another world is possible and the time to take action is now."

—Nathan Hall, author of *Path of the Moonlit Hedge*

"Rev. Wendy Rose Van Allen explores multicultural approaches to Nature spirituality, drawing on Wiccan, Lukumi, Indigenous, and myriad Pagan beliefs and practices. Along the journey, she dips into common tensions between our perceived dualities…to reveal that living as Earthlings is much more complex than we might realize. Through witnessing her unique perspective, we might each find inspiration to uncover the nourishing and limiting aspects of our own chosen spiritual paths."

—Sarah Bowen, author of *Spiritual Rebel*

"*Relighting the Cauldron* provides research tracing the evolutionary and revolutionary practices of Nature-based religion and spirituality."

—Eric V. Eldritch, Third Degree priestx of the
Tradition of Stone Circle Wicca (USA)

"*Relighting the Cauldron* echoes the passionate (and often desperate) call within so many of us to return to nature…Van Allen's meticulously researched work is an interspiritual explosion and crosscultural fusion of Earth-wisdom and nature-based spirituality…What makes *Relighting the Cauldron* uniquely special is Van Allen's use of spiritual practices (meditations, journeys, and spells) that ignite the reader's psyche, heart, and spirit in experiential processes that lift the material out of the theoretical and into the visceral. *Relighting the Cauldron* is a clarion call to the scared purpose within each of us to walk in gratitude and reverence upon this Earth."

—Jonathan Hammond, author of
*The Shaman's Mind*

"Wendy Van Allen captures the beauty and benefits of returning to our indigenous roots through nature-based practices and spirituality…*Relighting the Cauldron* is an ancestral call that provides pathways of reconnection to ourselves, each other, and Mother Earth before it is too late."

—Iya Rev. DeShannon Barnes-Bowens, M.S.,
founder of ILERA Counseling & Education
Services, Ifa priestess, and interfaith minister

# RELIGHTING
## THE
# CAULDRON

EMBRACING NATURE SPIRITUALITY
IN OUR MODERN WORLD

# RELIGHTING
## THE
# CAULDRON

## REV. WENDY VAN ALLEN

Llewellyn Publications • Woodbury, Minnesota

FIRST EDITION
First Printing, 2023

Book design by Mandie Brasington
Cover art by Erika Gutierrez
Cover design by Shannon McKuhen

Llewellyn Publications is a registered trademark of Llewellyn Worldwide Ltd.

**Library of Congress Cataloging–in–Publication Data (Pending)**
ISBN: 978–0–7387–7178–6

Llewellyn Worldwide Ltd. does not participate in, endorse, or have any authority or responsibility concerning private business transactions between our authors and the public.

All mail addressed to the author is forwarded but the publisher cannot, unless specifically instructed by the author, give out an address or phone number.

Any internet references contained in this work are current at publication time, but the publisher cannot guarantee that a specific location will continue to be maintained. Please refer to the publisher's website for links to authors' websites and other sources.

Llewellyn Publications
A Division of Llewellyn Worldwide Ltd.
2143 Wooddale Drive
Woodbury, MN 55125–2989
www.llewellyn.com

Printed in the United States of America

# ABOUT THE AUTHOR

Rev. Wendy Van Allen is an ordained interspiritual minister and counselor. She is a longtime practitioner of both Wicca and the Lukumi Afro-Caribbean tradition, and a practicing Spiritist. She is a faculty member for pastoral counseling at Grace Theological Catholic Seminary. She has a private spiritual counseling practice and is a cofounder of Soul Blossom Center, a nature-based spiritual center in New York State.

# CONTENTS

No tree, it is said, can grow to heaven unless
its roots reach down to hell.

—Carl Jung

# PROLOGUE

*In the Beginning...*

In the beginning, long after the last of the great reptiles died off or shifted their shapes into birds, a hairy, bipedal creature began its ascent to the stars. This creature was a mammal, living as all other mammals do: in Oneness with Mother Earth, in relationship with the other life-forms, in fear of the great cats and hyenas that made it their prey, and in wonder at the forces of nature and the bowl of heaven that embraced it in a dark cocoon each night. This mammal came in both male and female forms, mating as the other animals did when it was time to mate. They lived together, probably nesting in trees and safe, hidden places, on the great savannah of the continent of Africa.

These beings lived by foraging food sources such as fruits, nuts, tubers, and insects, and other small animals or animal carcasses they scavenged after the other predators had had their fill. They were communal creatures, with mothers and their young taking primacy, defended and fought over by the male members of the tribe. These family groups worked together to thrive, defend themselves, and reproduce. One group discovered if they cracked stones together skillfully, they could create tools to better process the bones of the animals they scavenged. This species reproduced and passed down their genes successfully, leaving their remains in the dust of the savannah and later becoming known to us as *Homo habilis*, the first toolmakers or "handy men."

Over many centuries, a great shape-shifting of these early people began. A taller, less-hairy form developed; the tools they created from carefully selected stones now included a heavy hammerstone, an axe, and flint blades. They left their home among the large mammals and dreamscape of the high African savannah and began to range farther. They came to be known as *Homo erectus* because they stood completely erect. They discovered fire and processed their food; the scavenging and foraging developed now into a more sophisticated knowledge base of what to eat, what to hunt, what grows where, what will kill, and what will heal, and perhaps even what made visions that brought dreams, knowledge, and insight. Over time, these early people continued to shift their shapes, to develop their tools and defenses, and to explore. Some new forms emerged, and many ages ago, more than one form of these early hominids lived and ranged and competed for resources in the ancient world. They traveled as far away from Africa as the southern continent of Australia, the high steppes of Asia, and the frozen terrain of Europe. Eventually, only one type of human survived; what happened to the others remains a mystery, lost in the great span of time.

These humans were skilled hunters of big game and advanced foragers of food and medicine. They lived a nomadic lifestyle, following the animals they relied on and seeing them as relatives who fed them and provided them with food, bones, and skins. Around the campfire, in caves, and in more sophisticated nomadic, skin-covered homes, they developed culture, language, song, and spiritual beliefs. To them, all the other life-forms, all the natural wonders that surrounded them, had Spirit, as they did. To them, all animals and living things shared in an innate knowledge for how to live well on the Earth; they shared in the original knowledge and interdependence with the Creator. Deep in the caves, they created masterpieces of art, paintings drawn in vision and trance by their holy people honoring the sacred dance of the hunt and their relationship with the animals and other beings. They buried their dead in the Earth, smearing their bones with red ochre—a reminder of the blood they, too, were born with—and returned the body to the Great Mother's womb for rebirth. Their lives were brief and difficult.

Eons of time elapsed. The ages of the Earth came and went; the ice receded, and with it, continents and mountains cleared and became habitable for people, while great mammals disappeared. The humans, too, evolved and changed. The wisest of them began to realize that seeds planted in the Earth Mother would create stable crops, and that some beasts could be tamed to live among them to raise for food and to help plant crops—a dramatic shift in lifeways that no longer required people to follow the herds.

Over time and with a new understanding of the cycles of seasons, settlements appeared, and with them, people began to build in stone. Large megalithic structures—circles to meet in to study, worship, and connect with the heavens—were created. As were earthen barrows in high and remote places, created with many stones and covered in earth to serve as repositories for ancestors. These burial mounds and circles oriented toward the rising sun at certain times of its cycle, which suggested the people now had sophisticated knowledge of the heavens. They may have revered the sun as a sacred being—a deity, perhaps; something to celebrate. The stone-building culture formed patterns over Mother Earth, possibly tracing currents of Telluric energies able to be recognized and utilized by a people who depended so closely on her for sustenance—a skill we, their descendants, have lost over time.[1] Language, song, dance, custom, religion, art, astronomy, science, medicine: all of these became part of the cultural fabric of these still-early people. The Sky Father emerged alongside the Great Mother, their Divine Child representing the eternal cycles of rebirth and fertility of the Earth. Human life spans extended; the role of elders began to emerge as important members of the tribes. They held the memory, knowledge, and wisdom of their ancestors; they were the keeper of the songs and were instrumental in raising and educating the young as farming community life was still hard for the strong, younger adults.

From small communities rose larger settlements. From shared communal resources, certain humans, through competition and competency, began to raise themselves to be a new ruling class. A people who would later be seen as a divinely ordained aristocracy: kings, queens, lords, and ladies. The new class system also created a priestly caste. From humble beginnings of the early tribal leaders known to us today in anthropology as shamans, a new class of dedicated individuals would become the priestesses and priests of these early civilizations. Complex societies were born; labor and resources now were divided between these classes, and the working peasants served them in exchange for protection from other competitive warring tribes. Spirituality transformed into religion. Humans invented writing and began to keep detailed records of resources, myths, legends, histories, beliefs, customs, laws, and property. Commerce, trade, and market economies were born. Others domesticated the horse, and entire clan

1 Janet Bord and Colin Bord, *The Secret Country* (London: Warner Books, 1976), 17–26.

groups rose to maximize the use of these animals, growing into warrior cultures, able to raid and plunder the settled communities with
great speed and efficiency. Within their own cultures, their leaders
were seen as heroes who were granted a divine right to rule.

New gods appeared among these people, no longer only forces of
nature, but deities representing psychological aspects of humanity.
Gods of love, wisdom, crafts, and war were worshipped, placated, and
revered. Humans themselves, those from the ruling class, demanded
worship. As these transformations took place, as the societies shape-
shifted into complexes of civilization, competition and conflict followed. Humans competed for resources, for mates, for wealth, for
ownership of land and for ownership of other humans. Through all
this, the older ways that marked simpler agrarian and nomadic communities, those of commonly shared resources and power, were rele-
gated to the status of outsiders, now considered a primitive and savage
people. It was determined that these should be the slaves, serfs, and
subjects of the ruling classes of civilization.

Metals were discovered deep within the Earth, and skilled crafts-
people called smiths began to work these metals into weapons and
precious jewelry for the gods and as status symbols for people of
wealth. The Stone Age gave way to the Neolithic and then the Bronze
Age, which developed into an Iron Age, where might made right. In
many places, women lost their status as rulers and their roles as priestesses and healers and became the property of men. Most humans
became servants and subjects of lords and kings, some were reduced
to slaves, but all became subservient to the rule of those who controlled the beliefs of the society, the priests. At this time, civilizations
began to embrace the idea of One God alone to rule all others. Even
where some old pantheons of gods remained, civilization furthered
this hierarchal and increasingly patriarchal ordering of humanity. The
paradigm of domination ascended and replicated itself across the

Earth. In most large civilizations, people embraced this as God's way, relegating the older ways to the hidden peoples of the jungle, countryside, and remote mountain plains.

Civilization marched on, and now the descendants of the early humans resided in urban areas, populations of skilled and unskilled laborers, and rural communities of farmers. Over time, the old ways of their ancestors were demonized, erased, or forgotten. The religions of the Book, of the One God, controlled all aspects of their lives—from birth to death. Here, nature herself was to be subjugated as a place of wild animals and dangerous predators including savage humans—something civilized folk must establish dominion over. Instead, service to king, tithes to church, and surrendering of resources and taxes took precedence. Life still was stubbornly hard. Between warfare and deadly pandemics like the Black Death, a new type of market economy was born. Peasants who survived began to earn more money and independence from their lords and kings. Capitalism began, and with it came new ideas of "the inherent rights of man." Slowly, the concept of democratic freedom for people began to spread and take hold. However, it wasn't meant for all humans. Those who didn't participate in civilization, who clung to old tribal ways, customs, and beliefs, especially those with darker skin tones, were deemed not worthy of freedom, or worthy of souls; neither were women. The domination paradigm needed slave labor to maintain its wealth, power, and status.

At this time, the priests of the orthodox religion were determined to put an end once and for all to the stubborn folk beliefs of nature, of Mother Earth, and of the old gods. They joined forces with warrior kings and lords seeking power, and over hundreds of years they held great crusades to purge and cleanse with fire, warfare, torture, and propaganda. Many perished and lost their lives. Much knowledge of ancient science, mathematics, herbal medicine, and birth control died with them, along with whole libraries on the pyres of intolerance. Despite this vacuum, modern medicine, now the sole profession of men, was born. Modern science was born. Modern law was born. Modern technology was born.

Societies grew, and after centuries of bloodshed, corruption, and warfare, the church began to lose its unquestionable grip on the minds of humans. The idea of divinely chosen kings also lost sway. Science and industry filled this void. The development of science and technology rose and became the new church. Through technology, humankind again began to look to the stars and contemplate our place in the greater universe. This technological age allowed humans to travel to all points on the Earth, to live in large settlements, to have heated and lighted homes, to create education, to have labor laws, and to establish democracy. But there was a steep price: a severed connection to nature. To the scientifically and economically minded, nature herself was reduced to inert matter, to resources for humans to master and mine in order to create wealth and civilization. The modern world either converted or decimated Indigenous societies worldwide, condemning the people they found as savages, who should convert to their way of life, become slaves, or perish. Their land was claimed as the property of the victors.

Which brings us to modern times. Some of the victors of modern humanity live in vast urban jungles of steel, concrete, and complex societies, or in nearby developed suburban communities. They enjoy miracles of warmth, heat, electrical power, modern medicine, technology, industry, easily accessible food, career options, and other modern resources. Others also live in these urban centers, but they are poor, often serving the others in service roles. They lack access to nutritious food, clean water, warm homes, medicine, healthy food, non-slave-wage labor, capital, education, and upward career opportunities. Instead, they survive, living lives of bare sustenance often in black-market economies, in communities that have been polluted by the refuse of modern living. This is true in most highly Westernized countries. Most Western people are dependent on large corporations controlled by fewer and fewer kings of capital who control food supplies, finance, resources, entertainment, politics, media, and military defense. Most people no longer grow their own food; many do not have a say if their food is scientifically altered or modified. Most have no knowledge of natural medicine and are dependent on medical doctors who treat illness as problem areas in the body. Disease is chemically bombarded or cut out, without considering treatment for the whole person and the relationship of health, lifestyle, and environment for prevention of disease. Even access to modern medicine to treat illness is limited by class and wealth.

Large corporations now control most food production and are planting monocrops, depleting soils, creating niche opportunities for devastating crop illnesses, and clearing huge swaths of forested lands. In these places, forests are replaced with pastures for cattle to feed people with non-nutritious fast food. With the removal of these forested areas, the Earth has lost the balance of her ecosystems that sustain other life-forms, and the conditions for global climate change have arisen, which threatens all life. So, too, the lands of the remaining Indigenous people also disappear. The waste of the cities and the refuse of the oil and gas industry that fuels our modern lifestyle now pollute the entire planet, including air, oceans, and soils.

Despite the wonders of modern technology and the comforts of modern life, many humans suffer from social malaise and disconnection. They have little interaction with the natural world. While many profess a belief in God, their religions preach unquestionable submission, vengeance on enemies, or get-rich schemes for power, money, and prestige. Many people have given up completely on modern religion, and most rely on connections provided to them through technology and social networking. They work long hours in unfulfilling service jobs at large corporations, making profit for others, creating dependency and debt by consumerism, or numbing themselves with social media, video games, television, or substance abuse.

What is the purpose of all this? Is this the apex of human civilization? Science has conquered many illnesses, has discovered so many life-enriching technologies, has even taken us back to the stars that have so long inspired us. So many people wonder, at what point did we lose our way? Is it too late to correct our path? What can we learn from those who still live the old ways? Surely it is time for the modern human shape-shifter to figure out a way to change our shape once again to create more meaningful and connected lives? How can we correct this destructive trajectory we have been on for so long? This is what we will consider in this book. This is where we begin this tale.

# 1

# THE DARKENED CAULDRON

On September 20, 2019, on six continents around the world, millions of children, young people, and activists marched to protest the inaction of world leaders to combat global climate change. Led by Swedish teen activist Greta Thunberg, the rallies had one objective—to stress the urgency to take action now.[2]

The Earth is under siege—by humans. For more than sixty years, the world's governments have conspired with transnational, multibillion-dollar fossil fuel corporations, oligarch billionaires, and all those who profit from technologies that have contributed to unsustainable greenhouse gas emissions and pollution, which has wrought widespread environmental

---

2  Greta Thunberg, "Climate Strike in New York City: September 20, 2019," YouTube, September 21, 2019, https://www.youtube.com/watch?v=GqEhLK7YWgI.

destruction and devastation.[3] This has allowed the damage and climate consequences to spiral out of control. Despite urgent warnings by scientists for decades, these governments, individuals, and corporations have put profits before the health of the planet, thus jeopardizing ecosystems around the globe.

After decades of state-sponsored denial and media propaganda, many people still blindly believe that climate change is not real or a threat, despite the fact that megastorms, biosphere hazards like rapidly melting ice caps, and life-threatening floods and droughts are happening all over. As I write this, Sydney, Australia, is experiencing the worst flooding and storms they have had in over sixty years, a scenario now played out repeatedly all over the planet, on six continents, with the glaciers of the North and South Poles melting at record speeds. If we continue this trajectory, many species may have to die for us to return to a balance, to a carrying capacity the Earth can sustain. It's a tragedy that this should be the case, as the children and activists fighting to combat global climate change around the world so urgently point out. They will be the generation to inherit what happens now. Will the damage we do to the planet, which is currently experiencing extinction of other species at alarming rates, be so grim that we, too, will become extinct?

The Earth is ancient, and while the idea of a sentient Earth can be dismissed, ridiculed, denied, and demonized, an understanding of her as Divine Matrix can only be pushed down into our collective subconscious. Psychologists understand that to the principles of conscious and subconscious mind is added a third: the superconscious greater self. The Earth is believed by many to be a conscious being, which is the concept of "the Gaia Hypothesis."[4] This idea, that the

---

3 Shannon Hall, "Exxon Knew about Climate Change almost 40 Years Ago," *Scientific American*, October 26, 2015, https://www.scientificamerican.com/article/exxon-knew-about-climate-change-almost-40-years-ago/.

4 Doreen Valiente, *Witchcraft for Tomorrow* (London: Hale Limited, 1983), 132–133.

Earth has a consciousness, says our planet may fight back to defend herself. Mother Nature can and will destroy a destructive species. As we exploit and deplete natural resources and disrupt the delicate ecosystem balance of crucial environments, she is simultaneously awakening those children willing to defend her. As global climate change worsens, it just may be that she is fighting to bring back balance to the world by destroying overpopulation and our destructive way of modern life.

We can imagine that within the Earth is an intelligence and life force, which holds the power of a solar fire burning at her core. We can envision this core as a cauldron of fire that, through human greed and indifference, is now threatened to be snuffed out. Let us start by examining the ways modern humanity is threatening this fire, endangering all life on Earth. To do so, we must recognize the systems that are creating the most harm, and Western culture, the dominant cultural paradigm and system of societal organization of humanity, is the one that holds the most responsibility for the problems we have created. Its problematic legacies and roots and their consequences need to be fully recognized and corrected to move forward.

## PATRIARCHY AND SEXISM

Death has been described as the greatest teacher of our race, in that through it, humanity realized a concept of the presence of an animating force in ourselves, and in all living things, which animates life.[5] Perhaps the only force in nature equal to death in how it has shaped ritual, religion, and worldview, is birth. Fertility, mating, conception, pregnancy, and child-bearing, as well as the survival the young, were equally primal and wrought with danger and were profound mysteries to early humans. Because of this, the first people who may have

---

5 Lewis Bayles-Paton, *Spiritism and the Cult of the Dead in Antiquity* (New York: Forgotten Books, 2016), 1.

held a sanctified role for the important tasks of life and death for their tribes and communities were women. To this date, in many societies, it is women who are the midwives of childbirth and also those who prepare the body for burial and cremation. It is women who give birth.

For a very long span of history, over four thousand years in Western culture, humanity has lived under a concept of a god who is male and all-powerful, whose rule includes warfare, religion, technology, machinery, and the family systems of humanity. Yet the idea of an exclusively male God hasn't always been the case. In the distant past, before the rise of modern civilizations, humans had a very different concept of deity. In the beginning, early humans had an idea of God that was female.

## The Goddess

Since the nineteenth century, archaeologists have uncovered female forms in the archaeological record dating back to the dimmest reaches of human prehistory. These statues of women, as misnamed by Western, patriarchal-biased museums, are over twenty-five thousand years old. They were found in caves in France and date back to the Paleolithic culture of Old Europe. Their imagery consists of curvaceous female bodies with large breasts, bottoms, abdomens, hips, and thighs, usually tapering at the top and bottom. The Venus of Lausel, for example, is approximately twenty-five thousand years old; she is a full-figured female holding a symbol that looks like the crescent moon, or a bison horn possibly carved with marks representing the passage of time.

In the 1970s, archaeologist Marija Gimbutas was instrumental in her research documenting the widespread and very long presence of Goddess Earth imagery in the archeological record. She demonstrated this deity's dominance from the Paleolithic Age to the Bronze Age.[6]

---

6 Marija Gimbutas, *The Goddesses and Gods of Old Europe* (Los Angeles: University of California Press, 1982), 152–163.

The goddess's characteristics, attributes, and what she presided over all grew organically out of women's roles as mothers, grandmothers, producers, educators, craftswomen, healers, cultural leaders, and communicators with the spirit world. Her mysteries represented creation, transformation, and the cycles of rebirth.[7] Because of this, it has been theorized that the settlements of Old Europe and the Near East may have been originally matriarchal. Through archaeological excavations of tombs and temple structures, it is confirmed that women held highly valued statuses and roles.

Poets and historians also recognize the goddess's presence in myth. Robert Graves in 1948 wrote *The White Goddess*, where he asserted that worship of her as inspiration and Divine Creatrix and her relationship to a Divine Son were the basis for all poetry. He believed her worship and evolution represented the evolution of humanity.[8] The ancient goddess evolved as humans evolved. By about the fifth century BCE, her images are often of a pregnant thronelike form, as with the image of Isis holding her son Horus, symbolic of the fertile Earth. With the onset of agricultural revolution, goddess worship expanded to view her as the mother of the grain, her worship finding expression in countless forms such as Demeter, Ceres, Rhea, Gaia, Astarte, Nerthus, and Danu or Don.

With the rise of Christianity in Europe, the Divine Mother was adopted within Catholic iconography and merged with the image and myths of the Holy Mother of Christ. This strategy—where the fertility cults, holy places, and folk customs of earlier Earth and nature goddesses found throughout Europe were adopted by the new religion—represented a concerted effort of propaganda, syncretization, and cultural appropriation by the fathers of the church who wanted

---

7  Monica Sjöö and Barbara Mor, *The Great Cosmic Mother* (New York: Harper and Row, 1991), 50–51.
8  Robert Graves, *The White Goddess* (New York: Noonday Press, 1948), 24–26.

to promote their new religion over all others. As the church gained power and became more imperial, dogmatic, and militarized, they replaced the Earth Mother everywhere with this safer and sanitized Holy Mother to worship instead. She was otherworldly and entirely removed from her natural functions, holy only through her relationship with her Divine Son.[9]

## From Goddess to God

The shift in the West from Goddess to God did not happen in a vacuum or without casualties; it was part of a long complex of change. In human evolution, early civilizations did perform barbaric practices including human sacrifice and infanticide. So, too, were present the violence of holy war, mass rape, and slavery. While we are certain about little of the most ancient, Goddess-centered beliefs and practices, we do know that over time and with the development of more militant civilizations, old beliefs degenerated. This period involved the supplication and placation of deities out of fear, where humans made offerings, including human sacrifice, to their gods to guard against natural calamities like famine and the loss of crops. In time, and for good reason, these practices were condemned. However, as civilization grew and lost the more complete, older beliefs, humanity lost the awe and connection to nature, which the earlier beliefs had engendered. They no longer revered the Earth.

Over time, as Mother Mary took on most of the attributes of Pagan Earth Mother goddesses wherever she was embraced in Europe, the Middle East, and Africa, she never quite regained the connection to Mother Nature that predominated in the consciousness of the Pagan mind. This disconnection severed humans' responsibility to respect and revere the Earth and is the legacy we inherit and live with today.[10]

---

9 Sjöö and Mor, *The Great Cosmic Mother*, 350–351.
10 Sjöö and Mor, *The Great Cosmic Mother*, 350–351.

Patriarchy determined then that God was male, and females were subordinate to males because of this. They believed the male Creator was above, outside, and apart from Creation, and while he is perfect, the world itself, the Earth, is flawed. We see this reflected in the sacred texts of the Abrahamic religions: records of condemnation for those who would offer cakes to the Queen of Heaven, with instructions to destroy the groves where Goddess was worshipped. Earth became inert resources to subdue and exploit. And this is where the rise of a formal and patriarchal orthodox and imperial church, while correctly outlawing some barbaric practices, managed to destroy beneficial knowledge and important ideas by condemning all aspects of the earlier faiths and social systems as diabolical. The goddess of the earlier beliefs was now an evil demon and temptress, as were the male deities associated with her.

## The Burning Times

Through this fanatical suppression, especially in the Middle East and Europe, the connection to the pre-Christian ancestors and to their knowledge, wisdom, and technologies became feared and lost. This mindset introduced a ruthless brutality against people who were otherized, which has lasted down through the ages into modern times. In the end, a great sacrifice of human lives took place again. In Europe alone, from the fifteenth through the eighteenth centuries, in the name of a religion that professed peace, by the power of a combined church and state, thousands were murdered, and the practices, ceremonies, and people of the old ways were exterminated, forgotten, or driven underground. Hence the survival of these practices became known in European culture as occult, or hidden knowledge.

Under this militant patriarchy, the character of priests became united with the authority of the state. The priest now was tasked with controlling the body, especially female bodies, which held the power of birth. The church policed the mind and spiritual life to maintain control. Freedom of thought, freedom of belief, or spiritual gifts that couldn't be controlled were demonized and suspect.[11] These included folk practices that fell outside the realm of what the priest allowed and could control: the midwife, the seer, the healer. Even art during these centuries was expected to only uphold Christian beliefs and ideals. Jealous of her initial role in birth, the priests relentlessly persecuted midwives, torturing and killing them in the thousands.[12]

While some have called this time the Burning Times of Europe and claimed millions lost their lives to the fanaticism of the church, scholarship has proven those numbers were greatly exaggerated. It was more like tens of thousands, most of whom were not witches or Pagans or part of an organized cult, but the victims of smear campaigns, ignorance, misogyny, and mass hysteria.

It was from the death of these individuals—who included those who had knowledge of natural medicine, midwifery, and folk healing— that modern science and medicine developed, as well as the legal profession. It is important to realize that the legal definition of the crime of witchcraft was crafted in the early fifteenth century by European lawyers interpreting biblical passages through an authoritarian lens. The inquisitors took legal opinion on witches, which marked the start of the witch burnings. They said a "magic-making woman must be burned, because Christ had said that whoever left his community must be cast out, like a withered branch that one burns."[13] Even historians who do not believe there was ever a sect of actual witches have accepted that the stereotype came about during and as a result of the Inquisition's campaign against heretics in Southern France and Northern Italy.[14]

---

11  Norman Cohn, *Europe's Inner Demons* (New York: Basic Books Press, 1975), 248.

12  Cohn, *Europe's Inner Demons*, 249.

13  Cohn, *Europe's Inner Demons*, 139.

14  Cohn, *Europe's Inner Demons*, 126.

The reality is that this campaign of religious cleansing happened within the European community over hundreds of years. Generations became infected with this idea that non-Christian people were demonic and worthy of torture and death. The church benefited from this greatly; they took the land, property, titles, and wealth of the people who died during the Inquisition and the Burning Times. This is one reason why the Catholic Church is one of the wealthiest institutions on the planet. This is also the reason why when European people encountered other non-Christian people in the lands they conquered, it was very easy to continue the barbarism, enslavement, killing, and demonization of non-Christian faiths and societies. It had become the norm; they had done it to their neighbors and their own people.

## Legacy of Sexism

This form of patriarchy was maintained through land ownership; the divine right of kings; access to education, wealth, and high status roles; and, most of all, through the church. Even though Jesus himself historically had female disciples in Mary Magdalene and her sister Martha, any concept of sexual equality within the early Christian church was suppressed. To this day, many branches of Christianity, including Orthodox, Roman Catholic, and significant portions of Evangelical denominations, still deny full female participation as priests and preach that ideal societal organization lies in women returning to their homes and submitting to the authority of their husbands. Orthodox sects within Judaism and Islam are equally repressive toward women. God himself remains exclusively male, and his system is enforced with punitive and guilt-projecting ideologies. As patriarchy became the dominant paradigm, even as the church ceded power to the state, its leadership was open only to men. These institutions remain male-dominated to this day. Later, with civilization came mechanization and the rise of military power, technology, and industry. This represented a concept of economic and societal organization where the strongest men dominated all others and the Earth. This laid the basis for all further alienated relationships—between people and God, between people and people, between people and the natural world. Between rulers and the ruled.[15]

The negative and controlling attitude toward women and the Earth as Divine Female is a reflection of the attitude patriarchy has taken toward women over long ages of oppression. Today, even in most Western countries, women still suffer under male domination, especially economically. In the United States, for example, one in four women lives with her children in poverty, while older women past retirement age are ten times more likely to live in poverty than their male counterparts.[16] Feminist counseling theory asserts that the primary cause of intimate partner violence in the United States is patriarchal ideology, which maintains male control of women's power and bodies through patterns of intimidation, violence, isolation, and economic and physical abuse.[17] Intimate partner violence remains a major public health concern; 22 percent of American women have experienced severe intimate partner violence.[18] The problem is worldwide and exacerbated wherever patriarchal social structures maintain dominance and control.

# RACISM

With the ascendency of European religious imperialism came the evils of racism, xenophobia, and the enslavement and genocide of peoples who were deemed inferior savages. With this strict hierar-

---

15  Sjöö and Mor, *The Great Cosmic Mother*, 231–232.

16  Riane Eisler, *The Real Wealth of Nations* (San Francisco: Berrett-Koehler Publishers, 2008), 76–79.

17  L. Jackson-Cherry and B. Erford, *Crisis Assessment, Intervention and Prevention*, 3rd ed. (Pearson, 2018), 237.

18  Jackson-Cherry and Erford, *Crisis Assessment, Intervention and Prevention*, 237.

chy of races, a completely new cultural phenomenon was born, with white Europeans at the top, and everyone else falling under in subjugation. Racism is a social construct that asserts humans are not one species, but separate races from each other. This allowed hierarchies based on this lie to be created, the purpose of which is to enrich the people who propagate it and establish their economic and spiritual dominance.

The motivation for brutality against those deemed inferior is an assumed sense of intellectual, religious, cultural, and racial superiority by an ethnocentric, dominant culture, which results in the taking of land and wealth and a cultural or actual genocide of subdued peoples. The Indigenous societies who survived were subjugated and became property, enduring rape, slavery, or forced labor. It is hard to say when this destructive paradigm began. Some believe it started with the empire of the Greeks and their conquest of the neighboring Middle Eastern, African, and European old kingdoms. Others point to the overrunning of Rome, Greece, India, and Anatolia by the nomadic Aryan tribes, which began to reorder their conquered lands with a hierarchy of caste and kings. One thing is for sure: by the time Christian Rome conquered most of Europe, the methodology of patriarchal militant colonization had mastered the template.

## A New World Order

From around AD 200 up through the twentieth century, imperial colonization created the same conditions for destroying Indigenous traditional and rural communities and culture everywhere it went. In Pagan times, the Romans often adopted the gods of the people they conquered into their own pantheon, but by the time Rome and the church had become one entity, their hunger for land and desire to stamp out the old ways was insatiable, as was their intolerance for other beliefs. There could be only one God and one empire. Over a thousand years, at least nine Crusades took place in Northern, Western, and Eastern Europe. During these Crusades, which were followed by the Inquisition, the Holy Roman Church brutally exterminated Pagan Europeans. This pattern was built into the European domination system of conquest and control.

We need to consider how terrifying living under this system must have been for the descendants of those who survived. The rule of the church state was absolute, and any opposition was heretical and had to be destroyed. If modern psychology is correct that generational trauma can be trapped, maintained, and continued in the minds and bodies of a people, this unhealed wound of cultural barbarism and terror has never been dealt with, yet it is the source for the racism and colonialism still doing damage to this day. This was the continuation of the wound begun and perpetuated over centuries by militant, patriarchal Christianity. Andras Corban-Arthen, a modern Pagan priest and scholar featured in this book, commented on this fact in his speech at the Parliament of the World's Religions in 2018, saying, "It isn't because the people who committed these atrocities against New World Indigenous people and enslaved African people were white, it was because they were Christian." It was this form of Christianity that allowed them to justify racist genocide and cultural destruction of non-Christians because they decided that they alone were fully human.

## One Human Race

We know from academic archaeology that humanity has evolved most likely from a common ancestor with the great apes in Africa over two million years ago. Since then, there have been no less than nine different related species of human ancestors and human-type beings—what anthropology calls hominids.

Human evolution began on the African savannah, with humans learning to make stone tools to scavenge the remains of big game hunted by large predators who also hunted us: the great cats of the African plains. Since then, our species has adapted, moved, interacted with other archaic humans such as *Homo neandertal,* and eventually ranged throughout the planet. The other hominids, as far as we know, have since died out and gone extinct; we may have successfully interbred with some of them. Perhaps our own prejudice and fears of people "not like us" is based on embedded racial memories from this distant past when we competed against other humanlike people for territory, food, mates, and game.

Since modern humans, *Homo sapiens,* emerged some two hundred thousand years ago, we have ranged throughout the globe, the most ancient of us in Australia and the South Pacific. In all places, evolution explains that nature created conditions where humanity evolved; adapted skin tone, body size, eye color, and hair color and texture; and created new language, culture, and customs. Yet we are all human, a diverse species sharing the same root race and African ancestry.

## New World

The prevailing theory of how the New World became populated with ancestral Native Americans holds that groups of fully modern humans followed migrating animals over the Bering Land Bridge that existed between fifteen thousand and twenty-three thousand years ago, perhaps even living on the bridge for centuries before it vanished beneath the waves after the Ice Age thaw. To some scientists, the area in and around the Bering Land Bridge is the most plausible place where ancestors of the first Americans could have been genetically isolated and become a distinct culture.[19] Called pre-Clovis, these

---

19  Fen Montaigne, "How Humans Came to the Americas," *Smithsonian Magazine,* January–February 2020, https://www.smithsonianmag.com/science-nature/how-humans-came-to-americas-180973739/.

waves of humanity came down into North America from the Siberian tundra, carrying with them their Stone Age technology, lifestyle, and belief systems. Over time, they followed the herds down into warmer and more hospitable climates in the New World, and it is interesting to make possible connections between the ancient Indigenous spiritual traditions of Far Eastern lands, such as what has become known as Taoism, with the belief systems of the Native American people, like the ancestors of the Hopi and the Quechua peoples of Peru.

There is evidence that early New World settlers may have also arrived in the Northeastern continent by crossing the Arctic Ocean. Tantalizing finds in Nova Scotia and Newfoundland, along with literary references to Vinland in the Scandinavian Sagas said to have been discovered by Eric the Red and Vikings traveling West, provide some factual basis to the idea that they arrived here earlier than Columbus. There are similarities and affinities in the folk traditions and oral stories of the Eastern New England Algonquin people and the Scandinavian deities.[20]

Some researchers in South America believe that ships of ancient African or Mediterranean seafaring people may have arrived during precolonial times in Central and South America as well; they may have left their imprint on the stone faces uncovered in the jungles inhabited by the legendary Olmec peoples. One imagines that in each case, these ancestral people brought their language, their customs, their way of life, and their cosmology to the new lands they found and settled. Yet these ancestral people—different in ethnic stock, body type, diet, language, culture, and religion—were still all modern humans.

Racism is endemic in Western colonial society, and all of us hold it to some degree, even those who have suffered the most from it. African-American scholar Ibram Kendi in his groundbreaking work *How to Be*

---

20  Charles Leland, *Algonquin Legends* (New York: Dover Publications, 1982), 1–13.

*an Antiracist* describes how African Americans and other marginalized people have internalized racism due to an illusory idea that black people and minorities can't be racist because they don't have any power. However, when racism is internalized and unconscious, it is then projected onto one's own communities, which reinforces its hold.[21]

# COLONIALISM

The horrors of racism and colonialism have left a traumatic wound on our human psyches, which is passed down collectively and intergenerationally when it is unhealed. This is true for all people, as all have suffered in some way. Resmaa Menakem explains in his book *My Grandmother's Hands* that this racialized trauma also leaves its mark in bodies and, when unhealed, is then "blown through" as violence onto others. As he calls it, this white body trauma, the collective unhealed wound of centuries of European internal religious strife and colonization, has been inflicted onto African and Native American people for centuries.[22] But this is not unique to tension between white and black people in North and South America; it is also present in Australia, New Zealand, and South Africa.

Colonialism is the political offspring of religious orthodoxy. Even after the church split into Protestantism and one by one countries freed themselves from religious rule, the now-powerful European states expanded their reach into other lands and founded colonies. As with Rome, they justified their domination because they believed they represented civilization and progress, or because they saw themselves as uniquely entitled through their God's grace. They fervently believed that the people they enslaved or killed to invade their lands were wholly barbaric and ungodly. From Africa, where the Portuguese

---

21  Ibram Kendi, *How to Be an Antiracist* (New York: Penguin Books, 2019), 136–150.
22  Resmaa Menakem, *My Grandmother's Hands* (Las Vegas: Central Recovery Press, 2017), 36–37.

began the slave trade, to the Americas, Australia, and New Zealand, all the Indigenous people—their languages, family structures, traditional beliefs and religions, farming and hunting practices, and knowledge of natural medicine and healing—were feared, demonized, outlawed, and forbidden. This is the process of colonization the world over that continued up through the twentieth century in places such as the United States, Canada, South America, and New Zealand.

Colonialism has the following traits: subdue the native inhabitants by force; enslave the population; establish the right to rule based on some imagined bloodline, divine right, or racial hierarchy; enforce male domination and protect wealth; control and usurp land and natural resources; and maintain the power and prestige of the rulers at all costs. Colonialism is not limited to European powers; it has included empires and peoples from the Middle and Far East, as well as in the Americas, who have used this system to overcome any and all Indigenous people who stood in the way of the ruling power's desire for dominance, resources, wealth, and control.

Even into the twentieth century, one area where patriarchal colonialism decimated Indigenous people, forcing mass migrations, was Eurasia. Rev. Arda Itez, an interspiritual and humanist minister featured in this book, who practices Indigenous Tuvan Shamanism, explained,

> My ancestors hail from the North Caucasus and as far east as Mongolia. We are Karachays, an Indigenous Turkic tribe, native to the land in Karachay-Cherkessia. During WW2, those who were not executed, exiled, or sent to labor camps by the Soviet regime fled to save themselves from Stalin's genocide of ethnic minorities. As a child, my mother and her entire family escaped to Turkey on foot, where they were taken in as refugees and given citizenship.

In other areas, we see that wound and its ramifications being played out in Israel, where the Israeli government and its policy of apartheid against Palestinians are continuing state-sanctioned violence and murder of entire families under the justification of stopping terrorism. The irony that a country founded to be a safe homeland for the Jewish people after centuries of worldwide persecution and the Holocaust having then perpetuated this intergenerational trauma through oppression of the native Palestinian people is a perfect example of the danger of obsessively holding on to unhealed cultural wounds and projecting them.[23]

## A Prison of the Mind

Colonialism is a fear-based, might-makes-right paradigm. Family, economic structures, and political power become rigid hierarchies maintained through the threat of violence. Females are subordinated to males, and there is usually a caste or racial hierarchy that places the ruling, dominating males on the top, with lower-caste males in subservient roles, including slavery. Gender roles are rigid and sexual norms are enforced. The cultures that have succumbed are required to give up their languages, culture, and societal structures. Demonizing and outlawing culture is always part of colonization, as is socially enforcing conformity to the dominant culture's family structures and conformity to state, education, and religious institutions and the way of life. The power of colonization then becomes a virtual prison in the mind of those who have been conquered. In the end, the survivors internalize the beliefs, systems, values, and customs of the dominant culture, so much so that they eventually participate in the destruction of their own culture and way of life, forgetting it completely. In this way, the survivors are forced to acculturate by losing every aspect of their identity, essentially forgetting who they are.

One recent example that illustrates this pattern well is what happened to the Indigenous people of Australia and New Zealand. Puáwai

---

23  Hadar Cohen, "Violence Done in Our Name," *Lilith*, May 13, 2021, https://lilith
    .org/2021/05/the-violence-being-done-in-our-name/?fbclid=IwAR3JWjNMljlrAhi-K
    _UPyVM64zoZmh-Wopvvrn-_Nmk8hLpzmMLmg0HTy2c.

Ormsby, a Māori elder, activist, and educator interviewed for this book, described this exactly when discussing her parents' generation:

> When I was brought up, my mother and father were a generation that was not allowed to speak Māori, not allowed to be Māori. So, they brought us up where they put us in institutions, they called them orphanages, but I wasn't an orphan, so me and my two other sisters were put in white institutions. If she could have bleached us, she would have. She didn't want me to be any Māori. There was no concept of Māori in my upbringing. There was not one word, I never heard one word of Māori, apart from the place-names. It wasn't until I gave birth to my son that I knew I needed to change things for myself. So, I don't have the fluency of our language because it's not total immersion. I can get by, I have prayers, I have greetings, I can introduce myself. I cannot sit and have a full conversation because of it.

All peoples from the continents of Africa, Asia, North and South America, and Europe were subjected to the process of colonization at one time or another. Considering how long and how effective colonization has been as a force on this planet, primarily through Western European and later American powers, it is amazing that Indigenous cultures and belief systems have survived at all. Yet in some places they have survived with resilience. All over the world, Indigenous people have stubbornly resisted colonialism, adapted, and preserved their traditions despite marginalization and oppression. As Barbara Means Adams so eloquently describes in her book *Prayers of Smoke*, "The teachers at Catholic School dismissed all my traditional ways as witchcraft, but they could not cause me to abandon my heritage."[24]

## Indigenous and Diasporic Tradition
For African people, the destruction was devastating. The West African lands, torn by internal tribal warfare, exported the defeated people to the slave trade, including many from the Yorubaland, the people

---

24  Barbara Adams, *Prayers of Smoke* (Berkeley, CA: Celestial Arts, 1990), 9.

of the Congo, and the Fon people of Benin. Here the sacred systems and knowledge were imported across the ocean and held in the bodies, hearts, and minds of the people who were enslaved. Despite their oppressors reducing them to nonhuman status, forbidding their language, religion, and songs, and breaking up their families, the Diasporic traditions of Orisha- and Loa-based spiritual systems resisted and remained, preserving much herbal lore for healing and the spiritual practices and technologies to access personal power that came from roots in Africa. The church and later popular culture and propaganda deliberately demonized and forbade these practices, associating them with black (term not a coincidence) magick, evil, and devil worship in the minds of Western people, including the descendants of the slaves themselves. At the root of these systems, however, remained traditional knowledge that was almost lost over centuries of brutal colonization and oppression.

The Diaspora traditions were born in Africa. Orisha-based traditions like Cuban Lukumi, Brazilian Candomble, and the Shango Baptist tradition of Trinidad and Tobago, all descend from the Yoruba Indigenous tradition of Ifa, brought to the New World from Yorubaland. The traditions of Vodou, whether they be Haitian, Dominican, or practiced in New Orleans, descend from neighboring Dahomey and the Fon people. Palo Mayombe is a tradition that hails from the Congo people. When these traditions came to the New World with the slave trade, they flourished in countries with Catholic versus Protestant religion, as Catholicism provided a cover for syncretism with saints; these adapted religions took on the name Santería. Today, they are thriving traditions within Latin American cultures. La Regla de Ocha (the Rule of Orisha) is the form this tradition took in Cuba, and is the primary form of Afro-Caribbean practice in the New World; its preferred name is Lukumi. Some practitioners today hold on to the syncretized aspects of these traditions, a method that allows for them to be combined with Catholic iconography and saints, but to others, this syncretic version is now considered pejorative. Many are increasingly abandoning that aspect of the traditions as no longer necessary.

## Effects of Colonialism on Diaspora Traditions

Being a practitioner of Orisha and Pagan traditions and an admirer of Indigenous belief systems, I recognize that there is stress, tension, and mutual distrust between these various nature-based groups. It is imperative to approach relationship with these communities with sensitivity, respect, and full awareness and acknowledgment of this destructive legacy of Western colonialism. Unfortunately, because racism infuses Latin America based on colonialism, resentment against white participants exists. There are some in these spiritual communities where African descendants predominate who resent the descendants of European people in their faith communities. They identify as the descendants of those whose culture and way of life were marginalized and demonized, whose ancestors were decimated or enslaved. The idea that money affords these newcomers access to something that should otherwise be the birthright of African people is painfully present.

This resentment is also shared within First Nation tribal communities, whose customs and practices have been culturally appropriated without considering the impact this has had on living First Nation people, still struggling from colonialism. To now allow the descendants of Europeans entrance into their traditions and access to the sacred knowledge preserved through initiation or apprenticeship despite great attempts at annihilation feels insulting. The negative effect of colonialism and its tendency to appropriate spiritual traditions of conquered people can also be seen with Yoga, from the religious and cultural traditions of India.

One aspect of cultural appropriation is that newcomers take what they learn from Afro-Caribbean or Indigenous traditions, then reject or change the parts they don't agree with and share knowledge indiscriminately, especially for money, prestige, and power. They may bastardize the beliefs and mix traditional knowledge of different cultures into a personal blend, where the original teachings and meanings are lost and unrecognizable. They then assert themselves as experts, leaders, or shamans, speaking over the voices of the original teachers while charging huge sums for trainings and workshops. This is cultural appropriation at its worst.

I once asked a well-known and highly respected Lukumi elder how best not to do this, and she said to me, "Orisha has welcomed you and you have the honor to belong to this tradition now, but it does not belong to you." I think it is fair to remember this, especially after so much hurt and damage has been done by people who look like me. When it comes to those who teach and represent Indigenous and Diasporic traditions, it is important to allow the voices of those native to these traditions, or who have been most affected by the forces of colonialism and oppression, to lead. And even for Westerners who sensitively and respectfully teach and share these traditions, it's important to consider how they can use their privilege and/or wealth to give back to the original people the traditions came from.

In some areas, many Indigenous peoples the world over are reclaiming their ancient heritage, values, and customs and revisioning their belief systems for modern times. In New Zealand, a great renaissance has taken place where the Māori people have reestablished full-immersion schools to teach children of all races the language, customs, beliefs, and culture of their ancestral people. This model is so successful, said Ormsby in her interview, that other Indigenous cultures from around the world are visiting New Zealand in order to learn from and replicate their success.

## Racism in Neo-Paganism

Modern Neo-Paganism is not free from destructive racism. Today, there is a branch of the Asatru Heathen Community that promotes the idea that only people who ethnically share the blood of Germanic peoples can practice their tradition. This mindset is being combatted vigorously by Pagan and Heathen activists, including one of the featured interviewees of this book, Robert Schweirer, founder of the Urglaawe tradition of the Pennsylvania Deitsch people and of Heathens Against Hate, which is based in the Philadelphia region of Pennsylvania. On combatting Heathen-identified racism, he says,

> Neo-Nazism and nationalist hate groups have unfortunately attached themselves to Heathen religion. I am the elder manager of Heathens Against Hate, which is a large effort which had been under the Troth's umbrella for a while; we put it back on its own as a sovereign entity because, quite honestly, it needs to have a free hand in order to confront some of the awful things that are happening in our society as a result of racism and other forms of bigotry. Within Distelfink Sippschaft, I had established In-Reech Heidische Gfengnisbedienunge, which is known in English as In-Reach Heathen Prison Services. In-Reach provides inmates who are trying to learn about Heathenry with information that can help them avoid the racist Odinism which is viral within the prison system. Our team tries to educate people as to what Heathenry is and what it isn't.

As a researcher, Robert finds the presence of white supremacy in the United States Heathen community ironic. He says,

> The funny thing is, I am currently doing a lot of studies of Pennsylvania Deitsch heritage, and one of the things I just wrote about is the fact that we weren't considered white when we arrived. We were considered "swarthy"; Benjamin Franklin hated us, and we were the first refugee arrivals on these shores. We didn't really become white until the Civil War, when we were needed, and then some people hopped on that racism bandwagon because it meant

advancement; but by the same token, we lost a piece of what we were. We were the largest ethnic group in the country other than the English at that point.

Another way racism and colonialism are being addressed in the Pagan community is by raising the awareness that European ancestral people, up until the time of Roman rule, evolved within a worldview that had a comparable approach to the relationship with nature as that which can be found among other Indigenous societies. Andras Corban-Arthen pointed to an illustrative incident that happened while speaking at a conference in Mexico:

Back in 2007, the Parliament of the World's Religions, which I am part of, sent me to this event in Mexico, in Monterey. They sent me specifically to talk about the Indigenous European traditions, which is something I do, but when you say that to people, they usually say, "What the hell are you talking about!" So, I went, we had this opening plenary, twelve thousand people came, all the speakers were invited to stand and introduce themselves and say who we were and what we were talking about. Because Spanish is my mother tongue, I said in Spanish who I was, and I talked about representing the Indigenous European traditions. So, there was some fuss; some people reacted in such a way that I couldn't tell. Well anyway, I was standing on the floor of the arena, and some people came up and asked if they could take their picture with me. And I said, "Sure." And then I started talking to my friends, and some other people came, and they wanted to take their picture with me. Suddenly, more and more people were coming, and they all wanted to take their picture with me! And I was feeling a little weird about this. The young woman who was assigned to be my assistant came running over because she said, "I saw you from a distance and there was this mob of like a hundred people around you, and I didn't know what was happening. I wanted to make sure you were okay." So, she came over, and they said, "Oh, we just want to get our picture taken with him," and she said, "Then go to his presentations, please, because he has to leave." So, I went to my presentations and they were all packed, standing room only, and at the end, people came up and asked to take their picture with me. You know, I don't like that kind of attention; I am very uncomfortable with that, it felt very odd and strange, and I asked them, "Why do you want to have your picture taken with me?"

Then one person told me, "It's because we are Mexicans. We are part Indigenous and we are part Spanish. We venerate our Indigenous ancestors, we love them, we try to honor their ways, and so they are very dear to us. But when we think of our Spanish ancestors, we think of these people who came here and massacred our Indigenous ancestors, destroyed their culture, turned them into slaves, did all kinds of terrible things to them, and so we don't know what to do with that. It's a conflict that we live with all the time. We feel like we should hate these people for what they did, but they, too, are our ancestors. But you are coming here, and you are telling us that if you go further back than the people who came here, further back in the history of Europe, we have other Indigenous ancestors on that side of the ocean, that were like our Indigenous ancestors here. Suddenly, we are thinking, oh, okay, that's who we should honor! That's what we should do, and suddenly, we are feeling whole, like a piece of us has been given to us that we never knew before."

# ECONOMIES OF DOMINATION

Western civilization can be defined as complex large societies with the following attributes: developed culture and language, centralized power and ruling class, the division of labor and economic classes, and a system of societal organization based on settlements and shared culture. The Western model of modern economy is based on a feudal system, and the economic paradigm inherited by this model has been a destructive failure for most of human society and the Earth. Communism and capitalism have failed to create utopian societies. This is a paradigm built on ruthless competition, yet competition is not the only inheritance we have from many centuries of early human evolution.

## Partnership Societies

When we examine the entire span and natural history of humanity and as we learn from the study of surviving Indigenous peoples, there are other models of societal organization and structure. Partnership societies, especially those that honor women as equal to men and value the care and education of the young and reverence and care for the old, may have been more successful over time than the relatively short-lived cultures of the current patriarchal paradigm.[25]

Throughout the world, from earlier hunter-gatherer and pastoral lifestyles to many other Indigenous societies, humans survived and thrived through cooperation, banding together to avoid predators, developing agriculture and the domestication of animals, and developing culture, art, music, writing, technology, and crafts. In cultures where a greater emphasis is placed on cooperation and collaboration, as well as on enjoying an equal and shared power between men and women, an emphasis on caring for the group as a whole and altruism is present. Sociologist Riane Eisler describes this partnership model of society as follows: democratic and egalitarian in both family and societal structures, equality between the sexes, and the valuing of feminine traits and activities, such as child-rearing, teaching, and caring for others, in women and men and in social and economic policy. These societies display a low degree of violence and do not need to maintain hierarchies of domination; power is shared, especially collectively.[26]

The basic building block of society is the human being followed by family structures. Contrary to dominant culture, family structures need not inevitably be dominator or patriarchal, and haven't been so uniformly throughout time and space.[27] Conversely, over time, more successful and stable human paradigms may have been egalitarian,

---

25  Riane Eisler, *Building a Partnership World* (Rhinebeck, NY: The Omega Institute, 2020).

26  Eisler, *Building a Partnership World.*

27  Eisler, *Building a Partnership World.*

based on partnership and collaboration as they are among many groups of living Indigenous people.

## Patriarchal Economies and Technology

In the West, modern science, despite great advances in medicine and technology, still works within the dominant patriarchal model, and this has resulted in us not being able to apply its main efforts to uplifting and caring for humanity as a whole. We still await a cure for world poverty, endemic and pandemic disease, devastating famine, and climate change. We still live under the constant threat of nuclear war and annihilation by rogue countries, intent on dominating resources and societal control. Under patriarchy, science still prioritizes creating weapons of mass destruction, including biological weapons, and enriching global markets with fossil fuel technologies and the pharmaceutical industry, where the majority of profits benefit a small number of powerful and wealthy men.

This is not all ancient history. If we are to break the hold of patriarchy, we must be willing to wake up from what Eisler calls the "domination trance," which is upheld by our institutions, both government and religious, as well as our financial and market institutions, family structures, and the cultural narratives that support them to embrace a partnership model of economic and familial structures.[28] As the world changes and globalism allows us to become aware of alternative educational ways and viewpoints, science may embrace a partnership paradigm that welcomes complementary, traditional, and alternative medicines, where brilliant scientific minds can focus on bettering the world as a whole and advancing into space.

---

28  Eisler, *Building a Partnership World.*

# ENVIRONMENTAL DESTRUCTION

The domination mentality of humans over the Earth has created a rupture in our relationship toward other species and the planet. Instead of realizing our interdependence on other species and our dependence on maintaining a healthy planet, Western culture sees the Earth as passive matter, the animals and plants subordinate to us as the superior species, which allows them to be exploited and dealt with as we see fit. Even at its most positive expression as divine stewardship, this still represents an accepted idea of dominion and superiority over the Earth and other species.

Because of this, in addition to the result of global climate change, which is an extinction threat for many species, we ourselves are contributing to our demise through the rise of chemical pollutants that saturate our soil, air, and water, along with genetic- and hormone-disrupting chemicals in food, health, and lifestyle products, which are increasingly being blamed for lower sperm counts, infertility, and shrinking penises in men.[29] We are allowing this all to happen in the name of civilization and progress. All of this is an outgrowth of a toxic and unsustainable patriarchal paradigm that needs to be abandoned.

## Learning a Sustainable Worldview

Indigenous societies can teach us a great deal about living a more sustainable relationship with the environment. I have attended the Parliament of the World's Religions twice when it has convened in person in North America: in Salt Lake City, Utah, in 2015, and in Toronto, Canada, in 2018. At each session, one of the largest contingents of

---

29 Erin Brockovich, "Plummeting Sperm Counts, Shrinking Penises: Toxic Chemicals Threaten Humanity," *The Guardian*, March 18, 2021, https://www.theguardian.com /commentisfree/2021/mar/18/toxic-chemicals-health-humanity-erin-brokovich?CMP =oth_b-aplnews_d-1&fbclid=IwAR28mT2L5DjtgurBioSu8 -0PC9vqdZEXIolq1k1mwaIvaM0TmkWnI6VDEDc.

faith communities came from First Nations people from North America and South America to the people of the Arctic and representatives from tribal communities of Africa, Asia, and the South Pacific. All came with the same message of urgency: Mother Earth is demanding we change our ways. Yanomami Chief David Kopenawa of the Amazon advised us that if we are to make progress in stopping the destruction of his lands, the jungle his people have a sacred duty to protect, Western Europeans and Americans need to learn how to listen to Indigenous voices and the wisdom of the Earth.

An Inuit elder from the Arctic region came to warn attendees that from his land in the deep reaches of Greenland, the polar ice caps have already receded past the point of no return. He wept as he implored those gathered that we must be prepared to listen. An elder from the Canadian Midwestern tribes described in horror how she received the message that we must stop polluting the Earth and waters of her land from the deer she still hunts for food. A sickly deer, filled with cancerous tumors, appeared on her land and stared deeply into her eyes, ready to die, imploring a message that we have to open our eyes and see the suffering of the animals around us. These are just some examples of the way in which nature is talking to us, as conveyed through people who still listen to what she has to say.

## OUR ONLY OPTION

Where has our insistence on a left-brained, male-dominated, Western-oriented world brought humanity? We are a species of billions of human beings, yet 1 percent of the world's population owns half of the wealth of the planet. Billions of others exist in deep poverty, and war and famine have continued unabated throughout the globe for centuries. We are in the midst of the seventh mass extinction event, our natural resources are depleted, and we now live under the constant threat of existential destruction due to climate change or nuclear war caused by unrelenting greed and disregard for other humans and life-forms.

Even in wealthy Western countries like the United States, most citizens live their lives in debt, with little work-life balance. We lack creative and spiritual outlets and nurturing community connection so that mental illness, depression, anxiety, violence, and substance abuse are rampant. While some church leaders try to blame these problems on our moving away from traditional Orthodox Christian patriarchal religion and male-dominated nuclear families, it was those beliefs that created and made way for the current conditions we are experiencing today. There must be a better way.

Awakening begins with unlearning the dogma and beliefs that reinforce these false values to begin to honor and listen to and learn from those who have preserved nature's way for thousands of years. Central to the beliefs of these way showers is nature spirituality. For those who pay attention to nature, one thing is clear: there is always diversity and abundance, and humanity is no different. We do not see animals of the same species segregating themselves off by any superficial division or standard. Even in the plant kingdom, healthy ecosystems are healthy precisely because of the diversity of plant, insect, and animal life sharing those spaces. Healthy trees are full of branches and leaves and homes to other species; healthy meadows are filled with grasses, brush, birds, and wildlife. Species come in a multitude of colors, sizes, shapes, and adaptability to different climates. We are no different.

## Creating Dialogue and Awakening

More and more in all the communities I participate in, a dialogue of sexual and gender equality, antiracism, and decolonization is taking place. Having this dialogue is essential if we as nature-based people are to speak with one voice as engaged protectors of the Earth. This process of decolonization that frees hearts, minds, and spirits and places humanity in full relationship with the Earth is an essential aspect of coming together now at this crucial time of change.

Evolving past false ideas of sexual domination, blood purity, and right is paramount because humanity will never advance or unite to care for and honor the planet if we stay stuck in the divisive cycle of sexual, racial, or religious hierarchy and victim-oppressor dynamic forever. Through respect for tradition, naming and cherishing the specific roots of religious ideas and practices, focusing on the higher good of caring for the planet, and creating healthy spiritual communities where we acknowledge and make restitution for harms and grievances, as well as create space for diverse participants, humanity can move ahead to a future that includes egalitarian and inclusive communities grounded in shared nature-affirming values.

The idea of awakening is often something described as a blissful, fairy-tale ending, yet in reality, awakening includes a jolting awareness and realization that we need to change drastically and recognize what in us must be discarded if we are to survive as a species. There are many paths out of this morass. Learning from surviving ethnic and cultural groups that have managed to hold on to their spiritual practices and beliefs despite centuries of sustained demonization and oppression by the dominant culture is one way.

Humanity must awaken from its destructive trance to create a new paradigm that works for us as well as for Mother Earth and other sentient beings. This doesn't mean we need to abandon the benefits of science, technology, and human progress that represent the best of Western civilization. We just need to get out of our comfort zones and be willing to let go of destructive patterns and embrace the more sustainable ideas present in a nature-based paradigm that realizes we are one race who shares the resources of one planet. Resources are not inexhaustible. By realizing this paradigm, we can build a bridge to the past, learning from beliefs and worldviews that worked, and from the Indigenous people who have survived. We also must bridge to one another and overcome the false divisions of religion, racism, sexism, and colonialism created and maintained by the current failed system. Other species must be considered and valued as we acknowledge we are interdependent with them and with the planet as a whole.

The future is open, but tenuous. I have written this book in an attempt to counter the destructive trajectory our culture is on regarding whether or not we will continue as a species. So, continuing with our metaphor of the cauldron representing the fiery consciousness of Mother Earth, may it also represent the awakening of humanity to the idea that, together, we can form a healthier family. The remainder of this book is intended to help you be part of bridge building and cauldron lighting toward a more sustainable, holistic, and united future. May we consciously participate in the relighting of the cauldron of Mother Earth.

# PURPOSE OF THIS BOOK

To create this new paradigm, we need to begin on the individual level, the building block of society, while also considering our relations with others. Beginning with the internal work at the individual level is the place where true transformation occurs. This book is designed to help us make these internal shifts, and it will draw on wisdom I have gathered from years studying anthropology, psychology, religion, folklore, mysticism, holistic health and wellness, and nature-based spiritual practices.

As we stand at the precipice where we decide if we wish to move forward or go backward, we must choose which parts of our collective human wisdom are worth keeping; which maximize our human knowledge, creativity, spirituality, and wisdom; and which we can apply to create a future where we survive.

By examining ourselves at the individual and collective levels and applying principles of esoteric and nature-based spiritual teachings, we can
return to a healthier way of living in relationship to the outer world.

Nature tradition teaches an animistic vision of reality, where Spirit
permeates and infuses all living things, even nonliving things like sea
and stone. Shifting the perception from a saving God somewhere out
there to an indwelling Spirit in all things, we return to the community
of nature, to the garden, a metaphor for Oneness and healthy relations with the Earth.

The time has arrived to fully reclaim nature-based spirituality as
a legitimate and valid path for spiritual wholeness and evolution as a
system that views the Earth as holy. Practitioners of nature-based traditions and Indigenous cultures have been tending the flame of the
Earth Mother's cauldron for many centuries and deserve credit and
encouragement to take center stage and lead humanity toward a more
sustainable, partnership-based, egalitarian, and democratic organiza-
tional paradigm. Earth herself has been waiting for us.

Nature-based religion and spiritual practices are an important
aspect of a return of Earth-centered consciousness as they allow
humans to make conscious and embody this connection. This book is
intended to guide you to seek and internalize these lessons into your
life, providing a closer communion and recognition of harmonious
interdependence with nonhuman relatives, the land, and the environment. This shift in attitude includes a shift in lifestyle choices as
well—values such as sustainable living, permaculture, recycling, and
reducing our waste and carbon footprints are essential. This approach
must happen on a mass scale for us to make the lifestyle changes
so urgently needed. With a nature-based worldview, these actions
become a genuine religious duty, a new paradigm, and a meaningful
way of life.

# WHO AM I?

I am from New York, and my ethnic heritage includes Irish, Dutch, English, and French-Canadian ancestry on my father's side, with a paternal ancestor who came from Ireland during the Potato Famine. These European ancestors landed in Canada, New England, and New York State over time since the seventeenth century. My mother was Puerto Rican and came to New York City in 1957. Her heritage included Spanish, Taino, and African ancestors. Our Spanish family there can be traced back to the sixteenth century. I feel I speak for many Americans whose genetic ancestry is European, Native American, and African that this mixture can be painfully conflicting. We are in the unique position to both benefit from white privilege from our European heritage and experience the pain of racism and prejudice directed toward our Indigenous, Latino, and African ancestors. We may feel guilt or anger for the actions of ancestors who participated in cultural genocide and slavery of other ancestors. This is the legacy of what it means to be a multiethnic American.

While I was raised Episcopalian, since my teens, I have embraced nature-based faith traditions of both European and Afro-Caribbean paths. I have been an active member of the Pagan community for over thirty years, self-dedicating to Wicca when I was eighteen and initiated into an eclectic tradition of Wicca in Seattle in the 1990s. I am an initiated Lukumi priestess of Obatala, making Kariocha in the Efunche lineage in Philadelphia in 2012. In addition, I was ordained as an interspiritual minister and received training in interspiritual counseling at One Spirit Learning Alliance, New York, in 2014 and 2019. I am an intuitive consultant and a Spiritist.

My personal and professional background has enabled me to be part of and learn from teachings of various spiritual and holistic communities. All these connections have afforded me a unique position of living as an expression of a diversity of Earth-based paths. I have lived a life belonging to multiple cultures, and I see myself as a bridge between them. By writing this book, my desire is to offer the reader this bridge toward understanding and mutual respect and to highlight the commonalities, shared values, practices, and beliefs of these traditions in order to develop greater appreciation for each, and to establish common ground in service to our beloved Mother Planet. This work is intended as a bridge to the past and out toward contemporary Indigenous communities as well, in order to learn from them and preserve their values for a more holistic and sustainable future. Finally, the practices shared in this book are intended to help you begin this necessary planetary healing by developing your own personal practices and commitment to nature.

## RECREATING AND RESTORING EUROPEAN-INSPIRED NATURE TRADITIONS

Many descendants of European peoples have reclaimed Earth-based beliefs and practices of their ancestors around the world. New traditions based on ancient Pagan beliefs have been established: Wicca, modern Druidism, and Heathenism, to name a few. There are many different branches of Wicca, from the British Gardnerian tradition to Celtic-inspired Wicca, Italian-based Strega, and Dianic Wicca, a form inspired by the Greek goddess with a focus on the Divine Feminine. There are other witches who do not consider themselves Wiccan and claim heredity descent or initiation: green witches, kitchen witches, hedge witches, among others. There are practitioners of Neo-Pagan modern reconstruction traditions based on Roman, Greek, Italic, or Egyptian pantheons.

Among Heathens, much scholarly research has gone into reconstructing and relearning the literary sagas and cultures of the ancient

Nordic and Germanic peoples. Likewise, among Celtic culture, there are Gaelic-inspired Druids who practice a modern interpretation reconstructed from surviving texts and traditions of the Celts of Ancient Britain, Wales, Scotland, Ireland, and Brittany. In Europe, there are surviving and reclaimed traditions gaining new adherents, like the Romuva of the Baltic Peoples and Rodnovery of the Slavs. These have revived the living religion of their ancestors. All these practices and traditions are open to all.

When it comes to most Neo-Pagan traditions, we realize today that despite claims by earlier scholars and researchers like Gerald Gardner and Margaret Murray, these traditions do not come from unbroken lines of practice as they do in African-based traditions of the New World or in the religions of the First Nation people. These are revivals and reconstructions, and it is important to acknowledge this is precisely so because the Europeans destroyed their own pre-Christian religious beliefs. Nonetheless, as a practicing Pagan for over thirty years, I can attest that these new traditions based on ancestral nature-worshipping Paganism are effective ways to revere the Earth, honor ancestors, and connect with mystery practices. Pagan and Heathen practices and religions provide practitioners a deeply meaningful and spiritual way of life connected to the Earth that honors the seasons, the Divine, and our relationship to one another and all creation.

## What Unites Us

Nature- and Earth-based spirituality has been the primary spiritual expression of humankind for millennia and remains the unifying force that connects all Indigenous traditions around the planet. It is the foundational commonality in most of the Neo-Pagan revival and reconstructionist traditions of Europe and the basic foundation of Diasporic belief. It is also central to Indigenous traditions from the

East, such as Taoism, and to many effective New Age practices. All of these share the idea that living in harmony with Mother Earth and the environment is a holy obligation.

My research for this book has identified that most nature-based practices, whether they be Indigenous or modern, share similar beliefs, practices, and attributes. In summary, these are as follows: an animistic view of the Divine that is indwelling to all of nature and a reverence for nature and the Earth; ancestor veneration and worship; working with nature spirits or elementals; techniques and practices that encourage altered states of consciousness for spirit communication, insights, and personal or collective healing; knowledge of natural medicine, herbal magick, and medicine; and, in some cases, energy healing. These traditions also often create like-minded communities that provide mutual aid and support to their individual members. Some are actively choosing to create more sustainable communities guided by environmental and sustainability goals. I will discuss each of these commonalities of nature spirituality later on.

## Guiding Principles

Mother Nature can serve as our guru, our own mystical guide. Through communion with her, she can teach us all we need to know, reclaim, and remember that will guide us forward. Ultimately, the survival of our species, as well as how fulfilling our own lives can be, lies in our own hearts and hands. My hope is this work will inspire some of you to seek out Earth- and nature-based community and practices. Perhaps you will deepen what you are already doing, research your own heritage, or implement some of the magickal practices and healing techniques presented here. You may not resonate with every tradition or practice, and that is okay. Even for those reading this book who belong to traditional religions like Judaism, Christianity, or Islam, you are not being asked to abandon your faith tradition, but only to consider expanding it to include a commitment to nature-based ideals.

# KEY TERMS AND CONCEPTS

It is important to clarify some terms I will be using in this book.

**Ancestors**—The generations of people who came before our current global population; they can be distant or more recent. In all nature-based traditions, the veneration of personal, familial, ethnic, and cultural ancestors is a central belief. Ancestors can also refer to nonhuman ancestors, such as ancestors of the land, the elements, or nature spirits.

**Diasporic Traditions**—The beliefs, practices, and religions that have emerged in the New World due to the enslavement of African people during the slave trade. These include Vodou, Shango Baptist, Candomble, Lukumi, the 21 Divisions, Quimbanda, and Sanse, among others. Within these traditions, the core roots retain African concepts, deities, and practices, while some also incorporate elements from European traditions, like Spiritualism, as well as Native American practices. The Lukumi tradition is known as *La Regla de Ocha* (the Rule of Orisha); members of the religion often refer to it as Ocha.

**Indigenous**—Refers to those who represent the original and earliest precolonial inhabitants of a land. They have in prior times been referred to as Indians, Native Americans, Aborigines, and individual and localized tribal people. They have endured colonial slurs and offensive stereotypes as well as cultural appropriation by the dominant culture for centuries. Today, many Indigenous people around the world have embraced the term Indigenous with a capital *I* to identify themselves and their traditional cultures and religious beliefs. In the Americas, the term First Nations is also preferred, especially in Canada. Where I am able, I will strive to specify which people or culture a belief, language, custom, or practice comes from. It is important not to generalize ideas unless these ideas are accepted across Indigenous cultures.

**Magick**—I will be using the term *magick* with the *k* as the nineteenth-century occultist Aleister Crowley, who coined the term, defined it, to distinguish it from the type of magic we associate with stage or sleight-of-hand tricks. Magick holds a belief that there are forces in nature that can be tapped into and utilized in conformance with intention to manipulate reality. Many of the traditions discussed in this book incorporate the belief in the ability to manifest one's will to affect magickal outcomes, facilitate change, or engage in a reciprocal relationship with natural forces and Spirit or spirit beings for direct aid. Mysticism and learning how to achieve altered states of consciousness are prevalent in nature-based traditions.

**Nature-Based or Earth-Based**—I will use these terms interchangeably. They refer to all practices, traditions, beliefs, and religions, which are not based on either revealed text, such as those found in the Abrahamic religions, or on religions founded by a holy prophet or leader, such as Buddhism. Nature-based and Earth-based spiritual beliefs are traditions that revere nature as the most sacred and holy expression of the Divine and that see the presence of the Divine or Spirit indwelling in all of Creation. Many are animistic, which is a belief that objects, places, and creatures all possess a distinct spiritual essence.

**New Age Practices**—New Age practices represent spiritual concepts, traditions, and practices that incorporate ideas and beliefs from Eastern traditions such as Buddhism, Taoism, and Hinduism, as well as techniques and lifestyle practices related to energy healing, health and wellness, and nature spirituality. The New Age movement has roots in the nineteenth century but became established by the 1970s. It is based on the idea that a new era for humanity has arrived with the coming of the age of the Aquarius zodiac sign. The themes of the New Age are a focus on humanity's awakening to a higher consciousness and the development of holistic, mind, body, and spirit practices. Some New Age practices borrow from Indigenous beliefs and concepts, and this can be problematic due to cultural appropriation or lack of context, revisioning without acknowledgment, and respecting the wholeness of the cultural milieu they are taken from. The New Age is really more of a philosophy than a religion.

**Pagan and Neo-Pagan**—These terms represent modern reconstructed, reclaimed, or revisioned religions based on the pre-Christian religions and practices of ancient Europeans. These terms are interchangeable and, most importantly, represent nature-based spirituality outside of the Judeo-Christian context. Pagan beliefs can be monocultural, taken from one particular cultural context, or experienced as a more eclectic expression of concepts. The form I practice is eclectic.

**Shaman**—I will use this word with a capital *S* to refer to those within Indigenous culture who refer to themselves as

Shamans. In the following chapter, I discuss the difference between *Shaman* and *shaman*. Elsewhere, I will utilize the term *shamanism* or *shamanic practices*, as defined by anthropology, to include beliefs and practices that are used to achieve various states of consciousness through trance or ecstatic religious practice and to increase personal power. The reason I choose to use these terms is simple: there is no other English equivalent as of now that captures the constellation of practices and ideas unique to their role.

## SHARING THE VOICES OF EARTH-BASED PRACTITIONERS

The intention of this book is not to serve as a primer to the traditions discussed, but to provide a survey as to where these practices, values, ideals, and worldviews share common ground and similarities both in form and function. In addition to my researched material, I present the voices of ten practitioners of various modern nature-based faith traditions. In these interviews, each discussed how nature inspires their deeply held practices and beliefs, how it connects them to the Earth, and how their spirituality helps them connect with their ancestors and other realms, providing them with an experiential and mystical approach to personal and collective spirituality.

Those interviewed all shared that their faith tradition is a positive and healing force for themselves and their communities and also the Earth. Nonetheless, I would like to clarify that their views are personal and are not meant to represent everyone who shares their tradition. In the back of the book, you will find fuller biographies for each practitioner.

The contributors to this book are as follows. For existing Indigenous traditions, I interviewed the Rev. Dr. Diane Rooney for Taoism;

Chip Brown, Pagan, who discussed how he incorporates his ancestral Native American tradition into his spiritual practice and worldview; Puáwai Ormsby, Māori elder, who discussed the revival of Indigenous spirituality and culture in New Zealand; and the Rev. Arda Itez, who discussed her practice of Tuvan Shamanism.

Next, I interviewed practitioners from African Diasporic traditions: Daniel Rodriguez, Lukumi priest and elder who is also a practitioner of the 21 Divisions, a form of the Vodou religion from the Dominican Republic; Ilan Chester, a Lukumi elder and gifted practitioner of Espiritismo, a form of Spiritualism practiced throughout Latin America; and Gloria "Glow" Okandekun, an Iya and elder within the tradition of Afro-Caribbean Lukumi.

My final three interviews are with those who practice modern forms of Neo-Paganism: Robert Lüsch Schreiwer, the founder of the Der Urglaawe tradition of Pennsylvania Deitsch Heathenry; Eric V. Eldritch, Third Degree priestx of the Tradition of Stone Circle Wicca (USA); and Andras Corban-Arthen, founder and spiritual leader of EarthSpirit Community, who shared insights and teachings from the Celtic-inspired Way of Anamanta.

## Practices

In addition to discussing these traditions, I will draw from practices and concepts from Eastern traditions, such as Ayurveda, Yoga, and Eastern medicine, which have nature-based ideas useful to self- and collective healing, as well as Spiritism and New Age beliefs. I will present spiritual practices from the traditions highlighted that are open to and able to be enjoyed by all. I also present meditations and practices I have created, which will allow you to explore themes developed in each chapter. Wherever possible, I have included which culture is represented in the specific practices shared. Practicing nature-based spirituality deepens the connection to divinity, ancestors, and the Earth.

I recommend following your inner guide and learning more about whichever pathway is inviting to your inner self. The main goal of presenting these practices and exercises is to encourage you to incorporate them for your own personal healing and spiritual growth.

When we work on our own personal healing, the energy ripples out. By doing so, a planetary healing can occur. We are then encouraged to inspire others with our renewed commitment to nature-based spirituality. My godfather in Ocha, Ilan Chester, explained this in this way:

> The job of the teacher begins when we understand ourselves. If you don't understand yourself, there is no way you can teach others the path to enlightenment. What I have seen in others is once they can tap into themselves and understand who they are, it begins. Most of the problem right now in humankind is most people don't even know who they are. How is it that most people don't know where they came from? Who their ancestors were or how their ancestors were able to survive? Once you disconnect yourself, like I said, you don't know who you are, then there is a total breakdown. You aren't connected to yourself or to Nature. But when we do make these connections, and we connect with what's been passed on through generations, we feel liberated. Not just in the physical form but in the spiritual form. We don't feel the same as the everyday person.
>
> What I have seen is once you can teach a person how to get to this next level, then there is this connection of energies; we make this opening. Like opening a sheet and then spreading out and covering with the sheet, we make this connection then with each other and we can all work together. That doesn't mean that I know you, but it means that you have tapped into the Nucleus—that's what I call the Divine, the energy; we are all connected to this Nucleus. The Catholic Church might call it God, but I call it the Nucleus. But once some of us make that connection, we all begin to work for one good purpose, and we can feel one another. We become One.

# 3HAMANIC 山NHERITANCE AND THE ☀QUARIAN ☀GE

On the Winter Solstice of December 21, 2020, the grand conjunction of Jupiter and Saturn took place, and many believed this particular astrological event signaled the dawn of the Aquarian Age. Astrologically, this meant we were leaving the Age of Pisces at long last, the energy of which has dominated for the past two thousand years. The Piscean Age was shaped by a worldview that embraced dualism, competition, water travel, orthodox religions, exploration, and emotional turbulence. The Age of Aquarius, as an air sign, signals a time of forward thinking, unity consciousness, individual spirituality, balance, and air-based technologies and progress for humanity, such as has already been ushered in by electronics, the internet, and the Space Age. The Age of Aquarius marks a shift from a rigidly male-female split in our collective psyches, instead offering a nonbinary, nondual way of being.[30]

Old paradigms are only replaced when they become obsolete, and we are witnessing now that the structures and corrupt institutions of the current paradigm are collapsing. This transition will not happen overnight and will not be completed in most of our lifetimes. However, it will complete. At this time in Earth's history, it is our role to reenvision and begin to build and create the new paradigm for future generations. This is what the dawning of this New Age predicts. One aspect of the Jupiter-Saturn conjunction, whose full energies won't be completed until 2023, is that we will preserve those ancient human institutions and beliefs that still serve us, while discarding and releasing those that no longer do. One of our most fundamental and enduring ideas is a return of sacred nature consciousness into the realm of everyday life for most human beings.

## THE ORIGINAL INSTRUCTIONS

In some ways, the understanding is humanity will relearn and incorporate teachings, practices, and beliefs of ancient times. This mirrors the concept of what First Nation people of the Americas call "The Original Instructions." Dr. Blair Stonechild, an Indigenous faculty member of the First Nations University of Canada, explained the concept to attendees at the Parliament of the World's Religions in 2018. It is the idea that all of humanity, regardless of continent, culture, or skin color, and all animals and plants, received the original instructions for how to live in harmony and peaceful coexistence directly from the Creator Spirit.[31]

---

30  Marion Weinstein, *Positive Magic* (New York: Phoenix, 1981), 17–25.

31  Manitonquat, *Medicine Story, The Original Instructions* (Bloomington, IN: AuthorHouse, 2009), xx.

These instructions are essential for us to relearn and implement into our way of life.[32] The instructions are within us as the natural way of being, but they have been forgotten over time and with human ideas born of greed, envy, and ambition. The Original Instructions include values such as mutual respect, interdependence, the cyclical nature of life and the circle of life, courtesy, gratitude, generosity, hospitality, humility, cherishing the wisdom of elders, and love for others and the Creator. Returning to our Original Instructions means a return to balance, to unity, and to partnership and cooperation between the sexes and humanity as a whole, both spiritually and economically.[33]

# INTERSPIRITUALITY

Another aspect of the Aquarian Age is that society will shift away from top-down, dogmatic, institutionalized religious beliefs and practices that dominated the Piscean Age, with priests serving as intermediators in the relationship between human and the Divine. The Aquarian Age instead embraces an individualized, directly experiential, and personally meaningful spirituality. The idea that there is one exclusive right way to God will become a thing of the past, replaced by openness and integration of what works personally for each one of us. We are now a global society, thanks to technology and the internet; the coming Aquarian Age will also be an interspiritual age, a time when we as individuals uphold the unifying core beliefs of the collective wisdom of human consciousness expressed and shared by numerous world teachings, Indigenous belief systems, and occult lore. People will mold their personal beliefs and values by personalizing what works for them from East and West, North and South, and throughout the world.

---

32 Manitonquat, *Medicine Story, The Original Instructions*, 9–43.
33 Manitonquat, *Medicine Story, The Original Instructions*, 41–101.

In the Aquarian Age, society will move away from the domination paradigm and embrace egalitarianism. By integrating this approach throughout society—including in family systems, religious institutions, economic systems, and day-to-day life—and preserving the best of modern science and understanding, humanity can weave together a partnership world.[34]

# INDIGENOUS BEGINNINGS

The word *shaman* probably derives from the Manchu-Tungus word *šaman*, meaning "one who knows." The word may also have originated from the Evenki word *šamán*, most likely from the southwestern dialect spoken by the Sym-Evenki peoples. The Tungusic term was subsequently adopted by Russians interacting with the Indigenous peoples in Siberia.[35]

In prehistoric communities, the shaman's role was broad and powerful, which was why they were both respected and feared. Their value to early communities was vital for survival. The shaman was the priest, the intermediary to the spirit world, the healer, the scientist, the counselor, the advisor, the artist, the visionary, the poet, the philosopher, and the spiritual guide. Today, in extant Indigenous communities, this role and its attributes are still found throughout the world, named specifically within each culture, and those who utilize the practices are thought to be able to heal, communicate with and journey to the spirit world, and raise energy and consciousness.

Because of colonialism, the use and overuse of the term today is not without controversy. Rev. Arda Itez, who is an initiate and practitioner of Tuvan Shamanism, said,

> I believe there are shamanic practices, like you said, with a small *s*, and there is Shamanism with a capital *S* for sure. People who pooh-

---

34   Eisler, *The Real Wealth of Nations*, 117–138.

35   Gary Doore, *Shaman's Path* (Boston: Shambhala Books, 1988), 33–34.

pooh it don't even know what it is, to be honest. Because if you go back far enough, to any of their ancestors, they were engaged in some kind of shamanic practices. Even later peoples, some sort of tradition they are holding on to is based in a shamanic practice. In my language, the word is *kam*. People get steeped in a fear-based theology that says anything outside of what they know is either to be pooh-poohed or is evil. However, although they are believed to have originated in Siberia, Shamans have existed in every culture, all over the world. Nordic, Celtic, South American, African, Asian—the list is endless.

Colonialism has contributed to the denigration of the word, however. Some feel strongly that the term has been misused and usurped by Western people, without respect to living, Indigenous cultures. Andras Corban-Arthen explained this:

We don't use the word *shaman* or *shamanism*: it's a very complicated word that carries a lot of baggage. I understand how you are using it; I know a lot of people who use it for the same reason you do, and I respect that, because I know what they mean. But, for other very good reasons, a lot of Indigenous people object to it. They feel it's a word that has been taken out of context and misused by anthropologists (many of whom are now distancing themselves from it). Because of those reasons, I try to be very clear that we don't use that term, and that I have never called myself a shaman.

## SHAMANISM ROOTS AND BRANCHES

The modern priesthood even within organized religion is descended from tribal shamanism. Traditional shamans still exist in Indigenous cultures around the world, wherever people follow nomadic, hunter-gatherer, or pastoral ways.

In Africa, shamanic practices are part of the Indigenous cultures of many native people, including the Yoruba. In Yoruba religion, the Baba or Iya, male or female priests, still enjoy aspects of this role. In addition to learning the use and application of natural medicine and healing, they lead the community in ceremony and prayer. Prayer is especially important for the Yoruba faith. To make supplications to one's *ori* (the Higher Self that lives in our head) or to ancestors, the Orisha, and Oldumare (God) is an essential aspect of Yoruba worship.[36] It is understood that prayers to the Orishas are essential to uplift, elevate, and purify baser human qualities. The highest form of prayer is for the devotees to make offerings, called *ebbo*, and to petition for transcendence and protection from negative forces. By means of sincere prayer, the devotee is better able to pass through the lower realms and attain an evolution of consciousness. Yoruba priests and priestesses assist devotees in their heavenly and earthly trials with the ultimate goal of helping the individual soul's progress toward Oneness with the Divine.[37]

Likewise, in the languages of the numerous tribes of the Americas, the elders are known by various names and as medicine women and men. As with other systems, they are the keepers of knowledge and tradition, as well as healers, artists, seers, counselors, and diviners. Prior to conquest, the Indigenous medicine people knew the knowledge of the plants and the ceremonies that connected their people with animal spirits whom they depended on for survival.

In the Far East in China, ancient priests and priestesses were also nature priests. In Siberia, these female priestesses were known as *shamankas*.[38] In the earliest available recorded material from the Chinese Bronze Age, the shamanka played a highly spiritual role. She was closely related to the fertile soil and the receptive earth. In Shang and Chou times, the shamankas were regularly employed in the interests

---

36  Baba Ifa Karade, *The Handbook of Yoruba Religious Concepts* (Newburyport, MA: Red Wheel Weiser, 2020), 37.

37  Karade, *The Handbook of Yoruba Religious Concepts*, 95–99.

38  Edward Schafer, *The Divine Woman* (Berkeley, CA: University of California Press, 1976), 13.

of human and natural fertility, above all in bringing rain to parched farmlands—a responsibility shared with the ancient kings.[39]

## The Shaman as Healer, Artist, and Visionary

During prehistory, by the time civilizations became more advanced with the shift to agriculture and large settlements, these shamanic practices were incorporated into more formal priesthoods and divided into other roles, such as statesman, advisor, bard, scientist, philosopher, poet, and artist. Over the development of the modern world in Europe, there were cultures who practiced a fusion of both a formal priesthood as well as a continuation of the shamanic ways of their ancestors, such as the Druids and the Celts, the seers within religious traditions of the Germanic peoples, and the oracle priestesses of the ancient mystery religions of Greece.

Druids were more than just priests and advisors to their communities. Anthropologists believe that the Celts may have absorbed some of the earlier Indigenous beliefs of the people they supplanted, but at the height of their religion, the Druid class encompassed Druid warrior, learned man, counselor to the king and the community, bard, judge, soothsayer, and shaman.[40] In Ireland, the legends of Tuatha da Danaan, the people conquered by the Milesians, described the Druids as wise magicians, skilled in the use of natural forces and mysterious powers. There were female Druids, which was surprising to the patriarchal Romans.

## The World Tree

The Saami in the Nordic lands had shamans who were hunters, midwives, herbal healers, dowsers, and seers. These are the people who left behind carved images of a White Goddess and other symbols and

---

39 Schafer, *The Divine Woman*, 13.
40 Jean Markale, *The Druids, Celtic Priests of Nature* (Rochester, VT: Inner Traditions Publishers, 1999), 28–38.

archetypes embraced and shared by later societies, one of which was the World Tree. The World Tree is a concept shared in all belief systems that arose from the ancient Indo-Europeans. It was associated with a goddess, or with a trio of goddesses, such as the Norns, who wove the fate of humankind at the roots of Yggdrasil for the Teutonic/Germanic peoples.[41]

Among the Yakut shamans of Siberia, the World Tree is a great fir that grows in the farthest north. In the branches of the tree nests the Bird of Prey Mother, who has iron feathers, an iron beak, hooked claws, and the head of an eagle. Shamans are born from the eggs she lays in the World Tree. She brings the shaman back to life after his ritual death.[42] This female figure, a bird goddess, appears in various forms throughout the mythology and spiritual practices of Europe, Tibet, and India over many centuries.

## Shamanic Abilities and Technology

As we have seen, the role of shaman in early societies became more complex and divided into numerous functions with the growing complexity of civilizations. In addition to the role of religious and spiritual leader, the shaman was gifted with certain healing and visionary abilities. Anthropologists include the following attributes: the individual works magick; creates art and ritual; performs healing; receives visions, messages, and inspiration through communication; and has the unique ability to transport into the spirit world through altered states of consciousness.[43]

The technology of the shaman is a complex phenomenon: the initiate uses ecstatic practices to draw themselves into alternate states of consciousness where they meet ancestors, spirit guides, and deities and gain access to powers not available to noninitiates nor during

---

41  Kenneth Johnson, *North Star Road* (St. Paul, MN: Llewellyn Publications, 1996), 19.

42  Johnson, *North Star Road*, 14–16.

43  Doore, *Shaman's Path*, 7–15.

everyday consciousness. Shamanism's mystique and social status is dependent on its cultural milieu. Where a shaman's powers are treated with reverence, appreciation, and awe or fear, they wield significant power within their communities. Those who utilize their services in return provide them with economic support, validation, faith, and legitimacy.

## Shamanism and Altered Mental States

Some researchers and scholars believe that shamanic practices, going back to prehistoric origins, may be responsible for early artwork and technological breakthroughs. Creative genius, mental illness, and spiritual peak experience may all be rooted in the same impulses of brain activity, through traits that are inherited in our DNA. In a 2013 TED Talk, archaeologist David Whitley theorized that the story of the birth of artistic genius is interconnected with the beginning of genetic mutations, which resulted in what we now define in the West as mental illness and mood disorders. He explained that during the same period the artwork of Old European culture began to appear in Paleolithic caves in France and Spain around forty to fifty thousand years ago, geneticists discovered a mutation in three variants of genes that control serotonin and dopamine systems. These mutations are responsible for the onset of mood disorders, mental disturbances, and significant creativity.[44]

In studying ancient cave art, archaeologists see that these masterpieces represent profound artistic and spiritual expression. The archaeological record also shows that during this period humans began making complex lithic tool kits, used for hunting, gathering, and processing food. Whitley believes that when these adaptations first appeared, their impact was transformational to society.[45] Those

44 David Whitley, "How Mental Illness Changed Humanity for the Better," YouTube, 2013, https://www.youtube.com/watch?v=yVwfJzZdkQ0.

45 Whitley, "How Mental Illness Changed Humanity for the Better."

with this creative genius gave cultural bursts in technological evolution and achievement. While appropriate economic and social conditions are required to foster art and religion, they are not the cause of innovation, and this first great art was made by shamans. Whitley's subsequent research confirmed that everywhere where the role of shaman still exists, they are the artists, poets, dancers, singers, and the original healers and scientists.[46]

This theory is confirmed by those who practice Indigenous shamanism today. Arda Itez, who practices Tuvan Shamanism, said this:

> Art of any kind—drawing, singing, dancing—is a shamanic practice! You need to engage the inner child to gain access to the spiritual realm, which is not unlike what Jesus taught. You must become childlike to open the door to a higher consciousness. You have to be willing to let go of binary thinking and everything you think you know. Uninhibited, creative expression is a wonderful way to do that.

## Mental States and Cultural Milieu

Shamans often describe their experience in terms of having visions, hearing voices, experiencing profound mood swings and sensitivities, and disassociating from their body to journey. When we examine modern diagnostic symptoms of mental disorders such as bipolar disorder, unipolar disorder, schizoaffective disorder, and schizophrenia and compare these to those descriptions, we can't help but notice similarities. As mentioned, substantial multidisciplinary scientific research supports the correlation between mood disorders, mental imbalance, and a high preponderance of creative expression and thought. The mad scientist, the melancholic poet, the suffering artist—these are all stereotypes that express this fact. Whitley concludes that while we can't deny someone with severe mental disturbance can suffer greatly, our choosing to see only the negative side of these traits prevents us from

---

46  Whitley, "How Mental Illness Changed Humanity for the Better."

seeing their overall positive contributions to human development, evolution, and society. They must be valued as strengths as well.[47]

Researchers from related disciplines agree. Philip Borges, a photographer and documentarian of many of the world's remote and Indigenous cultures, has spoken at length about his encounters with shamans and seers within communities of vanishing peoples. In his TED Talk discussion "Myths, Shamans and Seers," he described his interview with a seer who was responsible for advising the Dalai Lama of Tibet.[48]

The young monk said his gift began at twelve years old when he experienced a lasting illness and began to hear voices. The frightened youth didn't understand, but an older monk took him aside and explained he had a gift. The monk then spent one year with him to instruct him in the skill of going in and out of trance states and listening to the voices in order to bring their messages to others. The gifted monk then went on to become the medium for the Dalai Lama's Oracle, who later explained his importance to Tibetan Buddhist culture: "He actually gives us very important information. He told me when we would be invaded and when it was time for me to leave to go into exile."[49]

Borges described his encounter with the visionary of the Samburu people while documenting their tribe in Northern Kenya for Amnesty International. While there, his guide mentioned to him that their seer had foreseen his visit, describing in great detail the way he would hide to take photos. He didn't understand the reference at first, but then realized his equipment, a panoramic view camera, required that he hide himself beneath a sheet. Intrigued, he met with the thirty-seven-year-old female visionary, mother of five, who stated that her gifts

47 Whitley, "How Mental Illness Changed Humanity for the Better."
48 Philip Borges, "Myths, Shamans and Seers," YouTube, 2012, https://www.youtube.com/watch?v=q2VzhyIyGkA.
49 Borges, "Myths, Shamans and Seers."

also began as a young teen, receiving auditory and visual hallucinations after a lingering illness. Her grandmother comforted her and explained she had a gift that would be in service to her community.[50]

A third case Borges discusses in this video illustrates the link between shamanism and contemporary Indigenous culture from the border of Afghanistan and Pakistan. Borges documented the story of the elder shaman of a tribe known as the Kalash. The Kalash are animists who believe in all the various spirits that inhabit nature. The shaman shared with him how he learned the techniques from a mentor, connecting through these practices to the spirit world and inducing trance for healing.[51]

Borges has documented shamans around the world—in Africa, Asia, South America, the Arctic—in order to help Westerners understand their methods and importance in culture. He discovered that in most cases, the shaman had the experience of a mysterious sickness, which later resulted in new abilities. Where the culture offered validation for these abilities, they often then received training and guidance by skilled individuals who shared these gifts to take on this special and important role.[52]

Counter that with how mental illnesses, such as bipolar disorder and schizophrenia, are treated in Western culture from the onset and throughout a person's life. When people start seeing things, hearing things, or experiencing other realities, phenomena not shared by others, they are labeled mentally ill and believed to be in need of psychiatric care. Western culture only sees their gifts as an illness or as a chemical imbalance that must be aggressively treated and stopped with medication and therapy—something to control and block out, and certainly not as something desirable. We have come a long

---

50  Borges, "Myths, Shamans and Seers."
51  Borges, "Myths, Shamans and Seers."
52  Borges, "Myths, Shamans and Seers."

way from total institutionalization or treating these experiences as demonic. Many mental health practitioners today also understand that a person's delusions are real to them, yet most Western-trained mental health practitioners, and society, do not appreciate and may even fear delusional states and the people who have them. In Western culture, a person may end up homeless, institutionalized, shunned, and even incarcerated if they act violently due to their symptoms. If they had been in an Indigenous or a more sympathetic framework from the onset of these experiences, they might have been recognized as special and gifted and provided with training and status. How different would an outcome be for someone with that diagnosis in those cultures versus ours, where they are only told they are diseased? As Borges cautions, "Our culture gives us little permission to explore non-rational states of consciousness."[53]

## IN NATURE-BASED SPIRITUAL PRACTICES TODAY

In all the interviews I conducted for this book, one major communality is the use of various techniques to induce alternative states of consciousness. Whether the tradition was a preserved Indigenous practice, an African Diasporic religion, or a modern reconstruction of Pagan tradition, each of the interviewees mentioned that shifting one's consciousness through movement, drumming, chanting, meditation, or journeying is important to access insight, healing, and power. To the nature-based practitioner, shape-shifting and the power this can bring to one's being is magick, and it is real. Eldritch explained how The Stone Circle Tradition of Wicca (USA) develops and invites newcomers to welcome this experience:

---

53 Borges, "Myths, Shamans and Seers."

In our Wiccan training class on The Drum, we talk about prayer, about meditation, and going into trance. Within trance, we use aspecting, where you sense you are here, but Spirit is coming in back here [gestures to back of head] and coming into you. Or someone will draw down Spirit on you and the two of you coexist. At a deeper level in our practice, we acknowledge, but do not often practice, possession, where you give up and let a spirit ride you and guide you, letting a spirit act through you. As a regular practice, we teach using cloth as a veil or a shroud to enhance the meditative state you are in for the healing that you seek.

In the Dominican Vodou tradition known as the 21 Divisions, Daniel Rodriguez says trance work and possession are essential components:

The 21 Divisions is very possession-based. It is much more possession-based than Ocha. I would say that because it's almost necessary for things to happen; you need a possession. You can do an Ocha without having possession, but in the 21 Divisions, you have to have possession if you are going to do a baptism. Someone there, the priests, as they are called *Houngans*, somebody has to bring the Loa down to give instructions. One thing to remember, however, is possession comes in all forms. One doesn't have to be fully possessed to hear the Loa and know what they want; they communicate in different ways.

The idea that possession and altered states of consciousness are something to be welcomed, explored, and respected is certainly new to most in Western society where we have been taught to fear these states or dismiss them as superstition or delusion. However, as we have seen within societies who still practice shamanism, where these transcendent states are respected and the information and insight received during these states have a safe place to be shared and released, there is great value in them. It is helpful as well that those born gifted or who suddenly become aware of their gifts receive instruction and guidance from others who have learned to manage those gifts. This mentorship is present in cultures that make space for altered states and creatively express them, whether in artistic expression or in healing for self and others.

The nature-based practice of ecstatic union with the Divine through trance and shifting states of consciousness can help us relight Mother Earth's cauldron. When we reclaim this practice, we can build a new paradigm by bringing through creative ideas and inspiration to reimagine a whole new world.

## TENDING THE FLAME
### Urglaawe Heathen Tradition

Robert Lüsch Schreiwer is the founder of the Der Urglaawe tradition of Pennsylvania Deitsch Heathenry. Heathenry has enjoyed a resurgence of interest for many Americans, especially those of Germanic descent. In his interview, Robert shared some examples of how Urglaawe utilizes trance and journeying techniques for self-healing, ancestor work, and working with the spirits of the land. He also discussed how Heathens conceptualize working magick.

Robert pointed out that Urglaawe is inclusive to all; one does not have to be of Germanic ethnic background. Many in the Neo-Pagan and Heathen community do not refer to what they do as shamanic as they consider that cultural appropriation. In the Urglaawe tradition, members prefer to define the magickal and spiritual practices utilized in their tradition with their own linguistic terms. Some of what Robert and the Urglaawe tradition do is tease out the Heathen practices and deities from the later

Christian saints and overlays, which helps these practices survive through culture and folklore:

> *Urglaawe* is the Deitsch (Pennsylvania Dutch) term for "primal faith." It is the pursuit of the ancient Germanic religion using the lens of the modern Pennsylvania Deitsch culture. So, it's a modern expression of Heathen religion. The two organizations, Urglaawe and the Troth, are both Heathen, but they are somewhat different. The Troth is inclusive of all denominations and stripes of Heathenry, and Urglaawe is one of them, another being Asatru, Anglo-Saxon Heathenry, and other branches. Urglaawe then, obviously, is focusing specifically on Pennsylvania Deitsch traditions. We are talking about things that are already in our culture and bringing them back to life, or breathing life back into them.
>
> In the past, we would sometimes use the word *shamanic* because there was no other real word in the English language to describe it, but we have decided that henceforth, we are going to use the words *hexich* and *hexlich* to describe it because that is within our own tradition. The semantic between the two is very, very narrow. *Hexich* is like a witch and *hexlich* would be done in a witchy manner. It has cognate *Braucherich* and *Braucherlich*. There are two practices, and how you view them makes all the difference in the world.
>
> Taking the example of two coins: some people see one as Hexerei and one as Braucherei—two separate coins, very different. Meanwhile, many others might see the practices as just one coin—this side is Hexerei and this side is Braucherei. How you view that makes all the difference in the world because this is two sides of the same coin versus two separate coins; this can actually be one unit—meanwhile, this has to be two separate things. This latter comes down to Christian dualism, the idea that this is of God, this is not of God, Hexerei is evil, Braucherei is good. Hexerei is black, Braucherei

is white. But we are not a dualistic religion, we are a holistic religion. Even this one coin with two sides is not correct, because there really are not two sides, it's one thing.

In Urglaawe, the deities are certainly active. We honor the Germanic pantheon, but our perspectives are somewhat different on some of the deities versus that of many people in Asatru. That's a key factor. We know some deities that they did not know, and they know some of the deities that we did not know. For example, Frouwa is our cognate of Freya, and there is a belief within Hexerei that some of her attributes were grafted onto St. Gertrude of Nivelles. St. Gertrude's Day is March 17 and is still fairly widely observed with some very Heathen practices within the Deitscherei (Pennsylvania Dutch Country) today.

It is odd that a saint's day survived so strongly in the heavily Anabaptist and Protestant Deitscherei, but the observance is typically more secular or Heathen in content. To Pennsylvania Deitsch folks, it's St. Gertrude's Day. It's the day of Frouwa, it's our honoring of the goddess known to the Norse as Freya. Even in the Christian celebration, St. Gertrude's Day celebrations are loaded with Heathen elements. There is a special type of bread that the Christians and Urglaawe bake with the symbolism of their respective belief systems dictating the use—among the meanings being that bread is the completion of the potato cycle. The last of the prior year's potatoes are used to bake the bread that is offered to Frouwa and placed onto and into the soil as the new potato crop is planted.

Urglaawe definitely has a very strong set of goddesses; the chief goddess of our religion is the goddess Holle. She is an Earth Mother, and she also keeps the cycles of life, death, and birth. She keeps the cycles on all levels—the cosmic cycles of the returns and the beginnings and the ends—so we definitely have these concepts at play.

# ❋ A PRACTICE ❋

## Creating an Offering to the Earth

One common practice in nature traditions is creating formal offerings of food and libations, as the Urglaawe do with the bread offering to Frouwa, for expressions of friendship and gratitude to the Earth, ancestors, and nature spirits. An Indigenous example is with the Quechua, a native people from the Andean Highlands of Peru and Bolivia. Here, their medicine people, known as *paqo*, whose colorful traditional clothing and headdresses are known worldwide, have a tradition of creating prayer bundles of various flowers, grains, and offerings to express gratitude to their ancestors, power animals, and guides, known as *Despacho*.[54]

In the Lukumi tradition, there is also a ceremony known as Feeding the Earth, which is an offering, or ebbo, to the Earth, led by initiated priests and designed to help bring necessary changes to a person's life and destiny.

These are just a few examples of the practice. The following ceremony is inspired by these types of practices and is designed to express gratitude and prayers directly to your ancestors, power animals, and guides to help you cultivate a deeper and more reciprocal relationship with the Earth Mother.

This ceremony is best performed in early spring.

## Tools

You will need a round biodegradable planter pot of at least 4.5 inches in diameter. You will also need enough potting soil to fill the container and a packet of sunflower, pansy, or marigold seeds, which are easy to grow indoors if you will not be replanting outside. You will

---

54 *A version of this practice was shared by Qe'ro Peruvian Shamans with the Omega community in the Great Shamanic Initiation, October 2019.*

also need one cup of water, a half cup of breadcrumbs, a tablespoon of coffee grounds, and a tablespoon of brown sugar.

## Begin

Holding your hands over the empty container, declare your intention to create an offering to the Earth, your ancestors, and your guides.

> *I consecrate this vessel to be a sacred offering to the Earth Mother. I make this offering as a symbol of love and gratitude to my ancestors, the land ancestors, and my guides, to help deepen our relationship. This container is now a holy offering to you. So be it.*

Add a half inch of soil to the bottom of the container; this represents the deepest strata of the Earth Mother, where the ancestors reside. On top of this, sprinkle a small amount of the coffee grounds, asking the Earth Mother to share her fertility and your ancestors to receive this offering and continue to be in relationship with you.

Add more soil. Upon this soil, add the layer of breadcrumbs, saying to the ancestors and guides that this food represents your gratitude to them, and is also an offering to the Earth Mother, giving thanks to her for all the nourishment the plant kingdom provides.

Cover this layer with more soil, nearly to the top, and ask their blessing on the seeds you will sow here.

Next, add the seeds. While you are adding them, give thanks to each of the elements—earth, air, fire, and water—and the powers of nature. When this is complete, cover the seeds with a final quarter inch of soil.

On top of the completed planting, you will now sprinkle the brown sugar over the seeds to represent your gratitude for the sweetness of life. Give thanks for all the celebrations you have enjoyed with loved ones, and send loving wishes to your ancestors that they may have healing, joy, and celebration in the spirit realm. Give thanks to your spirit guides and invite them to enjoy this nourishing sweetness and to continue working with you. Cover the sugar with a thin layer of potting soil and pat it down.

Place your hands over the planted pot. Call in the energy of the Sky Father, the Earth Mother, the ancestors, and the guides and ask them to please bless your seeds with life, light, and nourishment so that they may take root and your relationship with them will grow and flourish. Make a final offering of the water as a libation to seal your offering, completing your work by saying out loud, "Let this be so!"

Place your potted plant in a bright and sunny window or space and water it when the soil is dry. You may want to put the biodegradable pot in a ceramic pot to avoid it leaking on your windowsill until it is replanted. When your seeds sprout, you may plant the new flowers in the biodegradable pot directly into your garden, once again stating that these flowers represent your offering to the Earth. You can also enjoy them in your home. When the plants bloom and blossom, it is recommended that you save the seeds to repeat the ceremony again in the coming spring as a form of honoring the cycle of life and rededication to the Earth Mother, your ancestors, and your guides.

# 4

# JOURNEYING TO THE ASTRAL PLANE

How do traditional shamans induce alternate states of consciousness? Most shamans may be innately gifted with a natural ability to shift consciousness or receive it after an illness. But these abilities can be aided and enhanced in various ways, and learned. From sacred singing, dancing, and drumming to fasting and vision quests, lucid dreaming, or the use of herbs or the smoke of plant-based psychoactive entheogens, practitioners use their tool kit, often combined with ritual ceremony, to work their way into trance. From here, they will journey or astrally project where they encounter realms beyond this one, alternate dimensions, in order to meet intelligent entities and receive visions, messages, and the ability to heal.[55]

---

55 Doore, *Shaman's Path*, 34–36.

What type of power do they have? How do they get their power? Do they tap into a parallel universe? Is it the use of the collective unconscious? Is it using the powers of the nature spirits that surround us? Does a subtle part of them physically leave their bodies? These are mysteries not easily answered by modern scientists or observers but understood deeply and experientially by those who participate in these activities.

# SHAMANIC HEALING

Healing brought through from altered states of consciousness can not only be personal, or only for sick people, but it can also be for nature and the planet. In a video shared on social media in 2021, Noah Green, a nine-year-old Cree singer and drummer who learned his skill by the time he was eight from his grandmother Carol Powder, creates songs to heal Mother Earth. Powder is a traditional powwow hand drum singer, and together they visit powwows and conferences throughout North America to raise awareness, energy, and prayers to combat climate change. Noah was inspired to join the climate change fight after he heard activist Greta Thunberg speak about climate change urgency. Powder expressed that the method of singing and drumming is a practice of healing, and the healing can be directed toward humans and the Earth. She is also grateful that people are paying attention now, ever since Greta's appearance on the world stage, but native people have had this message forever as the voice of Mother Earth.

## Magick

A shaman uses ritual and ceremony to manipulate the spirits of nature or the dead. They will attempt to affect this world with non-rational means, mostly in the form of ritual actions to affect guides, helpers, and spirits from the otherworld. This manipulation of forces can be termed *magick*. Shamans also journey, leaving their bodies and this realm of ordinary being. The use of symbolism is very important in the shamanic/magickal complex. The symbols give the ceremonies meaning and purpose and become representative of important concepts as well as vehicles of power as the shaman works to manipulate the forces of nature—for example, to ask for a strong harvest or help with the hunt or to dispel sickness and disease. The symbols themselves vary within each culture, but most include universal archetypes, such as references to Mother Earth, the forces of nature, animal totems, the spirits of ancestors and the cosmos, and other dimensions. These symbols then are preserved and disseminated through art, myth, song, poetry, and legend by the communities themselves.[56] An example of a magickal symbol can be seen in the colorful decoration of Pennsylvania Deitsch barns for protection with ancient symbology. When asked about these common Pennsylvania Dutch barn decorations, Robert explained,

> A lot of people will tell you that it's unconscious and it's just for decoration. Everyone is free to believe what they want to believe. Ultimately it goes back to the person who painted it who knows what it was originally intended to do. But there are plenty of people who do paint these things and do so in an Old World context. And even if they didn't have them before, they certainly have the meanings now.

# THE JOURNEY TO THE OTHERWORLD

In the Urglaawe tradition, practitioners of Hexerei utilize a form of journeying that helps them perform individual and communal healing through connecting with the spirit world to ancestor and land spirits. Robert discussed this:

---

56  Doore, *Shaman's Path*, 43–52.

Heathenry is about making connections: to yourself, to your family, to your community; connections to your ancestors; connections to the deities. Once people establish those connections, it helps them recognize that they are really not alone.

We are not just in this linear station, we are in this big, cosmic, interdimensional, multidimensional universe, where, as overwhelming as all that is, there is still really only one of each of us. Even though we do believe in partial soul rebirth, part of you will be back again, but it's not going to be you, it's not going to be the same you. It's going to be a different you with a different makeup, so every single life is precious. And every single life has an opportunity before it. Even if you screwed up your entire life, that doesn't mean you still can't tap into those connections and find the strength from your ancestors. In Hexerei, you can find it from your descendants by going out and finding out if your descendants are talking to you.

Making the connections does help people. Like with addictions, especially with things like alcoholism, you can talk to the spirit of Hops and get them to intercede on behalf of clients. When you get into synthetics, it becomes much more difficult, because there is essentially no spirit to talk to. But even there, when you dig deep enough, they are still part of the animistic matrix, they are still made from something natural, so related spirits can haunt them. Primarily, we journey in one of the realms.

In terms of working with land spirits and entities, Urglaawe has certain practices that are very shamanic. Robert explained one unique practice:

One of the biggest events for this is in February, when we activate our scarecrows. When we step out under the World Tree—and "step out" is our phrase for entering the trance state—we become a bridge between the western leaves of the world tree and this realm. Which invites the ancestral spirits of the plants to cross over through us and go into the scarecrows and awaken the dormant spirits that are in them. Allegorically speaking, we are activating them, and quite literally in some cases. The scarecrow is built from last year's crops. So that scarecrow becomes the father of this year's crops. That scarecrow's job is to spiritually patrol his turf.

These practices access personal power. They are a technology that uses connection with nature and the spirit world to not only help community, but to also pursue personal and communal growth and transformation. When a practitioner begins their journey, they are able to access realms of the subconscious and supraconscious that bring forth individuation and evolution.

## Journey for Mental Health Healing

The technique of journeying is being utilized by some in the modern mental health arena. Michael Harner was a pioneer of shamanic journeying and used drums or recordings to guide clients to access guidance, healing, and wisdom through journeying to non-ordinary reality. His legacy, the Harner Method, is designed to help the client become their own shaman to restore personal power and heal old wounds and trauma. One key requirement to be a shamanic counselor is a strong desire to help others. The aims of shamanic experiences are ultimately identical to the aims of mindfulness and contemplative practice; they help us rise above our normal waking self to spiritual mastery and ascendance.[57]

## Embracing the Role of Guide

Many have reclaimed the term *witch*, instead of *shaman*, along with *priestess* to describe this magickal role today in Pagan practice. Essentially, this role really is as a guide and an expert in manifestation and transformation. For them, freely accessing the deep well of nature practices and mystical heritage of what came before modern Judeo-Christian religion is empowering.

---

57  Doore, *Shaman's Path*, 179.

Perhaps it is enough to recognize that these practices and technologies shared by multiple preserved or reconstructed traditions have commonalities, regardless of the title given to the role. As we've explored, the practice of journeying to other realms for power, wisdom, and healing predates modern religions. What's most important is that it offers an approach to knowledge and experience that counterbalances the rational mind and provides opportunities for direct revelation and unique insights, which can facilitate profound healing for individuals and the community served.

Releasing our minds through ecstatic states of consciousness lifts us out of ordinary consciousness and creates space for new wisdom, creativity, and insights to emerge. This practice from nature spirituality is a fruitful way to help the Earth revitalize by freeing ourselves from the paradigm that currently locks us into a materialistic and deterministic, often destructive, outcome. The tools of drum, rattle, song, dance, meditation, and inspired creative expression are available and open to all. The shamans of the Amazon rainforest believe that the world around us has been created by the dream of Western minds and it is now a nightmare. Those who wish to create a better way for the future can utilize these techniques to encounter new visions and possibilities for humankind. In this way, we can dream a new dream.

## TENDING THE FLAME
### Tuvan Shamanism

Rev. Arda Itez is a humanist, an interspiritual minister, and a social justice activist. She has Anatolian, Caucasian, and Mongolian ancestry and is trained in and practices a traditional form of Tuvan Shamanism. In Tuva, a land in Southern Siberia bordering Mongolia, Shamans are formally recognized and required to register with the government. It is a living tradition that sees reality as multidimensional, with a hierarchy, and composed of a variety of entities a Shaman connects with through their work in the spirit world.

In our interview, Arda discussed an important aspect of shamanic practice: reciprocity. In most shamanic traditions, there is an absolute need for reciprocity and relationship between those who wish to work with these energies and forces themselves. It is the idea of exchange and interdependence between the practitioner and the spirit or natural world. There is an understanding that when we ask for something (healing, knowledge, etc.), there must be a return offering. One cannot do without the other; when we take, we must give something in return. The idea of sacrifice and offering, so common in the world of Indigenous people the world over, began here:

> I was raised Muslim, but my ancestors, as recent as my mother, were Indigenous people to the land in the Caucasus. We are Karachay, a Turkic tribe that originated, like all Turks, from the Altai Mountains thousands of years ago. We were a shamanic people who carried our ancient practices and traditions through generations. Of course, much of our practice has been absorbed into what many see as modern religious or cultural tradition—similar to the Christmas tree, which is Pagan, not Christian, in origin. The guiding principle of my practice is to live in balance with Nature. Shamanism has a hierarchy, and Shamans see themselves as a middle person—a bridge between this world and the spirit world. As teachers, it is their responsibility to help others connect, heal, and grow. It's a role; they are the connection

for the average person who maybe is not in tune. But it is their responsibility as teachers to help them connect.

A Shaman's life is lived straddling both of these worlds at all times. They are never alone. In fact, none of us are, as we have entire teams that work with us (or are waiting to), such as our ancestors, power animals, and spirit guides. It's even said that each of us is born from the consciousness of a specific deity. Therefore, their mythology, characteristics, strengths, attributes, foibles—everything about them is relevant and available to us. All the aforementioned is available to us—if we can relinquish our need for logic and control and can, as my teacher used to say, allow ourselves to "get uncomfortable." So, we have our power animals, gods and goddesses, ancestors, spirit guides; some people will include fairies. My teacher will tell you there are fairies and all kinds of creatures, like elementals.

In order to have a relationship with them—and this is very, very important in Shamanism—if you expect the favors of any of these energies that are within you or assisting you, you have to appease them. There's no free ride, essentially. It's a reciprocal relationship, and it takes time to develop. I began with Shamanism, like anyone would start a spiritual practice, with meditation. When you do it for an extended period of time, things start to happen. You start developing certain skills you may not have had before, and it's exactly the same with Shamanism. But the way it's described in Shamanism is all your energies, your team, they're kind of sitting around waiting for you to invite them in. So, you have to appease them, and that means showing them that you are serious, that you're developing a real practice.

It can begin in meditation, but the real practice is in rattling, it's in drumming, and it's in moving the body, moving meditations. In order to shift reality, and we believe that in Shamanism you can shift reality, you have to move it into a new reality. You have to literally move, and you shift reality by being uncomfortable. So that means moving in a way you find unnatural, or you would be embarrassed to do it in front of people, but nothing happens in a space of comfort. So, it's training your mind to accept the unacceptable, which begins with making yourself uncomfortable. Allowing your body to move in ways that don't look attractive, it's very jerky and awkward.

Drumming is a portal. Your drum is a portal. I knew that my practice was shifting when I was going over my teacher's house one day. She happens to live not even a mile away from me and she said her guide told her to have me bring my drum, and she said we were going to activate my drum. She then told me that there are two spirits who live in my drum, male and female, and when I use the drum, they are there to assist me in whatever way is needed. There are the four directions on the drum, and those four directions relate to mind, body, emotions, and intuition, as well as the elements—earth, air, fire, water—on each area on the drum. So, when you look for answers, the area that you drum in is very important.

For me, it's really intense. If I sent you pictures of the altars I have had in my house that were built to appease all of my team, you'd be amazed. My team likes specific things; this is the way it works. I know in a lot of other forms of Shamanism, they kind of put out this generic stuff: cornmeal, or tobacco, or this or that. But the way I was taught to practice is that it's very specific. Each team member wants something very specific. The more power animals you have, we believe, means the more spiritually attuned you are. I have eight of them on my team, and each one is very specific about what they want. One wants sugar cubes; one wants Skittles, believe it or not; one wants peanut butter. So, I very intentionally prepare and make the altar beautiful. I buy them flowers, and whatever candy or food, and baked goods. There are always baked goods for your ancestors, so it's a lot of work.

In Shamanism, if you are not consistent with your practice, you essentially lose contact. You can lose contact; your guides will be like, "Meh, she's not taking us seriously. So, we won't bother with her." My teacher said to me, imagine your team, this group of people who adore you and are waiting to serve you hand and foot and to assist you, but you pay no attention to them; how are they going to feel? Also, who are they more apt to pay attention to—the people who ignore them, or the ones who pay attention to them? Your practice is key, and if you don't practice to keep yourself protected, you open the door to illness. We believe illness is brought on energetically.

# ❀ A PRACTICE ❀
## A Meditative Journey to the Underworld

You will need to find a comfortable and quiet location to do this meditation. It may help for you to record the journey first and then listen to it while meditating.

## Tools

A rattle, a comfortable chair or bed. Your journal.

## Begin

I invite you now to close your eyes and get comfortable. Begin by seating yourself in a receptive and comfortable position, perhaps cross-legged on the floor with your hands in your lap, or in a chair.

Take five deep, cleansing breaths, counting slowly to four on the inhale and to four on the exhale. Allow yourself to let go of your day-to-day cares and bring your awareness into the present moment. Allow the deep breathing to continue for as long as you need.

Connect with your breath; check in with your body. Feel its solidity. Connect with your body, beginning at the top of your head, relaxing down into your face, shoulders, arms, chest, torso, and down into

your seat, down through your thighs, and into your legs. Allow yourself to connect to Mother Earth, feeling her solid form below you.

Envision a circle of light around you. Let that light be bold and
bright; feel its warmth, feel its light surrounding you, keeping you
safe. Take three more deep breaths. Call in your guides to surround
your body and keep you safe as you prepare to journey.

Knowing your body is safe, allow your spirit to begin the journey.
Begin to rattle.

Let the sound of the rattle and the rhythm of your breathing allow
your soul to release from your body. Know your body is safe in the
circle of light, surrounded by your guardian spirit guides.

Continuing to rattle, you find yourself on a path in the woods. You
are surrounded by a forest. Beneath your feet, a path winds its way
through these trees. Around you are plants, flowers, herbs, mushrooms, and the myriad scents and sounds of the deep woods. You
deeply breathe in the earthy smell. Above you, a sunny sky lights your
path, which you begin to walk down.

You continue down the wooded path; the sunlight gives way to
more shadows. You enter a very dark place in the wood, where the
trees are tall and wide. Beyond the trees, you can make out what
looks like cliffs and steep walls rising. Continue to rattle.

Begin to look around for a hole. The hole will be in a tree or
appear as a cave or crevice in the cliff walls; it could appear beneath
you on the path or in the forest floor. Take your time, noticing any
creatures or living things associated with this place.

When you find the hole, it is time to enter the underworld. Continue to rattle. Enter the hole and allow yourself to experience what
you experience beyond this liminal space. It may be sensations, colors,
feelings, or a knowing. You may come out into a whole new space or
dimension. You may be greeted by animal spirits or other types of
beings, even ancestors.

Continue to rattle and allow the sound of the rattle to guide you along your journey until you receive whatever experience is meant for you at this time. Pay attention to any and all messages from Spirit you receive here. In the meantime, your body may feel the need to lie down or roll up in a ball. Either way, know you are safe.

After you have journeyed into this realm, you will know when you have journeyed far enough and be prompted to return to ordinary consciousness. Thank whatever beings you have encountered here and your guides for this experience.

As you rattle, begin your return journey back through the hole, up through the forest, back along the path, until you arrive at the sunny spot where you entered this realm. With deep, releasing breaths, return now into ordinary consciousness.

Stand and stretch if you are able, perhaps eating a light snack and drinking to ground back in your body. Be sure to journal all the details of the experience you can remember.

This is a meditation you can repeat again and again when you need to connect with your guides and helpers on the other side. It is very important to begin the meditation in a protected state and end with a grounding back into everyday consciousness. Your skill at journeying will increase as you practice each time.

# ANCESTOR REVERENCE

In the Lukumi tradition, there is a saying about the primal importance of recognizing and venerating ancestors first before all other avenues of spiritual practice can be realized or aspired to. In Lukumi, it is said, "Iku lobi Ocha," or, *We first need to die to become Orisha*. The translation means "Death gives birth to Orisha."[58] The dead must come before all. It is believed that when one is crowned through initiation with the energy of the guiding Orisha, they will eventually return to that whole constellation of energy. We become Orisha.

This concept of the importance of ancestor veneration is exceedingly widespread; it is shared in the tradition from the Congo known as *Palo Mayombe*. In Palo, the dead are seen not as bringers of sterility and

---

58  Todd R. Ochoa, *Society of the Dead* (Berkeley, CA: University of California Press, 2010), 36.

finality, but as the fertile component of the life force. Much like in nature, the organic material of dead living things creates the conditions for new life to emerge. The dead literally surround us and are known as *Kalunga*; they envelop our world, seeking rebirth into their family lineages and inspiring their descendants for their life's missions. When we die, we become part of this sea of imminence.[59]

Ancestor veneration is a practice that connects the living to the dead and locates us through space and time: Puáwai Ormsby, Māori elder, explains,

> When we come together, the men have a woven mat to speak words of eloquence, of welcome. Also, we, as women, do a chant, do that action with our hands [waves hand rapidly]. It's not that we are scared! This is our sign language for Spirit. This represents the shimmer of light on the ocean—when you look at light on the ocean, it shimmers. It represents the breeze and the leaves of the trees, so we do this to represent Spirit. When we do that ceremony, we are activating Spirit, we are bringing in all our ancestors, they are all part of the ceremony. So, all your ancestors are part of that ceremony, too. As soon as we activate that weave, they are on board as well. So, all the ancestors are meeting. So, you can understand there is no separation in anything we do. Your ancestors, they walk with you. Every person I meet, I actually meet their ancestors.

This is a universal concept in Indigenous and nature-based traditions. Ancestral people, including ancient European Pagans and modern Indigenous people of Asia, Africa, Australia, New Zealand, and the Americas, all continue to venerate and honor their ancestors. What is remembered is preserved. It is believed that connecting to ancestor spirits brings healing to individuals and the community. It also helps to move personal consciousness outward, moving beyond this level by creating a solid foundation, reaching back in time, and

---

59 Ochoa, *Society of the Dead*, 37.

then moving forward through our lineage and our descendants. This runs counter to the dominant Western culture that teaches fear of the dead, replaced with an idea that any communication with spirit beings from the other side is really with demons. Or, Westerners dismiss this practice altogether, a result of materialism that says this is all there is—when our bodies are gone, we are gone.

# PREHISTORY OF ANCESTOR VENERATION

Some anthropologists believe ancestor veneration may have predated modern humans. Archaeologists have uncovered Neanderthal burials from Europe as old as 50,000 BCE, where the bones of the dead were lovingly buried, placed in the fetal position, covered in red ochre, with flowers and offerings of primitive grave goods. Perhaps they had a belief in reincarnation, that the bodies of the dead were being returned for rebirth in the womb of the Earth Mother. Cro-Magnon burials of Old Europe were similar. The dead are found placed in sleeping positions. Perhaps death was believed to be a longer trip into the dreamtime?

Over time, burials related to status and rank increased, with higher-status individuals often buried with grave goods, along with their horses and other humans who could have been their slaves. These are found in mounds throughout Europe, which were the temples and holy places in their day. In some places, like Northern Europe, homesteads, communities, and stone megalithic structures were often placed directly over the gravesites of earlier people. Ancestors were buried in the ground where the homes of their descendants later stood. It was clear these people did not fear their ancestors, but rather chose a close relationship with them literally and figuratively.

The continuation of burial practices that honor and revere the ancestors with love and devotion is worldwide. Among North American tribes, totem poles of Pacific coastal people depict ancestors and animal spirits important to clan and community.[60] The legends of the Hopi people of the Southwest and the Navajo preserve an oral tradition of creation myths, and it is said that their ancestors emerged from the Grand Canyon, this being a burial ground. In Australia, ancient cave art depictions of Aboriginal ancestral spirits have been found, showing them descending from the stars during their journey of creation. In Africa, ancestor veneration is prevalent throughout the continent and serves as the basis for many Indigenous beliefs.

In traditional African religions, the community is the most important part of someone's life, and community is essential to remembering family and tradition. African Indigenous peoples such as the Fon and the Yoruba believe their ancestors should be recognized at all major events, such as weddings, births, and deaths, as well as minor ones, such as getting a job and finishing university. During these events, usually an offering—in pastoral societies, a cow, sheep, or chicken—may be slaughtered to honor, please, and thank them to invite their blessings.

This practice continues around the world. In India, Hindu and native Indian cultures offer food and offerings to their ancestors at specialized shrines on holy days throughout the year. In the Indigenous religion of ancient China down through the present day, Chinese people create shrines to their ancestors and make regular offerings of joss sticks and food to invoke blessings for prosperity, health, and success. In Mexico and in other Latin American countries, folk tradition blends with Catholicism to celebrate Día de Los Muertos, or Day of the Dead, on November 1, to recognize and celebrate departed loved ones. Elaborate displays of foods, sweets, marigolds and other flow-

---

60  David Fontana, *The Secret Language of Symbols* (London: Duncan Baird Publishers, 2003), 37.

ers, candles, and photos of the deceased decorate home shrines, and families gather for the evening, visiting with relatives in cemeteries. This is cognate with the ancient holiday of Samhain from European countries, which continues in the present-day holiday of Halloween, celebrated today as Samhain by many modern Pagans.

The church could not stop these practices among the cultures they encountered, so instead, within Roman Catholicism and continuing into the Episcopal Church, they made room for them in their own calendar with the holidays of All Saints' Day and All Souls' Day, on November 1 and 2. In a sense, the church chose an intentional strategy of syncretism with earlier faith traditions to increase acceptance. For believers, praying for the dead is a sacred duty.

Ancestors are not just blood ancestors. Many cultures honor ancestors of land and ancestors of religion, as in the holy people within lineages, like the veneration of saints. Others recognize the concept of ancestors to include nature spirits. Andras Corban-Arthen, founder of the EarthSpirit Community, shared this expanded viewpoint:

> When we say we honor our ancestors, we are very conscious of the fact that we have human ancestors, but they are not all our ancestors. Trees are ancestors, mountains are ancestors, fire is an ancestor—all these beings that are nonhuman are still our ancestors because they also created the life we share. So, they are very powerful and ancient.

## ANCESTOR REVERENCE RATIONALE

Why should ancestor reverence be important to a modern person? Honoring the beloved dead makes sense; we wouldn't be here without them. Honoring ancestors shows respect for them, their struggles, and their sacrifices. Science now understands the importance of ancestral heritage on who we are today in fields like epigenetics, behavioral science, and psychology. It is now widely accepted that many if not most behaviors in animals and humans are under significant genetic influence, connecting us to our ancestral heritage whether we believe in the spiritual aspect of this or not. Physical traits, our phenotype, eye color, hair color, height, and so on, as well as aptitudes in music, social skills, mathematical abilities, and so on, are inherited. Anthropologists have observed that even in our primate cousins, relatives inherit personality traits. We also inherit negative family patterns: tendencies toward mental illness, behavioral problems, maladaptive social strategies, genes that increase the risk for cancer, disease, obesity, and so on. In addition, we each inherit a cultural inheritance and values as well as the conscious and unconscious beliefs and programming that come down to us through our ethnic and national heritage.[61]

It may be cliché that forgetting or denying history guarantees it will be repeated. However, this concept can be related to the occult understanding that one cannot evolve spiritually until they know who they really are. Learning both the positive and negative aspects of your heritage and ancestry fulfills the concept inherent in the adage "know thyself," which can be very useful.

An example of this is the work of therapists and psychologists engaged in family constellation work. This counseling approach is designed to address cognitive or relational errors that are systemic in nature and contribute to patterns in families that repeat generationally. These might include family of origin issues, parent-child relationship difficulties, intimate relationship challenges, or difficulties with finances. Family constellation work is helpful for people who want to address negative or harmful patterns. Understanding the patterns inherited by family and community as well as intergenerational thinking habits can help us heal unconscious behaviors tied to the wounds of our family or cultural past. Working spiritually to connect with one's ancestors can aid in this process.

---

61  Ian Tattersall, *The Monkey in the Mirror* (Orlando, FL: Harcourt Press, 2002), 171–180.

# MUNDANE WAYS FOR WORKING WITH ANCESTORS

What are some practices to help you begin working with your ancestors and heal old patterns and wounds? There are mundane practices you may start with. One way is the simple process of learning and preserving cultural heritage in things like family recipes and traditions. Learn and retell stories from your ancestors' culture, learn songs, folk music, and dances. Be sure to cherish your living elders; listen to stories of their childhood and their memories of deceased relatives. If you have children, bring them to spend time with their grandparents and older relatives. For deceased relatives, try to write down their names and life histories, create a family tree, or learn to speak their original language and preserve important cultural traditions. If possible, you may go on a pilgrimage to the lands where your family originated.

Learning ancestral language is a doorway to unlocking the culture of the past, and this can make a difference when trying to get to know who your ancestors were. As my aunt explained to me in Spanish, "La lengua es la idioma," which translates to "The language is the culture." Eldritch, who has a master's degree in applied sociolinguistics, understands how deeply important accessing ancestral wisdom is and how the intentional extinction of language in the colonization process causes the loss of ancestral culture:

> I teach a class called Ancestral Paganism and open with the common quote: "When you learn a new language, you gain a new soul." Well, I also think the opposite is true. In the extinguishing of our family languages where we cannot speak the languages of our ancestors, our great-great-grandparents, we lose a part of our soul. It's so important. Teaching these classes about Ancestral Paganism shows it. I think it's important for me and for everyone to know where they came from for their spiritual healing.

Science allows us now to trace our DNA, which for Americans is especially helpful since many of us have DNA from various people around the world. African Americans in particular, due to colonialism and the slave trade, had their heritage torn from them. A DNA test can help you find out which part of Africa your ancestors came from. If you wish to honor the ancestors of your spiritual lineage, you can visit their shrines or burial grounds. If you wish to honor the ancestors of the land you live on, you can make offerings in nature. In the United States, you may offer tobacco, cornmeal, sweetgrass, or sage smoke, which are traditional offerings to the ancestors of the Indigenous people who were the first to inhabit this land. For yourself, you can go further, researching the prior Indigenous inhabitants of the area you live on, researching local flora and/or fauna, to discover what offerings may be traditional to that culture.

## BENEFITS OF ANCESTRAL VENERATION

The benefits of connection are many! When you are in an active, reciprocal relationship with your ancestors by inviting them into your life and regularly attending to this relationship, your whole life can change. Most of us may have had difficult relatives and may not wish to invite them into relationship with us after they have died. This is a personal decision only you can make. However, working with your ancestors in this way—especially with those you may not have known, and praying for those who may have harmed you, offering forgiveness and prayers for their evolution—can help them as much as it helps you. It is a way to attract good karma and feelings of gratitude from them and to them. You will also get to know yourself better.

Whether or not you believe in the continued spiritual presence of departed relatives, their influence on you and your family will always be with you. By creating intentional relationships, we heal patterns and behaviors going forward to descendants by going backward in time. Regular prayer and attention to ancestor spirits heal negative patterns and unfinished business, allow us to grieve them fully, and create better vibrations for future generations, breaking negative patterns from continuing. This in itself can bring about healthier future generations. These future generations will, when this practice is shared with them, venerate their ancestors in turn, creating a beneficial circle of life, healing the past and creating a healed future for humanity. Ancestor veneration nourishes Mother Earth's cauldron. It helps the evolution of consciousness by bringing light and progress to all beings in the spirit world, who then provide the soil where the new world can take root.

## TENDING THE FLAME
### The Way of Anamanta

Andras Corban-Arthen is the founder and spiritual director of the EarthSpirit Community in Western Massachusetts. Originally from Galiza in Northwestern Spain, Andras follows the Celtic-derived path of Anamanta. He learned the Anamanta practices from teachers he met while in college in the late 1960s and who hailed from a Gaelic-speaking region of the Scottish Highlands. As with many Indigenous survival traditions, their families and way of life had been uprooted by colonialism in Scotland in the mid-nineteenth century. Andras is emphatic that EarthSpirit is pretty much open to anyone who wants to practice—or even just to explore—nature-centered spirituality. Here he speaks about the survival of Indigenous European Pagan traditions and the importance of keeping these ways alive for those today who hunger for Earth-based spiritual practices and ancestral connection:

> I met my teachers seemingly by coincidence through a mutual friend who thought we would have a lot in common. They told me that, in their family, there was a long list of people who had been healers, who had been seers, who could make things happen—who had spiritual or psychic gifts, as people might say nowadays. They had knowledge of herbs, they had knowledge of all kinds of things of that sort, and some of their ancestors had been accused of witchcraft back in the day. They didn't really call themselves witches, but what they were called has been usually translated to English as that word, as *witch*. I met them because I was looking for some sort of spiritual path and didn't know what I was looking for, but once I met them, the moment I met them, it was like that was it; I just knew I had something very strong in common with these people.
>
> It took me a while to fully get what these teachings were really about; in fact, it wasn't until they had left, after about five years and I was on my own, that I slowly began to understand the fullness of what it was they had taught me, and where it came from, and the context of what it was. And it was actually a Native American man from Western New York with whom I'd had some long conversations about our spiritual practices who unexpectedly helped me understand it. We both came to the realization that we had a lot in common, except for the fact that we were coming from two very different cultural contexts. He was the first person to say to me, "It seems like what your teachers taught you was a Native practice, Native in the same sense that my practices are, only Native to Scotland."
>
> I hadn't really put it context up to that point, and then it struck me that there had to have been Indigenous peoples in Europe. Nobody at all ever talked about them, but it made sense that there had to have been; if so, who were they, and

what were they like? If my teachers were part of the remnants of a European Indigenous cultural or spiritual tradition, were there more? Were there others, other things that survived substantially enough, as was obviously the case in their family? Since the mid-1970s, I have done a lot of work in an effort to answer that question, traveling to Europe and trying to find if there were any other similar survivals—initially in Scotland, and then going from there to other parts of Europe.

I found that, even to this day, there are remnants of these traditions, of these cultures and practices that can be found in some out-of-the-way places, such as remote farming communities, isolated fishing villages, or up in the mountains: places where people still speak the old languages, in most cases. A lot of the ones I've found are people who keep their practices alive under a very thin veneer of Christianity, very consciously and deliberately. To be sure, throughout Europe, you can find a lot of syncretism, a lot of blending of Christian and old traditional practices—that's everywhere. But in some other places, there are people who often hold a great deal of animosity toward Christianity and are hanging on to their traditional practices by carefully living a double life, and they have done it for so long that it's become second nature to them. And it's very easy for them to slide back and forth, depending on what they are doing and who they are talking to.

In this tradition, the teachers had a concept of two kinds of human ancestors: the little ancestors, small ancestors, first. Those were the ones most recent to you: parents, grandparents, great-grandparents, and so on—people who were most immediate in bringing you to life, people whose names you knew, and maybe some of their stories, and what they were about. But beyond a certain point, once you go further back, most of our ancestors are anonymous.

They also had a concept of the so-called big ancestors. These were the really old early forebears, the tribal ancestors who gave birth to your people, to your culture, to your history. These would be the beings who, in other settings, would perhaps be called gods. In my teachers' tradition, they were seen not as deities, but as ancestors—the earliest human beings who gave birth to the rest of those we are descended from; figures such as Brìghid or Lugh, for example, and they had a particular Gaelic term for such beings. They didn't see them as being gods in the sense of supernatural, superhuman beings with all these amazing powers and possibly immortality, but they saw them as human beings who had really stood out for important reasons in their time—their valor, perhaps, or their beauty, their sense of justice, their wisdom, or other skills. And once they left this world, their names, stories, and exploits were told and retold by subsequent generations, and their status and renown grew, which is why they thought of them as big.

So, those are some of the ways my teachers related to their ancestors, all the while keeping in mind that some of our ancestors most likely were people we wouldn't want to honor. In some cases, they might have been downright evil people, but they are still our ancestors, and we need to acknowledge them, though we don't necessarily need to be proud of them, much less emulate them.

I think that for a lot of modern people of European descent, that is a factor that has to be strongly considered in the work we do with ancestors. We all most likely have, in our past, Christian ancestors who engaged in the genocide of our Pagan ancestors and almost completely wiped them out. Some of them were people who came here and committed all kinds of atrocities against the Indigenous peoples of this land, as well as Indigenous peoples elsewhere. Some of those ancestors who committed massacres, who were slave owners, slave traders—what do we do with people like that? The reality is that there isn't much we can do about them. We can't undo what they did, because it's done. And we can't take responsibility for it because we didn't do it, and we may not even know who they were. But we can take responsibility to work to change the effects of what they did, in modern times, as a way of making some kind of contribution toward healing those wounds.

Spirituality is very much related to death because spirituality is the process of engaging the mystery at the core of our existence, and death is the ultimate manifestation of that mystery. But we don't dwell too much on that mystery, because to do so scares us. This is why so many religions are premised on what happens after death: they provide a very convenient, reassuring explanation to shield us from the existential fear of the unknown. So, people latch on to the explanation and ignore the mystery that engendered it.

As an animist Pagan, that mystery *is* my religion—more specifically, how that mystery manifests throughout the natural world. To me, the awareness of death is not something to be avoided or repressed; it is, rather, something I embrace along with the fear, the uncertainty, and the powerlessness it provokes, and that has been part of my spiritual practice on a daily basis for over half a century. Because, unless we embrace the mystery of death, we cannot fully experience the wonder of life. So, maintaining that awareness of death—and particularly that death is always with us, that it can come when we least expect it—can have a profound effect on our awareness of life, and on what really matters.

To maintain a constant awareness of death—and, in the process, to explore the fullness of our existence and to make whatever changes we need to make in our lives as a result of that exploration—can be very difficult; it can be frightening, it can make us feel very uncomfortable. But that discomfort is important, and I would go so far as to say that if your spiritual path does not cause you some level of discomfort, then it's probably not taking you deep enough. That discomfort shows us our fears, and our fears show us the places where the flow of our souls gets stuck. We can use that discomfort as a tool to crack ourselves open to see what's really there.

# ❋ A PRACTICE ❋
## Creating a Boveda

All people have ancestors, some whom we knew and loved, some who may have been challenging, and others whom we did not know. Creating a boveda is an ancestral practice that can be very effective for connecting to your ancestors and is open to all. It comes from Espiritismo, a syncretism of the Spiritist tradition, Roman Catholic prayers, and Indigenous and African practices. Espiritismo is commonly practiced in Latin American culture. Spiritism is a branch of a Spiritualism popular in countries such as Cuba, Brazil, and Puerto Rico.

### Tools

You will need a table, a white tablecloth, and three to eight clear glasses and white candles. Depending on your own background, you may wish to have a copy of Allan Kardec's *Collection of Selected Prayers* (see recommended readings at the end of this book). Or, you may create your own prayers that are more appropriate to your personal beliefs.

The table is used to create a shrine to honor your dead by making a sacred space that becomes a doorway and link to your family of spirits. Spiritists understand that ancestors are those who are most helpful to connect with for help from the spirit world, as they continue their love and care for us from beyond. We are their living link to this world; inspiring us toward personal and family healing helps them evolve by seeing their mistakes corrected.

**Begin**

Decorate the table with the white cloth, white candles, and glasses of water. You may add flowers, fragrance, or sacred objects. Before adding water to the glasses, it is recommended to clean the glasses with cigar smoke by blowing the smoke directly into them. Tobacco is both an offering and a purifying smoke. Then fill the glasses with water. The element of water becomes the conduit for the spiritual forces to take form. Allow your intuition to guide you as to how many glasses you place on your altar; eight is traditional, with a ninth glass placed in the center as an offering to the Creator.

When you have cleaned your glasses and assembled the table, sit before the altar and invite in the highest emanation of the Divine and your ancestors. Welcome them to this space that is dedicated to them. You may play them soft or uplifting music they love, offer prayers or psalms, poetry, or songs. You can also speak from your heart about your life, your needs, your family, your hopes and desires, asking them to help you. If you have ancestors you wish to connect with, pray for their individual spirits by name and ask that they have light, love, healing, and spiritual progress in the spirit world. Then release and let go.

After this, allow yourself time in silence and meditation to listen for any messages in the form of thoughts, mental images, or feelings from your loved ones. It is my experience that messages will often feel like strong inclinations or thoughts that seem to arise out of nowhere, but are very pressing. When you are complete, thank your spirits for coming with words of gratitude and love and blow out the candles.

The main point about a boveda is that it should be attended to regularly, so your family spirits know you will be meeting with them on a regular basis. It is very important to keep the space clean and fresh, changing the water in the glasses and not allowing it to get stagnant. By praying here on a schedule, the ancestors have a point of meeting in both time and space and are made welcome into the life of your family.

A good rule of thumb is to pray and meditate at your shrine at least once a week or at the very least monthly. Regularly attend to your boveda with prayers for your departed loved ones, for your family, and for whatever needs come to your heart. Use this as a place of meditation and communication.

Over time and regular practice, you will establish a psychic link with your loved ones and will enjoy open intuitive communication with them, and a change in your life reflecting this connection will become apparent. Even if you, as most people do, had difficult ancestors, by praying for them and their spiritual evolution, the dead will welcome this exchange as it allows them to correct their own mistakes and assist us as we address negative ancestral patterns forward in time through us and for our children and descendants. It is believed that for even the most difficult ancestors, their perspective changes when they arrive on the other side, which creates a space for healing.

# THE ELEMENTS AND SPIRIT

When we reach back with reverence and curiosity to ancient concepts, both exoteric and esoteric, we arrive at the sacred circle. This circle represents the building blocks of the universe itself. It is formed by the four directions and the four primary elements of earth, air, fire, and water, and to these, we may add the fifth, which is ether, or Spirit.

Science tells us that the composition of our bodies, our planet, and everything in the universe is made up of stardust, the residue of the big bang of creation, the same building blocks of chemicals and matter that are distributed throughout the universe, creating all forms of matter. Esoteric wisdom stories from the world's collective consciousness say this universe is really a thought in the mind of the Divine, the language and expression of these thoughts being mathematics and probability. Modern physics says all is energy and that matter is just a different resonance of energy vibration. While scientists have provided us with a chemical table of elements, the ancients grouped these into five basic elements, and this knowledge was known and shared by civilizations as far apart in time and space as Europe and the people of the Americas.

# OCCULT LORE

The occult lore preserved from ancient traditions of the past links us to a form of knowing that reverberates with meaning and purpose in our lives on multiple levels of consciousness, from nurturing our physical well-being to how we relate to these traditions on the mental, spiritual, and otherworldly planes. To the esoteric preservers of this mystical knowledge, the elements are the forces that sustain the world. Alchemists represented these elements in symbols, and each of them signified vibrations that make up all material things, including the human body and the rest of creation.[62] By reclaiming this elemental wisdom from these esoteric and holistic systems, one can be grounded in nature herself.

In Eastern traditional concepts, vital energy is the most fundamental force. Called *qi* in Chinese and *prana* in Sanskrit, its cognate can be found elsewhere in the world. It is similar to the concept of ashé in the African Yoruba culture and found in all Orisha-based traditions. The Yoruba believe that all human beings are born with this vital force of energy that, when used, allows us to manifest change in our life and interact with spirits and the forces of nature. For Yoruba-based systems, the natural forces are expressed as the Orishas. An initiated priest or priestess learns how to make offerings and devotions or ebbo in order to utilize this force for healing and change. In the

---

62  Fontana, *The Secret Language of Symbols*, 180–191.

religion, an initiate aspires to a closer relationship with their guiding Orisha to align themselves to their personal highest destiny.[63]

According to Chinese Taoist wisdom, energy and matter are two sides of the whole, complementing one another, represented by the yin-yang symbol. Yin is receptive feminine and dark matter, and Yang, the positive pole of activity and light. The primary aspect of these energies together is constant change, moving and transforming; as physics confirms, energy can never be destroyed, it can only transmute itself.[64] To the Taoist, from the wholeness of yin-yang, this energy finds further expression in energies within the five elements of water, wood, air, metal, and earth.[65]

# THE ELEMENTS

Let's examine some basic concepts for each of the elements from the esoteric tradition and recognize how these are all encapsulated in our bodies and ourselves.

## Air

The air element on the collective level is the sacred air we breathe, that gives all sentient beings on this planet life. Humans cannot live without air, and we are in a symbiotic relationship with the plant kingdom, especially trees, which receive our exhaled carbon dioxide and return it to us as oxygen. Breath practices to stimulate the health of our prana are instrumental to the ancient science of Yoga and to the Buddhist path of meditation and enlightenment. For Eastern practitioners, prana is carried through the air. Focusing on the breath, meditating on its centering qualities, is the key to mindfulness practices.

---

63  Miguel De La Torre, *Santeria* (Grand Rapids, MI: Eerdmans Publishing, 2004), 112–118.

64  Daniel Reid, *The Complete Book of Chinese Health and Healing* (Boston: Shambhala Publishers, 1994), 24–28.

65  Reid, *The Complete Book of Chinese Health and Healing*, 49–53.

In the occult Western tradition, air was personified in Pagan times by air deities. Even into medieval Europe, the four winds were known by Pagan names: Boreas, the North Wind; Eurus, of the East; Notus, from the South; and Zephrys, god of the Western Wind.

In occult lore, air represents the mind, thought, ideas, communication, and all beings that fly, including the bird totems. Birds' ability to fly to other realms is a power that was sought and cherished by shamans. Seafaring cultures like the Greeks would pray to the beings that controlled the winds, which enabled them to colonize and trade with distant lands. For Germanic peoples, it was Njord who favored sailors. Air is changeable and represents the winds of change in our lives.[66]

## Water

The element of water on our Earth is probably the most important element as far as creating the conditions for life on this planet. All beings share bodies of water and water-filled bodies. During the Standing Rock political protest of the Dakota Access Pipeline in the United States between 2016 and 2017, the rallying cry of those who came together to protest was "Water Is Life." They held the ground for months because they were moved to protect the waters of the areas, as they believed the pipeline would be a grave threat to the land, the waters, and the local way of life. This rallying cry rang true for many.

The element of water is feminine and represented around the world by female goddesses and guardians: "Before birth, every child develops in its mother's womb before taking its first breath of air."[67]

In Africa and in the African world, people recognized the essential and sacred nature of water by honoring and celebrating feminine water spirits, incarnations that are ancient and mysterious. Some examples are Olokun, the goddess of the ocean depths; Mami Wati,

66  Fontana, *The Secret Language of Symbols*, 18–183.

67  Henry John Drewal, *Mami Wata* (Los Angeles: Fowler Museum, 2008), 23.

a water spirit venerated in West, Central, and Southern Africa; the river goddess Oshun from Western Africa; and also Yemaya, who represents the fertile sea for the Diasporic community. All these represent aspects of water. African water spirits are often personified in the form of a mermaid, an image that moved from Africa around the world.[68] In the Diaspora, these forms are venerated in Lukumi and other Orisha-based traditions as well as in Vodou and the 21 Divisions in the icons of Santa Marta Dominadora in the 21 Divisions, and La Sirene in Vodou.

In Chinese poetry, goddess archetypes appear as dragon ladies and rain maidens who represent the forces of mist and water, rainbows and mountains.[69] In Australia, the Aboriginal people view the goddess as a rainbow serpent, similar to how African Indigenous people view her. She lives in the dreamtime and created the entire universe in her dreams. This serpent, Julungull, is associated with fertility, rain, water, initiation, and rebirth.

To the ancient Greeks, Aphrodite was a sea-born goddess, engaged in sexuality and fertility, and was depicted emerging from a shell on the waters. For Celts, the goddess as Mother of the Waters gave her name to Don and many rivers, which were important to early settlements such as the Danube in Central Europe. Even within Christianity we see echoes of her in the image of the Virgin Mary, who appears in Catholic iconography riding on a seashell. The symbol of water as Divine Feminine, with water, shell, and moon, preserves an ancient aspect of the Divine Creatrix.

To the Western occultist, the water element represents the flowing energy of our emotions and our subconscious mind. To the Taoist, water is often used as a symbol of the Tao itself, the nature of the

---

68  Drewal, *Mami Wata*, 28.
69  Schafer, *The Divine Woman*, 7–10.

force of life, which is ever flowing and on which we should model our behavior. Water is creative, renewing, fluid, and sensual. It can be dramatic and bring destruction and storms, but it can also bring purification, calm, peace, and healing. Meditating with water can help us return to inner balance and equilibrium and reclaim our fertile, creative flow.

## Fire

Mastering the element of fire is one of the triumphs of humanity's evolution. Humans alone among Earth's creatures were able to tame this natural force to use. Its warmth keeps us alive in cold climates, keeps predators away in the dark, and cooks our food. This adaptation by our most distant ancestors in Africa was presumably the foothold to what set us apart as a species.

Fire is the element that best symbolizes the cosmic creation, that flame of power that embodies the symbol of light. Fire is destructive and purifying. Fire represents will, desire, passion, and the fire of spiritual enlightenment. Fire is the home of the solar deities: Ra of the Egyptians, Sol Invictus to the Romans, Lugh to the ancient Celts, Inti to the New World Incas, and countless more. But not all fire deities were gods; some were goddesses, like the Celtic Brigit, the divine goddess of fire, smithcraft, and poetry, who was Christianized, her lore and symbology preserved in the myths of St. Brigid. In pre-Christian European folklore, the beings known as dwarves used fire beneath the Earth to craft legendary swords and weapons of great magick and potency.

By meditating with fire, we connect to the inner flame. Yogic tradition calls on this power in the pranic practice known as the Breath of Fire, connected to the god of fire, Agni. In this practice, the breath heats and energizes the body and helps activate the Kundalini enlightenment energy at the base of our spine. To occultists, meditating on the esoteric purple flame is a key toward spiritual ascendency and mastery. To the alchemist, this Violet Flame of St. Germain represents the goal of alchemy, which is more than just transmuting metal into gold, but on the inner planes represents the transmutation of the human being into a more refined, purified being of enlightened consciousness.[70]

## Earth

The earth element is the element of our Mother Planet. Earth is *terra firma*—matter and manifestation. We share the living Earth with the trees and plants, which provide us with our nutritional needs, our homes, our medicine, and the animal and insect kingdoms. Earth can also be active, as in the power and majesty of volcanoes, and in the power released in the regeneration of spring.[71]

Earth energy as an element represents this divine force: fertility, abundance, manifestation, matter, prosperity, all things that grow. One can explore earth energy by exploring the caves and caverns of ourselves and our souls. The womb is dark, but from here souls emerge reborn. Meditating with earth energy is a contemplation of solidity. Caring for earth nature inside of ourselves provides a focus on taking care of one's body, the temple, as Jesus stated. Through the earth element, we recognize our mortality. Earth energy is the form of our bodies, bodies that will someday return to her as compost.

In folklore and myth, earth elementals are represented by gnomes, elemental beings who tend to the life of the stones, crystals, and Tellurian forces that keep the Earth in balance. They are protectors of the Earth's treasures.[72] Mountains are places where we can connect with the part of Earth that touches the heavens, which reaches out to

---

70  Fontana, *The Secret Language of Symbols*, 256–254.

71  Fontana, *The Secret Language of Symbols*, 190–191.

72  Fontana, *The Secret Language of Symbols*, 181.

the cosmos. Obatala is the Orisha who represents this energy, and he is said to be the father of all the Orishas. Climbing the mountains of Earth can inspire connection to the cosmos.

## Spirit

Spirit is the life force of the universe. This force was identified and cultivated by many ancient peoples. In the over-five-thousand-year tradition of Taoism, the three treasures are essence (jing), energy (chee), and spirit (shen).[73] To the Taoist, balancing these and seeking harmony represent the goals of life. This is equally true for those who practice Orisha traditions. A practitioner whose life is out of balance may seek a consultation with a priest or priestess to see how best to have their bodies, minds, and spirits aligned with their soul's purpose and return their aché to positive flow. A Lukumi priest consults the Diloggun, a form of divination with kola nuts or cowrie shells, and may then recommend a prescription that will involve a cleansing bath, a change in diet, behavioral modification, and prohibitions against certain foods or situations, or making an ebbo to Orisha.

In Chinese medicine as well as in the Ayurvedic tradition of ancient India, optimal health and well-being can be cultivated through nourishing one's health to prevent illness rather than fighting it when it has already manifested in the body. Germs, toxins, and negative forces are always out there, but through maintaining healthy lifestyles, a nourishing diet, and balance of the five energies, prevention is achieved.

In nature-based practice, Spirit is manifest in all creation, in all living things—even seemingly inanimate objects like crystals are planetary beings. The indwelling Spirit is connected to the higher-vibrational forces that exist all around us, to each other, and to the Divine Spirit of all.

---

73  Reid, *The Complete Book of Chinese Health and Healing*, 337–339.

# INCORPORATING THE ELEMENTS FOR HEALING

Ultimately, the goal of nature spirituality is to bring ourselves back into balance with these elemental forces within us, the universe, and all sentient beings.

For practitioners, the Earth herself is our temple. Connection to the plants and the animals, as well as to the land, is vital. Nature-based spirituality is rooted in the understanding that separation is an illusion, and the best way for us to awaken from this illusion is to make space for reconnection in our lives to the natural world on a regular basis.

There is no substitute for time spent communing with each of the elements—listening to the wind on a stormy night, feeling snow fall on our face, walking barefoot to recharge, keeping a garden, or caring for the birds in our backyard. These can be mundane but deeply effective methods to make nature communion part of our daily life and practice. When we do so on a regular basis, a shift in perception and consciousness can occur. Doing so can create a more embodied and grounded existence and help us find fulfillment and purpose for ourselves in this lifetime, in service to the Higher Self and to the Earth.

## TENDING THE FLAME
### Stone Circle Wicca

Wicca is a modern religion that is a big part of the twenty-first-century revival of European Neo-Paganism. Eldritch is a Third Degree priestx of the Tradition of Stone Circle Wicca, which is based in the mid-Atlantic region of the United States. Stone Circle Wicca embraces an inclusive expression of deity that includes One/Many, God/Goddess,

All/Neither, and is very inclusive. Wiccans believe this idea is reflected both in humanity and throughout sentient creation. Members who formally initiate are recognized by three terms: priest, priestess, and priestx, to reflect nonbinary gender inclusion. Eldritch spoke with me about Stone Circle Wicca and how a central practice of Wicca is working with elemental forces:

> I feel that every time we Cast a Circle, which I think of as casting a sphere, it's like the grand bubble of Glinda the Good Witch. We build a protective sphere, but we aren't separate from the whole. We take time to separate ourselves out, but we never leave the Circle or the shield up. We return to the whole of humanity, the whole of the Earth. It's natural for Wiccans to think about the Earth, the Air, the Fire, the Water, and to realize that they are part of something greater than themselves. We make sure that we live with respect and take responsibility for caring for the planet.
>
> I see Wicca as an intuitive religion. When we listen to our inner voice, we read the signs, we get information that directly reflects the Divine. We also pay attention to what is going on behind, beside, above, below us in order to live holistically and to be able to orient ourselves. I think about it as an internal gyroscope guidance system that kind of oscillates inside of us and steers us, compels us. Now, in an intuitive religion, you also have to be extra responsible, because you can also make stuff up. You have to be careful with the conversations you are having in your head and balance them out. You are following an intuitive religion with direct revelation and responsibility.
>
> In our version of Wiccan cosmology, we think about the North, the South, the East, and the West, and how we find balance. We can find reminders for balance in the elements.

Considering the East, I consider: Am I breathing enough? South: Do I have the passion and drive I need? West: Am I crying enough, or maybe too much? Am I experiencing all my emotions? People always think about the West as crying and water flowing, but there is a whole range of emotions we can experience. And in the North: Do I need to be grounded in the Earth? Do I need to be still and consider the bones of my ancestors?

I wrote a song honoring the elements:

*The blowing of the wind, the breaking of the dawn, inspires creativity.*

*Sun's heat! Flames leap! Intense! Attention to intention!*

*Welling up inside are tides that provide a knowing flowing deep inside.*

*Stones of Earth! Bones of Birth! Wisdom worth! All without within!*

We find balance in a Wiccan cosmology by understanding this and by considering the directions of above and below. These six directions help you scan your energy physically, emotionally, and spiritually. We also visualize a World Tree, where our body is the trunk rooted and drawing up from the Earth and our branches are in the sky drawing down the stars. All of that flow needs to be in balance, to be able to keep your life in balance. In these exercises, you get lots of clues just by sitting and asking, where do I have tension? What's that about? Paying attention to the different layers of ourselves, different layers of energy. In my view, this Wiccan cosmology is like having a gyroscope as a guidance system in your soul.

# ✪ A PRACTICE ✪
## Wiccan Meditation with the
## Directions and Elements

This is a gratitude meditation we practice at Soul Blossom Wiccan Circle. Our tradition is an eclectic form of Wicca, which I teach, that utilizes shamanic practices and techniques, which allow us to connect with nature and spirit guides. You may wish to record this in advance and play it back for yourself as you perform the meditation.

### Tools

A comfortable space to meditate in (a chair or on a bed). A candle and a light source. Your journal. A table that serves as an altar, dedicated with items that represent the four elements and Spirit. Air can be represented by incense or a feather; water, by a glass of water; earth, by a crystal or a bowl of salt; fire, by a candle; spirit can be your own choosing.

### Begin

Take a moment to center yourself before your altar so you will not be disturbed. If you are able, sit comfortably on the floor or in a chair. Light the candle and incense. Allow yourself some deep breaths to center yourself and ground your energy down into the Earth, connecting with Mother Earth, and then out through the top of your head into the sky, connecting with Great Spirit, God, or Father Sky—whichever works for you.

After some deep breathing, imagine yourself seated in the center of a bright orb of light that surrounds your body tightly, and the orb is filled with stars as you yourself are filled with a universe of stars. When this image is clear, imagine the circle is surrounding you snugly and burning away any attachments, worries, and stress, and you are in a very safe and holy balance of earth, sky, and stars.

Now let the circle's glow move slightly away from your body. As you do this, the circle expands so that it surrounds you about three feet away, and it is glowing and strong.

Begin to connect with the direction of the east. In the east, allow your mind to associate with the element of air—wind, thoughts, ideas, words, expressions. Also connect to the spirits and animals that inhabit the air. Now notice one of them comes forward. Who is your eastern animal spirit? Do not judge or question who comes forth. But in your mind's eye, see this animal clearly. Think about this animal: What does it eat? How does it live? What quality does it wish to share with you? What gift does it have to share with you in your journeys, in your life, and in your work? Name this gift and claim it as your own. Thank this animal spirit.

Return your energy to the center, reconnecting with the darkness and the starlight. When you are centered again, turn your attention to the south and connect with the element of fire. The energy of fire represents the flames, heat, warmth, light, passion, will, desire, and clearing and cleansing energy. Focus on the feeling of fire and then allow yourself to connect with an animal guide from this direction and element. Notice what appears without judgment or second-guessing. Who is your southern animal spirit? In your mind's eye, see this animal clearly. Think about this animal: What does it eat? How does it live? What quality does it wish to share with you? What gift does it have to share with you in your journeys, in your life, and in your work? Name this gift and claim it as your own. Thank this animal spirit.

When you are complete, return your energy to your starry center. When you are ready, turn your attention to the western ward, to the element of water. Allow yourself to hear, touch, smell, and observe this element with all your senses. Beyond the physical aspect of water, water is emotion, subconsciousness, and flow. Pay attention to what animal spirit comes forth from the western waters. See this animal clearly. What does it eat? How does it live? What quality does it wish to share with you? What gift does it have to share with you in your journeys, in your life, and in your work? Name this gift and claim it as your own. Thank this animal spirit.

Return once again to the center, feeling the presence of each animal guardian and the energies of the three directions you have connected with. Now turn to the final direction, north. From this direction, connect with the elementals of earth. Here we connect to four-legged animals and/or to the plant and tree beings and to crystals and stones. In this direction, see who or what being appears. Who is your northern animal spirit? Do not judge or question who comes forth. Clearly note all you can about the animal or being. Think about its presence. What does it eat? How does it live? What quality does it wish to share with you? What gift does it have to share with you in your journeys, in your life, and in your work? Name this gift and claim it as your own. Thank this animal spirit.

Now return to the center, to the stars, and feel yourself surrounded by the power of your animal spirits, the directions, the elements, and your connection to Mother Earth and Father Sky. Embrace this sense of unified consciousness, of Oneness with the universe, and take note of any other sensations or wisdom that comes especially to you. From this space, allow yourself to feel deep gratitude and thanksgiving for all. When you are ready, return to ordinary consciousness. You may make offerings to the animal spirits that came forward to strengthen those connections. These may include what is suggested in visionary journeys or the type of food they would prefer in nature. Water is also a standard libation.

Return to your body and blow out the candle. Be sure to write down the visions and messages you received from your journey. This meditation can be repeated as needed whenever you wish to reconnect with each of the elements and directions.

# DIVINATION, REVELATION, AND SPIRIT GUIDANCE

An important aspect of many nature traditions is the practice of communication with spirits, elementals, and other dimensions. Among Indigenous cultures, the role of the diviner or shaman utilizes non-rational states of consciousness by developing methods and technology that harness and connect them to alternate states of consciousness and allow astral projection into alternate realities. Through internal vision, nature-based practitioners access energy and wisdom from the unseen world for healing of community members, guidance for leaders, prophecy, revelation, and transcending the earthly realm. Various forms of divination and spirit guidance influence and inform modern nature-based practices.

# SPIRITUALISM

Spiritism is a form of Spiritualism popular in Latin American countries that began in the nineteenth century in Europe, and it is based on the study of *The Spirit's Book*, published in 1857 by Allan Kardec, the pseudonym of the French educator Hippolyte Léon Denizard Rivail.[74] His work took place during the height of the Spiritualism explosion among European elites who began exploring communication with spirits through the use of séance and mediums who entered trance to channel messages from the dead.

In the United States in the 1840s, the Fox sisters, Margaretta and Kate Fox of Rochester, New York, began hearing tapping sounds in their home. They figured out how to communicate with the entities through a series of knocks and raps, which created a social sensation. Soon, many intellectuals and middle- and upper-class Europeans began to meet and hold séance circles to communicate with spirits. Allan Kardec wished to investigate this phenomenon and began to collect information received from numerous séance groups after asking questions on the nature of the universe, God, and reality and questions of faith, progress, and technology. He codified his findings into what became the foundational work of Spiritism, *The Spirit's Book*.[75] Kardec renamed Spiritualism, Spiritism, formalized it, and suggested that the entity Jesus was a master teacher and guide. As with Spiritualism, Spiritism affirmed the truth of reincarnation, as evidenced by continued conversations through mediums, and identified spiritual evolution as a goal of our earthly existence. The purpose of incarnation is to evolve from the lessons we learn from multiple lifetimes. Spiritists believe the universe is populated with other planets and realms where spiritual beings evolve further, eventually becoming one with the Godhead.

---

74  Allan Kardec, *The Spirit's Book* (Guildford, UK: White Crow Books), 2010.
75  Emma Bragdon, *Spiritism and Mental Health* (Philadelphia, PA: Singing Dragon, 2012), 23–24.

Today, modern Spiritists study Kardec's book and use mediumship and energy healing. They believe practicing Spiritism helps humanity evolve spiritually and morally and heal from illnesses. The philosophy defines existence here as temporary; the nature of our planet is one of evolution, trials, and expiations. As our spirits evolve, we will evolve to planets with higher vibrations. Disembodied spirits, who have not attained an enlightened state of consciousness and who are trapped between planes, can affect the living negatively, while highly evolved spirits can affect us positively through inspiring us to improve our health and moral nature. In doing so, they themselves evolve further.

In Brazil and other Latin American countries, Spiritism has influenced a social movement of charity and integrative healthcare institutions that treat mental and physical illness with a worldview that accepts both a spiritual and Western medical approach.[76] Spiritist centers throughout Brazil offer childcare, education, and assistance to the poor. Charity and the gift of service are seen as the best way for Spiritists to help ourselves achieve enlightenment and clear negative karma and attachments.

While Spiritism is not a nature tradition per se, many who practice Afro-Caribbean traditions, like the Lukumi religion, incorporate Spiritism into their worldview. Spiritism claims the human soul is immortal and reincarnation factors into why suffering and disease affect us here on Earth. Trained mediums utilize healing passes in mediumship circles, and believers usually believe this type of healing complements Western medicine and therapy; they are not incompatible. However, Spiritists do not believe treatment of the mind, brain, and spirit are all the same, thus treatment through Western medicine without addressing the spiritual component can prove ineffective.

In Latin American Kardecian Spiritism, the main activity is studying the messages received to help ourselves evolve morally. After the

---

76 Bragdon, *Spiritism and Mental Health*, 24–25.

study, mediums who have been selected because of their development and moral commitment will give specialized passes of energy to those in attendance and share energized water. Kardecian Spiritism does not rely on ritual, ceremony, icons, or religious symbols and saints, as they believe these are unnecessary for moral development. The major objective is to recognize the work we are meant to do while we are alive, so that we may be received and prepared for our reentry into the spirit world and grow as a soul.

At American Spiritualism centers, such as the community at Lily Dale, New York, which has been in existence since the nineteenth century, the central practice is spirit communication. Spiritualist services may include prayers, hymns, energy healing, and mediums who are able to deliver messages to the congregation from relatives and loved ones on the other side. This brings comfort to the living and assurance that life continues after we die. Modern Spiritualists have incorporated many of the traditions and practices of nature-based beliefs—such as working with energy, elementals, and nature spirits—and offer classes and workshops on these topics.

## AFRICAN DIASPORIC TRADITIONS

In the African Diaspora, non-Western healing methods are embedded in the practices of African descendants in religions such as Vodou, the 21 Divisions, Candomble, and Lukumi. Ecstatic states and trance are achieved through drumming, song, and sacred dances at gatherings known as *fêtes*, *tambors*, and *bembes*, and at ritual feasts dedicated to celebrations of one's guardian Loa or Orisha, or initiation rites of new priests and priestesses.

Through the heartbeat of the drum, practitioners enter into trance possession, where the guardian spirit of the Orisha they are crowned with may inhabit their bodies. Thus entranced, the worshippers provide counsel, healing, make predictions, and offer admonitions and advice to those in attendance. The Orisha itself may enter more than one initiate, and the energy of these moments and the transformative effect on the celebrants is an electrifying experience. A similar experience takes place in celebrations for the Loa in Vodou and the 21 Divisions when practitioners are mounted as divine horses by the Loa.

This concept of possession was discussed with Lukumi priestess Glow Okandekun in her interview:

> I think that every time our Orisha get close to us, every time a spirit gets close to us, we call that *arrecostar*—it's not a full manifestation. *Arrecostar* means "to lean on you," and I believe that's a valid form of possession. Sometimes you might be dancing at a drumming, or you are sitting in a *misa*, and all of a sudden you feel a certain way, or you are dancing and drumming and this energy takes over you, and you don't know what happened. You feel it, and you are wondering, why am I dancing this way? You may think you have to stop. But when you try to stop, you continue, so to me that is a very valid form of possession because that's the spirituality of that Orisha who drew close to you, touched your spirituality, and created this new experience for you to feel the warmth of that Orisha, still conscious. I come from elders who used to say, "They touched you." A lot of people might negate that as a valid form of possession, but through my years and through all I have learned and experienced, I now see it as very valid. The Orisha or the spirit doesn't have to fully possess your body.

For practitioners, the experience of possession can be intimidating and initially frightening. Glow explained her own journey with it:

> When I was younger, I didn't like the whole possession experience. I made Ocha, and I used to get angry with the possession type of thing. I don't like to be out of control. I wore white for my first ten years in Ocha, pure white, because I made a pact with Obatala. I did not like what happened to me in my Kariocha, and I made a pact in Ita, that he would leave me alone. "Please don't dance in my head!" I was thinking I was really smart when I agreed, "I will wear white

for ten years if you leave my head alone for twenty years," because never in my mind at that time did I think other than, "Oh, twenty years is forever!" So, I said that, and the Oriate said, "Are you crazy? You are going to do that kind of pact?" They asked Obatala, and they kept looking at me: "You are going to try to make a pact?" My Padrino knew I was very strongheaded and he entertained me, and so it took ten years to leave me alone for twenty years.

And it did. I would go to drummings, and I didn't feel one chill, one nothing, and I had a good time, because I love to dance! But when I turned twenty-one years old in Ocha, I went to a drumming in New York for a little Korean girl. She was to be crowned to Obatala, she had issues with her bones, the disease where her bones would break. This was about thirteen or fourteen years ago. I was just twenty-one years old in Ocha now and it happened again, and I was like, "Wow, Obatala can count!"

From there, I still don't like it. I do enjoy when people get possessed, and I will transmit messages, but I know I have no more choice anymore. So now with years of experience, I have learned how to do things, maybe tend to my godchildren, but now I know it's going to happen. I believe, and I tell my godchildren, this: when we make Ocha, we kind of sign our lives away to them. We surrender, because that's what we serve. We serve them, and they can do with us what they will, but I believe they have the best interest for us involved.

## Specialized Priests

Within Yoruba culture, the system of Ifa includes the consultation of a divine oracle through priests known as *Babalawos* who serve the Orisha of divination, Orula. The title *Babalawo* means "Father of the Mysteries," and these priests receive years of specialized training, learning how to read the *ikuele*, or divining chains, or a person's destiny through the manipulation of a system of sixteen kola nuts. From the patterns that fall, they will be able to interpret specific stories of the Orishas that are used as guiding parables called *patakis*. The patakis describe instructional tales of the Orisha. Their lessons are applied to our lives in specific ways through these divine consultations.

A Babalawo is required to memorize all the possibilities of the patterns and the related patakis. A Babalawo will consider the entirety of a person when consulting the oracle, and in Yoruba cosmology, that consists of the physical aspect, or *ara*, the spiritual aspect, or *emi*, and the personalized soul or head, the *ori*. The Yoruba believe in reincarnation, most likely the spirit of an ancestor, and they believe a person has chosen this family, place of origin, and destiny in order to best work out their own personal soul's progress. In consulting with a Babalawo, the consultation is intended to bring the client back into alignment with their individual destiny. When we incarnate on Earth, it is easy to be distracted by trials and tribulations or suffer from bad decisions. It is vital, therefore, to take heed of the prohibitions and recommendations given during consultations.

Babalawos have lineages both in Africa and in the New World, and while they are an integral part of the Lukumi tradition, they are not required for all ceremonies. In my lineage, I was told Ifa and Lukumi are two rooms in the same house. I was brought for a consultation and ceremony with an Ifa house of Babalawos who determined my guiding Orisha was Obatala before I was crowned. After that, initiates receive divine guidance from experienced Oriates, who are gifted readers of the Dillogun, the consecrated cowrie shells. These are also cast and read. How they fall determines either a positive aspect, or *ire*, or a negative aspect, or *osogbo*. The patterns also relate to the patakis of the Orisha. Important guidelines and taboos that are specific to a person and the reading will be recommended. They should be followed.

Finally, an Olosha, or Lukumi priest who has received initiation, can do a reading with Obi, or coconut shells. One pataki teaches that Obi, the coconut, was actually once an Orisha. He had wealth, beauty, fine clothing, and fine speech. He had glistening white clothing and became very proud, and this offended Oldumare himself, as he elevated himself as high as the highest Orisha, over his subjects who needed his help. His punishment was determined then that he would become a humble coconut, through which, while he no longer speaks flowery language, he must provide advice, mostly in the form of answering yes-or-no questions, to everyone who consults him. In all cases, Babalawos, Oriates, and Olorishas (Oloshas) require training and practice developing their psychic gifts and aché. It isn't enough to memorize how to cast these oracles; a commitment to training and ceremony is invested in to get it right.

## Espiritismo

A misa, or Spiritualist Mass, is the central practice of those who practice Espiritismo. In Espiritismo, this practice is not something taken lightly; it is an exercise in moral development. Its purpose is to develop mediumship skills and elevate consciousness to connect with the Divine, ancestors, and guides for communication and spiritual elevation for them and for the participants. It is believed these skills can be developed through practice.

At a misa, the room is prepared with a circle of chairs, and a simple altar is set and draped in white. Participants wear white, as the energy of white is attractive for purification and elevated spiritual consciousness. On the table are usually white candles, a vase, flowers, and a bowl of water. Optional items are cigars, scented floral water and perfume, and *cascarilla*, or powdered eggshell.

The leading experienced medium begins by reading prayers, which are a combination of Catholic prayers and Spiritist prayers. The correct order of the prayers is traditional and available in Allan Kardec's *Collection of Selected Prayers*. Attendees enthusiastically join in the prayers as they are able, clearing their minds to enter into a meditative and attentive state. They prepare themselves to be open to the spirit world through guidance and intuitive messages.

While the lead medium guides the misa, offering suggestions to the attendees of the mass, all are welcome to share the impressions they receive. Spirits then make themselves known through the lead medium or others in the circle, whose attendance helps them manifest. Often, the spirits of deceased loved ones will come through with guidance or messages of love or warnings that a person in attendance needs to hear. When someone is prompted by the attending spirits to deliver a message, it is important to give these with a sense of love and care for one another, and to avoid fear-based or doom-laden delivery. Even if the message is a warning, it should be delivered with hope, comfort, and encouragement.

During the session, participants share messages received from Spirit, and some people receive guidance for spiritual cleansing, which is done with the assorted items on the altar. The fragrances, for instance, are believed to help attract benevolent entities; scented floral waters and perfume can clean participants and help generate positive energy and vibrations. Cascarilla, which is powdered eggshell, clears the aura. Rum and water may be drunk by some mediums as they work through their guides.

In Latin American Espiritismo, no hierarchy or initiation ceremonies are required to participate in a misa, or Spiritualist Mass—all are welcome. There are, however, some guidelines. One is that a person come to the mass with good intentions, sober, clean, and with serious intent.

Spirits offer messages that encourage behavioral modification, such as eating healthy, abstaining from drugs and alcohol, and deepening our prayer life. It is believed that the entities that communicate from the other side in this way do so out of love for us and a desire to help. The trade-off for them is spiritual evolution and relationship with us, their loved ones. The most important idea is that a person's demeanor is respectful and conducive to learning and growth. Being healthy in our mind, body, and spirit and abstaining from self-destructive and negative behaviors toward others is considered essential for spiritual evolution. At the end of the misa, the leader closes the ceremony, and all thank the spirits in attendance. It is important to end with prayers for the spirits' elevation and continued protection from the other side.

# NEW AGE CHANNELING

Another example of a modern expression of this type of knowledge and being is the emergence in Western cultures of the phenomenon of New Age channeling. This practice became popularized with the writings and work of Edgar Cayce during the early twentieth century; Cayce was known as the Sleeping Prophet, as he received his guidance during sleep. He may also be the first person to be considered a channel. During his trance states, his guiding entity helped people from a distance by diagnosing illnesses and prescribing natural remedies. Because of this, he is often credited as the father of natural medicine in the West.

Cayce also gave many messages regarding the origins of human life, the mythical land of Atlantis, and the existence of multiple realities and soul incarnations. Today, there are many New Age personalities who claim to receive information for human enlightenment and evolution from interdimensional beings and ancestors from the stars. These beings are known as Pleiadeans, Arcturians, Lemurians, Lyrians, and Syrians, among others, and all have human channels.

Many believers say that their trance channeling began spontaneously or through an accident or other abrupt experience. But like the medieval witch with her familiar spirit, the Indigenous shaman with his spirit guides, the Lukumi practitioner drawing down their head Orisha, the channelers feel the entities who guide them have a consciousness outside of themselves.

# PAGAN PRACTICES

In Neo-Paganism, divination is widespread and takes many personalized forms, including working with tarot cards, watching nature for omens, working with a pendulum, and crystal gazing. Many Heathens become students of the runes.

The runes are a system of divination that comes from the Germanic peoples. Folklore says these are symbols received by Odin himself when he sacrificed himself on the Tree of Knowledge. The symbols known as the Elder Futhark can be used as instruments to learn the will of the Divine in one's life and also to invoke certain elements and energies. It is said that when we consult the runes, we are consulting our inner guide, who is the Higher Self.[77] Learning to read the runes is a self-knowledge tool that can help one make better decisions and gain insight into a situation and the consequences of our actions and decisions.

Many Pagans and New Age practitioners are gifted readers of the tarot. This is a practice that comes out of Medieval Europe. The cards are believed to come from the region now known as Italy during the Middle Ages and are loaded with esoteric symbolism that relates to human archetypes. There are twenty-one major arcana cards that represent these archetypes, and fifty-six minor cards that represent the trials, triumphs, and tribulations encountered in life.

Studying the cards, learning different ways to read them, and allowing for intuitive knowledge when we read for ourselves and others is a commitment in time and a lifelong practice. It should be

---

77  Ralph H. Blum, *The Book of Runes* (New York: St. Martin's Press, 1993), 13.

noted, however, that the cards are intended to provide deeper insight into our life actions and situations. Free will acknowledges that with new insight and information, someone's destiny can always change and transform. In this way, tarot readings are not fortune-telling. They are guidance from the Higher Self, both from ourselves and from the reader. They represent a soul map for the journey of our souls toward enlightenment.

## TENDING THE FLAME
### Mediumship in Espiritismo

Ilan Chester is an elder Lukumi priest from the Northeastern US Ocha community. He is also an initiate and practitioner of the 21 Divisions and Palo Mayombe; his readings are sought out in his community. Here, he speaks about how Espiritismo is a folk tradition passed down in families in Caribbean cultures based on inherent spiritual gifts recognized and nurtured in young people by experienced relatives and elders. He affirms the positive benefits of this nature-based practice:

> In Spiritism, you are born with a gift. It's passed on through family as a traditional set of beliefs. You are following your family tradition. My first encounter with Spiritism was at the age of seven when my great-grandmother, Inez Jimenez, noticed there was some type of gift. She started introducing me to the different energies, how to tap into these energies. It's something I cannot talk openly about because it is something that is passed on through family. The set of beliefs is to follow ancestor practices, how to connect with the energy that's basically, one way or another, within your DNA. So, it's like you awaken these ancestors and, somehow, they begin to

communicate with you. It's a connection between ancestors and yourself, and we tap into different elements of Nature.

Depending on our level of sensitivity, we may go further than our relatives who taught us, because everything has to do with how you tap into energies. Some people have a better ability, and we have different levels. It doesn't mean that they are higher, it just means that certain people are prone to have a different sensitivity on how to communicate the message.

For example, some people have the sense of touch, and they will somehow feel what the other person feels. Some of us connect by the voice; in my case, it's the voice. And for some, they get connected through pictures, through writing. It all depends on how strong that connection can be. One thing I have noticed through my years is that the person needs to be empathic; it's the only way that allows us to feel what the other person is feeling. Some people are more connected to the pain. They feel it and can feel every part of that person's body.

Espiritismo has helped me in the sense that I have evolved as a person. A person is guided to make changes that help them develop unique talents and see life differently. You become an advisor to people, you learn through helping others, and at the same time you are helping yourself. You have a better understanding about life, not just the physical life that we see around us out there, but more the spiritual life that we feel. It's an expanded concept of yourself as a being beyond what's on this planet. When we grow, we teach others, and the job of the teacher begins when we understand ourselves. If you don't understand yourself, there is no way you can teach others the path to enlightenment. What I have seen in others is once they can tap into themselves and understand who they are, it begins. Most of the problem right now in humankind is most people don't even know who they are.

It's a profound disconnection. Once you disconnect yourself, you don't know who you are, then there is a total disconnection. People who live this way aren't connected to themselves or to Nature. But when we do make those connections, and we connect with what's been passed on through generations, we feel liberated. We don't feel the same as the everyday person. You are connected not just to your past, but to the future, and we become connected to a better version of ourselves, and hopefully the world. But we need teachers who are willing to pass on the tradition. That's the problem so many of us are seeing—the new generation, they don't want to be involved.

Modern technology has taken away a lot of things from us. One of them is, we are not going back to the basics, we aren't going back to the structure where we follow or learn our parents' beliefs, and, of course, the government and everyone else have detached themselves from Nature, what I say is the true religion.

We are human first, with this spiritual energy within us. The human part of us, I say, we must contain. We can be good for the world. People with gifts, we can see things that others cannot, so it's something that we always need restraint in, ourselves. We practice meditation so that we can tap into self-control and balance, self-discipline, and self-control. We can do a lot of damage if we don't learn this.

# ❀ A PRACTICE ❀
## Divination with a Pendulum

One popular and simple divination tool is working with a crystal pendulum. The choice of crystal is important; for example, a quartz crystal with a point on one end is a universal tool for focused energy. When selecting your crystal, you may choose one of two methods. First, if you have a certain vibration you wish to attract, you can select your crystal based on the properties traditionally associated with the stone. Or, you could allow your Higher Self to intuitively select the stone based on its inherent vibration.

What color is it? What does that color's energy mean to you? How does it feel when you hold it in your hand? By listening intuitively to the answers to these questions, you will personally attune with your stone. After selecting your crystal pendulum in this intuitive manner, you can then research the stone's traditional properties. Often, they do align with the vibration you most need to attract at that moment.

Pendulums can be found online or in person at many Pagan and New Age stores. Some suggestions are the following:

**Quartz**—Quartz crystals are universal, highly energetic, like a battery. Focuses, amplifies, transmits.

**Amethyst**—The sobriety stone. Increases spirituality, enlightenment, psychic development.

**Aquaramine**—Increases communication and effectiveness.

**Fluorite**—Absorbs negativity, removes energy blocks.

**Malachite**—Banishing stone, purging stone. Great aid to spiritual growth and healing on all planes.

**Rose Quartz**—Self-love, lifts depression, peace.

**Smoky Quartz**—Grounding stone, improves intuition, survival power.

**Tourmaline**—Rainbow bridge, healing stone, cosmic life force.

**Citrine**—Stone of the sun and happiness. Attracts abundance.

## Tools

A pendulum with a crystal that most speaks to you. A quiet place to do this meditation. Your journal.

## Begin

Center yourself with a few deep breaths. Sit quietly doing this. The pendulum should suspend from a chain, and you may invite in guidance from your personal guide or guardian angel. Then ask that your guardian spirit help you consecrate this pendulum for communication, and that the messages you receive are truth and for the highest good.

Next, you must establish the pattern that works for you for affirmative or negative answers. For instance, when I consult my pendulum, when it moves up and down, it means yes; when it moves side to side, it means no. When it moves in a circle, it is unknown or undecided. Be sure to be still when consulting your pendulum and do not try to manipulate your answers; you would only be fooling yourself.

Begin to communicate with your pendulum. This will take practice. To build up confidence, begin with simple yes-or-no questions. Journal the answers and see how accurate they are. Over time, you will develop rapport with your spirit guide, and you may begin to receive a more complex messaging system that includes spelling out words or phrases. Be sure to thank your spirit guide after each session for their assistance.

# ENERGY HEALING

A common theme of occult and Indigenous beliefs is the idea that the human body is a microcosm of the greater cosmos. The occult saying "as above, so below" references this knowledge. Nature-based practitioners see themselves as more than the physical body; most embrace a concept of a spiritual or etheric body that is pure energy or less heavy than our physical form. Our etheric selves unite with the cosmos, and one can raise consciousness through various methods to leave our bodies and to invite spiritual forces to promote healing and growth not only for individuals, but also for the collective. One such method is by raising energy for healing.

# ENERGY HEALING AS A FORCE FOR BALANCE

The nature of the cosmos includes the concept of unity and duality. Within the Asian yin-yang symbol lies a constantly changing polarity. It represents the balance of the complementary, dualistic energies of our known universe. Each side has a center within where the opposite energy is present. This yin-yang field is in a state of eternal transformation, always spinning and changing; the dance is a spiral. The relationship is interdependent and infinite, complementary and not antagonistic or opposite.[78]

Dualism also includes the Jungian idea of the anima and the animus within our psyche. The anima is a man's inner feminine aspect, and the animus is a woman's inner masculine aspect. Either can turn malignant when drained or overused. The healthy integration of the inner self with the rest of the psyche is the aim of Jungian psychotherapy. Ultimately, to develop health, a person must strive for flow and balance between these poles of being—harmony without stagnation. Internal alchemy is transforming yin into yang, silver into gold, base human self into our Higher Self, connected with the cosmos. One, then, is in the world, not of it, able to transcend the vicissitudes of life more easily by learning to go with the flow of what is. Energy-building exercises such as Tai Chi and Qi Gong help rebuild what has been lost through living a life out of balance and indulging in unhealthy mental and physical habits. Energy drain is a symptom of low Qi.[79]

In Taoism, the body has infinite wisdom that embeds us in nature; we are part of all that is. Taoists divide the body into three components, or *dan tiens*, our bodies becoming symbolic of the universal World Tree. The lower dan tien is connected to Earth, vitality, and

---

78  Reid, *The Complete Book of Chinese Health and Healing*, 26.

79  Diane Rooney, "Internal Alchemy," workshop presented at One Spirit Learning Alliance, New York, January 2021.

our physical body. The middle dan tien is connected to humanity, compassion, and the middle Earth we dwell on and share with our nonhuman relatives. The upper dan tien, beginning at our necks and continuing up behind the eyes and into our crown, connects us to the cosmos, to transcendence.[80] The Tao means the way, a journey; its flow is like water. We accept this as a reality that is consciously changing, and this change affects our being and is reflected in our lives. What connects these aspects of self is the energy body. And it is this aspect of self that many who practice nature spirituality believe can be affected by energetic healing techniques.

## Scientific Research and Support

Psychotherapist Dorotea Hover-Kramer in her book *Creative Energies: Integrative Energy Psychotherapy for Self-Expression and Healing* defines wellness as "a state of being of optimal health for an individual, physically and emotionally, with the ability to meet life's challenges with hope, resiliency, and creativity."[81] Today, practitioners of alternative spiritual healing, particularly those with a holistic philosophical orientation, are incorporating nontraditional energy healing into their wellness practices.

There is a growing consensus of interest and support for energy healing techniques today in Western culture. Energy healing is based on the concept of the human biofield. In a peer-reviewed paper published regarding Healing Touch (HT) therapy, the authors of the paper defined the human biofield as "the physical aspect of the individualized field of energy in which electrical activity functions as a complex organized system or whole."[82] Today, medical and psychology professionals

---

80  Reid, *The Complete Book of Chinese Health and Healing*, 6.

81  Dorotea Hover-Kramer, *Creative Energies* (New York: Norton and Company, 2002), 1–2.

82  K. Reeve, P. Black, and J. Huang, "Examining the Impact of Healing Touch Intervention to Reduce Post-Traumatic Stress Disorder Symptoms in Combat Veterans," *Psychology Trauma: Theory, Research, Practice and Policy* (2020), http://dx.doi.org/10.1037/tra0000591.

who incorporate energy healing techniques into their practice argue that they align well with ideas of quantum physics, which differs from classical physics in that it includes an understanding of particle and wave duality. The concept of the human biofield can be understood with this added insight into the vibrational nature of reality.[83]

The use of energetic healing modalities has made significant pathways into modern medicine. Acupuncture is probably the most well-known and well-respected energy healing technique. Energy is directed along energy paths, known as meridians, in the human body and amplified through the insertion of small needles at precision points. Large hospitals like Sloan Kettering Cancer Center in New York City now use acupuncture therapies to treat patients.

Reiki energy healing has also received widespread acceptance. Duke University Hospital in Durham, North Carolina, incorporates Reiki healing into its wellness practices. Energy healing techniques are used by nurses, end-of-life doulas, and mental health practitioners in a variety of ways, including the use of HT therapy, Therapeutic Touch (TT), Reiki energy healing, and sound healing. How a person responds to advanced illness and their own mortality is influenced greatly by their beliefs and worldview regarding spiritual matters. A recent article in *Beginnings: The Journal for Holistic Nursing* examined the used of HT therapy for patients with advanced illness in end-of-life care. During this difficult time, patients experience not only the debilitating pain and suffering of their physical illness, but they also suffer significant mental and emotional distress. The healing technique was reported to assist the patient energetically to clear and adjust their energy field to either physically help the client heal from illness or assist their mental and emotional field to ease the transition between life and death. The practitioners mentioned in the article claim that the most significant response to the HT technique is an

---

83  Hover-Kramer, *Creative Energies*, 17.

increase in the relaxation response by patients in their care, which can aid in self-healing.[84]

Another study examined the use of energy healing techniques with combat veterans suffering from PTSD.[85] In a qualitative and quantitative study, researchers examined the theory that PTSD affects the individual's ability to clear the energy system as trauma impedes their biofield, remaining trapped in thoughts and emotions and manifesting in the debilitating symptoms of PTSD. This study examined the use of HT to help clear the combat veteran participants of unwanted energy and decrease their symptoms in tandem with conventional Cognitive Behavioral Therapy (CBT). The researchers performed a two-armed, randomized, crossover, waitlist-controlled trial with two groups of veterans who self-reported statistically significant improvement to the severity of their symptoms after receiving ten treatments complementing their therapy. Overall, participants reported a range of positive physical and psychological effects. The researchers concluded that this study implies energetic healing techniques and practices can have a clinical impact and can be effectively applied in tandem with other therapies for treatment for patients suffering from a range of psychological imbalances and disorders.[86]

## WIDESPREAD USES FROM VARIOUS CULTURES AROUND THE WORLD

Energy healing is an ancient and universal practice. From Hawaiian Kahunas to South American Peruvian shamanic healing, to African Bushmen who perform tribal dances to raise healing energy, a variety of energetic techniques can be found worldwide. Elders or Indigenous

---

84  Donna Adams and Melinda Chichester, "Integrating Healing Touch for Advanced Illness and End-of-Life Nursing Care," *Beginnings: The Journal for Holistic Nursing* (2019): 14–26.

85  Reeve, et al., *Healing Touch Interventions*, 2020.

86  Reeve, et al., *Healing Touch Interventions*, 2020.

wisdom keepers are often described in anthropology as the original doctors and psychologists; they incorporate various methods to raise, direct, and clear energy centers to promote healing.[87] An example is the San people, an Indigenous society living in Botswana, Namibia, who still live a hunter-gatherer lifestyle in inhospitable regions of the Kalahari Desert. Here, they practice energy healing techniques with their primary cultural ritual of ecstatic dance.[88] In the dance, participants generate energy and direct it back toward their community. It exemplifies the egalitarian values of the community, which sees healing as a renewable resource, available, valuable, and shared by everyone.[89]

In the different cultural milieu of modern-day Paganism, energy-raising circles utilizing drumming, dancing, and ecstatic trance can be found today at both large and intimate gatherings. While the culture and purposes of the activities may differ, the style and purposes of these practices are similar. They represent an ancient technology. It is not new; it has been part of human culture for treating illness and imbalance and raising energy for thousands of years.

Energy healing is well established in the East in traditional Chinese medicine with Qigong, a well-known practice that relies on a series of movements that stimulate the meridians of the body, bringing healing to internal organs and regulation of the body's natural abilities to maintain optimal health. Various forms of energy healing are present in other existing Indigenous spiritual practices. While discussing the Māori cultural revival of New Zealand, Puáwai Ormsby said energetic hands-on healing is popular with New Zealanders from all backgrounds today.

---

87  Richard Katz, *Indigenous Healing Psychology* (Rochester, VT: Healing Arts, 2017), 294–310.
88  Katz, *Indigenous Healing Psychology*, 93.
89  Katz, *Indigenous Healing Psychology*, 93.

There are also healing clinics here that have been set up so that they can practice the medicine elders practice, known as their *Mirimiri*, their massage, a hands-on healing. They use the stones, the ancient rock massage. This is a green-stone, the heart stone of this land.

## Spiritualism and Spiritism

In Brazil and Latin American countries, Spiritism utilizes healing passes of energy to affect physical, mental, and spiritual health and well-being at centers and in smaller groups, a practice found here in the United States at Spiritist centers throughout the country. At these centers, energy healing plays a large part in the treatment for people suffering from mental illnesses like depression, anxiety, fatigue, and medical conditions that are resistant to Western medicine alone. From a Spiritist perspective, mental imbalances may be cured by applying spiritual forces to effect change. Individuals who are able to channel the energy of spirits are mediums and view this gift primarily as a way to help others; mediumship should not be misused for fame or wealth. Those gifted offer healing through energy passes and may receive training for how best to utilize their gifts.[90]

## New Age Energy Healing

Energy healing is part of New Age practice. Some healers work within traditional Japanese Reiki lineages, while many more purport to have received their energy healing techniques directly from spirit guides, ascended masters, or the universe itself. They claim their practices harness Earth energies or light frequencies and can help clear the mind and body from blockages, mental imbalances, and disease. Learning to channel these energies requires training and direct transmissions of energy, which come from the practitioner accessing them during altered states of consciousness.

---

90 Katz, *Indigenous Healing Psychology*, 85–86.

One such lineage is the Magical Awakenings system of energy healing, a direct transmission received and taught by energy healing master Brett Bevell of the Omega Institute.[91] In this system, Brett teaches a direct transmission lineage that relies on the three energy centers, or cauldrons, within our body, which, when activated, generate divine energy that can be directed toward healing of self, others, situations, and our surroundings. Within the system, the guides known historically as Merlin and the Lady of the Lake are believed to be divine avatars of magickal energy healing who assist the healer to access and transmit the cauldron energies. They also direct the practitioner's mastery for using the energy of the elements: air, water, earth, and fire.[92]

One aspect of natural wisdom is to recognize these internal universal rhythms and energy forces within us and to develop practices and technologies that promote balance so we in turn will lead a balanced life, in rhythm with the Earth's energies and our relationship with our world. Although this is a brief survey for energy healing techniques among various cultures, it is clear that practicing nature spirituality embraces an understanding of the value of these practices.

A desired goal of energy healing for all nature-based practitioners is to raise consciousness to elevate our thoughts to a higher plane and to heal our bodies and minds from the residue and stressors inherent in modern life that can create illness. When we raise consciousness, we can transcend change to arrive at a state of nonduality, of unity, and to access the power of the universe itself. As the universal energy of nature and consciousness is ever changing, we become part of the change of the universal biofield as well. Energy healing techniques allow us to tap into these forces. Collectively, we can help the evolution of planetary

---

91  Brett Bevell, *The Magical Awakening System of Healing* (Rhinebeck, NY: Monkfish Book Publishing Company), 2015.

92  Bevell, *The Magical Awakening System of Healing*, 2015.

consciousness, which is another step toward relighting the cauldron of Mother Earth.

# TENDING THE FLAME
## Taoism

Rev. Dr. Diane Rooney is an interspiritual minister, a professional acupuncturist, and a practicing Taoist. She teaches Eastern Taoist philosophy and Qigong. Here, she discusses Taoism as an ancient, Indigenous tradition from China, rooted in Earth energy for balance and healing:

Taoism is one of the original Indigenous traditions, dating back so far that they don't even really have a date because this predates writing, so anywhere from 4,000 to 5,000 BCE to 10,000 BCE—that's how long it has been around. The roots go back to the Wu people, who were the shamans at the time who saw Nature being not only the water, the air, the earth, the dirt, the animals, but also cosmology, the stars, the planets, and their movements. They did not separate themselves from nature; they saw themselves as part of it. They reasoned that what they saw outside of themselves had to also be inside. So, they followed the cycles of the cosmos and the cycles of the Earth's seasons as an example to follow the cycles within oneself, to become one with, and by becoming one with, one remains healthy.

I have been practicing my career as Taoism, my vocation, because I'm an acupuncturist, a Chinese medicine practitioner, and that falls under the umbrella of Taoism because we look at the body as whole, as the Tao, as a perfect harmony of Yin and Yang. When somebody comes into my office and there is something that's off, their Yin and Yang are imbalanced, so my job is to find out where in them the cycles of Nature are off, and then I balance the cycles with the meridians and with the needles at the acupuncture points to bring back the balance of Yin and Yang, to bring them closer to Tao.

Taoism is a philosophy. It later became a religion, but that was much later. It was originally a philosophy and a way of being, and it slowly started to become a religion with temples and things like that, but basically it got pushed to the background because the Chinese wanted to establish Confucianism. After that, the temples started popping up, and Tao became more of a religion with ritual, but really in the ancient philosophy there is nobody you give reverence to because you are the Tao. As a religion, it's communal. You go to the temple, you make offerings to the cauldron, you either put fruit down or you burn something. It's an offering to the spirits; you feed the hungry ghosts all that stuff before you enter the temple and share your reverence to different archetypes. So that's communal, but it's not necessary. I practice alone; it's not about the group. It's about one's individual connection to the cycles of Nature.

Tai Chi is part of Taoism. It started with the teacher; he was watching a cobra and a crane fighting each other, and he was mesmerized by their movements. They were both so graceful. He was so mesmerized, and neither of them lost; they separated. He formed Tai Chi after that. So, the movements we do are based on movements in Nature, like upholding the moon, for instance; we have animal movements, like dragon, that we get from Nature, that represent different aspects of our being.

I am not talking only about our psyche, I'm talking about our organs as well as our psyche. There is a very physical relationship we have with each other; for instance, stagnation of water, stagnation of water within us. The damming of a river or a stream can cause damming up within us. We watch water, which is a huge metaphor in Taoism, to see how water survives in life, and then we become that, because water flows.

Everything that is alive is seen as having Spirit. The trees, for instance. I mean, we don't call them the tree people or the two-legged or the winged ones, as in Native American traditions, but they are seen the same way. They all have souls; they are all part of who we are and health and healing.

I said there was no real goal at the time of the Wu people, but later on a goal did develop, and this is where Taoism overlaps with Buddhism. Awakening, enlightenment, and immortality are the goals in that order. To be awakened is to do these practices, is to quiet the mind and to remove the mind out of the equation, because the mind is the slayer of the real, the mind gets in the way, the mind never stops, the mind hogs the Qi. Meditation is also a big part of it, as is acupuncture. We have highways that are energetic streams within us. Sound is part of it.

The goal of Taoism today is to evolve. We evolve through discipline, practice, diligence. By undoing rather than doing. It's about undoing. What can you undo today, what can you unlearn today, is the saying and the practice of Taoism. Let go of all that noise and all that preconceived this or that and the worry and anxiety of living in this world and work on unlearning and going back to Source, knowing and trusting that it will flow. Even when we come up against something that is debilitating for us, that's not good or even horrible for us—it still is part of the flow. You come up with it, you feel your genuine feelings, and you keep going. You know that it, too, will change and shift.

There is a lot of pain that comes up when you are consistent with Taoist principles because we have to undo all those things we have constricted in our mind, body, and spirit. But when you are consistent, you will come up against yourself, you will come up against your darkness, your pain, your aches, your fears. But if you stick with it, you will then flow like any spiritual path in life, because we are spirit beings. Tao is no different. Taoism just broke it down for us, but we are really Tao beings, which are primordial forces or vapors that separated and became this Yin and Yang thing in order to observe itself. And we are that; we are just one step away from the Divine. Taoism, from my perspective, isn't even the One. It is the animating force behind the One. It's the breath of God, the animating of the One that became the Two. It's not even a Thing, it's a No-Thing.

# ❂ A PRACTICE ❂
## Drawing Earth Energy

This meditation is designed to help you connect with the Earth energy, which vitalizes plants, animals, and all living things. Select someplace comfortable outside to sit and relax. It could be in a wood or forest, or this could be on your front porch or before an open window. You may wish to record this meditation beforehand and listen to it when ready to practice.

### Begin

Sit comfortably, either directly on the earth or in a chair. Allow your mind to relax by closing your eyes and breathing in and out slowly. Count slowly to four on the inhale, and exhale slowly to the same count of four.

Now bring your awareness to your body. Feel your breath as it goes in and out; feel the beats of your heart and the rhythm of your breath. Bring your mental awareness to connect with your body.

Now shift your consciousness to an awareness of the space a few inches outside your body. This is your aura. Imagine this is where your spirit resides. Feel yourself connected through your mind with your body and your spirit. Allow yourself to feel centered here.

As you continue to breath rhythmically, begin to shift your awareness down through your feet. Imagine your feet or your bottom have grown roots, and these roots begin to penetrate down through the Earth's soil. As you do this, feel them intermingling with the roots of the grasses, trees, plants, and mycelium that dwell beneath the surface. Feel as your roots connect you with this network of roots; feel the electrical currents that flow here. Feel your awareness pass through layers of soil where animals and insects make their home.

Imagine that your roots continue down now until you reach the bedrock of the Earth's crust. Continue to breathe slowly, knowing your body, mind, and spirit are safe and connected down through the soil to the Earth Mother.

Now allow your root thread to continue down to the Earth's crust. Feel yourself pass through minerals, rocks, and crystalline stone until you arrive at the molten center of the core of the Earth. Here, allow your consciousness to tap into Mother Earth's cauldron of fire. Feel this fire as it connects all the way back through the layers of the Earth and comes back to you.

Begin to draw this energy up. In reverse order, feel the fire rise, pass through, and gain energy from the crystals and minerals; feel the electrical currents of the mycelium network, and the living power of the plants and roots. If you are able, imagine how this energy feels, smells, and tastes. Bring it up and through the layers of your body. Allow it to penetrate through your feet, your legs, up through your torso and into your heart. Feel the Earth fire flow into your heart fire. Stay here in your heart with this fiery energy for a few minutes.

Now bring that energy up further, through your chest, your arms, your hands, then your shoulders, neck, and finally your face. Remember to keep breathing slowly and allow the energy to flow out with your breath until it flows out the top of your head, up until it connects to the sky.

Imagine yourself now, connected deeply to the core of the Earth and connecting to the sky itself like the branches of a tree. The fire extends out through the sky, up into the stars of the universe itself. Become like a tree of pure energy. Feel this flow as you keep breathing deeply. When you are complete, return your tree's branches and roots back into your body, and return to ordinary consciousness. Be sure to ground back to ordinary consciousness with a light snack or by standing firmly on your two feet.

This exercise should leave you feeling energized, relaxed, and refreshed. Return to it regularly to connect to the Earth for rebalancing, especially whenever your energy feels drained.

# THE HEALING PATH OF THE CHAKRA SYSTEM

*Chakra* is a Sanksrit word from the ancient language of India, and it means "wheels of light that denote energy centers within our human energy field." It comes from the Vedic cosmology of ancient India, which has existed for over five thousand years. These centers within our body and around our astral or energy bodies represent the flow of what the Indian masters called prana, or nature's energy throughout our body and into the cosmos. The Eastern tradition of Yoga is steeped with this understanding of the human biofield and aims to promote health and healing through the maintenance, development, and balance of energies.

The idea that within the human body there are energy centers known as chakras is also shared by Indigenous people like the Hopi of North America, who believed the energy field of Mother Earth resonated through our bodies from the living Earth and natural forces.[93] By practicing regular connection and ceremonies with these forces, humans can be connected, balanced, and ecologically responsible to the ground on which they live and that they share with nonhuman relatives.

The Hopi had an understanding of the evolution of our species related to the energy centers of our bodies, and for each chakra, they assigned an appropriate animal totem. The root chakra, they oriented with the snake; the second, fish; the third, bird; the fourth, with mammals; and the fifth, with humanity.[94] Biologists today recognize that these are the precise evolutionary cycles that humans have passed through over the great span of our evolution and the development of our species. The Hopi did not perceive a higher and lower dichotomy, or place a negative value on the lower chakras. They recognized that developing all of them was necessary for balance and full human consciousness. This is also true to the Indian practitioner. Imbalance in any of the energy centers leads to disharmony and disease.[95] In terms of being able to perceive chakra or energy centers, in his books about Yaqui shamanism, Carlos Castaneda often spoke about how his teacher Don Juan stressed that a man of power must learn to see.[96] This way of seeing provided the ability to psychically and intuitively tune in to the physical body and see the astral or spirit body, or see into other worlds of reality. It was a gift of the awakened practitioner.

Our aura, which is the visual dimension of our astral bodies, visible to those with open psychic senses, specifically relates to the dominant color scheme we vibrate on. The quality of the energy produced by a chakra or group of chakras determines a person's dominant auric

---

93  Rosalyn Bruyere, *Wheels of Light* (New York: Simon and Schuster, 1994), 25–26.

94  Bruyere, *Wheels of Light*, 53.

95  Bruyere, *Wheels of Light*, 53.

96  Carlos Castaneda, *A Separate Reality* (New York: Washington Square Press, 1971), 10–12.

color or field. Our chakra mirrors our lifestyle. It is affected by what we think of ourselves and others, what we ingest both mentally and physically, and how we live our lives.[97] The auric field is a metaphor for life. A person's energy field reflects how healthy we are.[98]

# CLEARING AND BALANCING OUR CHAKRAS

Maintaining healthy chakras, therefore, is an important aspect to living a vibrant life, and those who practice nature spirituality can do exercises toward this end. Let us examine each of the chakra centers as a pathway toward keeping ourselves healthy. We will focus on examining each energy center or chakra, both individually and collectively.

For this section, I am grateful for the work of Anodea Judith. In her 2004 work *Eastern Body, Western Mind: Psychology and the Chakra System as a Path to the Self,* she describes in detail how working through the chakra system is a specific modality for the helping professions. In this chapter, to the brief description of how blocked and open chakras are reflected in an individual person's body and psyche, I have added my thoughts on how these energies are also expressed in collective culture. I also provide suggested activities that may be used to bring balance and healing.

As a comparison to another nature-based system of divination, I discuss the major themes of each chakra to ideas relative to the study of the runes from Germanic/Scandinavian Heathen systems. The purpose of the comparison is to help you recognize the commonality and wisdom embedded within very different nature-based traditions as they may relate to one another.

---

97 Castaneda, *A Separate Reality,* 21–22.
98 Bruyere, *Wheels of Light,* 84.

## First Chakra—Root Chakra

The first chakra is the root chakra, located at the base of the spine. It is the source of our life force. It is associated with the color red, which is the color of our blood. In the World Tree of humanity, from this chakra come the roots of our ancient civilizations, our DNA heritage, and our cultural beliefs. A rune to match this chakra would be Perth, or initiation. This rune reflects "the deepest strata of our being. The bedrock on which our destiny is founded."[99] The root chakra is the base center of our foundation, survival, nourishment, trust, health, home, family, and prosperity. Here is the element of earth. This is the chakra of the Great Mother, the Matrix, the matter from which we all come.

For the World Tree, this chakra represents the place of all manifestation, the solidity of our Earth home. When it is a strong foundation, our root chakra helps us stand balanced and firm, not only in our sense of survival and nourishment, but also in the foundation of core values and our belief system.[100] These we inherit from the cultural teachings and structures that form our worldview.

The root chakra connects us downward, to Earth and to Source, and back in time to all those who came before. Through this link, we are transported back to the beginning. Here is where the energy of those who passed their genes into the evolution of humankind is kept. Here lives the most basic sense of what makes us human and how we know who and what we belong to.

The energy of the root chakra is the drive to survive. At this level of consciousness, we are concerned with food, water, resources, community, our family, home, and safety. When in balance, a healthy survival foundation allows us to raise our consciousness to higher levels. When our survival is threatened, this need dominates all other concerns.[101]

---

99 Blum, *The Book of Runes*, 104.
100 Anodea Judith, *Eastern Body, Western Mind* (New York: Celestial Arts, 2004), 61–64.
101 Judith, *Eastern Body, Western Mind*, 71.

If one's lifestyle is constantly under attack from threats at this level, it is difficult to ever relax or be at peace and to rise in consciousness. Imbalance here leads to illnesses related to stress, anxiety, and failure to thrive. A person who is traumatized due to an imbalance in their root chakra will continuously face trials in life related to lack of money, resources, economic security, safety, and home.[102] A depletion in this chakra can manifest in a lack of connection with one's basic being and core self and leave a person in a chronic state of depression and discontent.

At the individual level, it is of paramount importance to bring healing to this chakra if it is out of balance in order to realize fundamental survival needs, according to Maslow's Hierarchy of Needs, and to not be ruled by fears of lack. At the collective level, it is the same. If a society does not provide for and create a safe space for its citizens to feed, house, and thrive, there can never be stable peace and fulfillment.

Fear is present in human evolution because it helps us be aware of threats, respond to them, and improve our chance of survival and create safety. Yet, individuals and societies that rule by fear instead of love or reason are defined by poverty, cruelty, and tyranny.

## Practices for Strengthening the Root Chakra

One way to strengthen the root chakra is through an understanding and embrace of one's roots and genetic or cultural heritage. Early people understood this, which is why ancestor veneration is found all over the ancient and Indigenous world. Through remembering, sharing stories, and honoring ancestors, one can honor and become acquainted with values, traditions, and beliefs that offer a sense of belonging. By honoring those who came before, whether they be ancestors of blood, land, or lineage, we lay claim to them as foundational and as our connection

102 Judith, *Eastern Body, Western Mind*, 64–65.

and sense of belonging to the Earth and humanity as a whole. A healthy root chakra and connection to one's roots allows one to be grounded and beliefs and values to be firm and solid. It is essential, therefore, to make a connection to one's roots to bring balance and healing to the root chakra.

Additional practices that can help strengthen and affirm the health of our root chakra are physical healing modalities, such as Yoga, Qi gong, Tai Chi, or other body-based practices, or other regular physical exercise and/or dance, which brings us into our bodies. Another method is practicing grounding exercises to connect us with Mother Earth, as well as spending time in nature, gardening, hiking, camping, and all outdoor activities.

### Second Chakra—Sacral Chakra

The second chakra or sacral chakra is located in our sacrum and encompasses our sexual organs. This area governs relationships, emotions, and creativity. From this chakra, which is associated with the color orange, one dives into the experience of feelings, sexuality, and creativity.[103] In this chakra, a soul becomes aware of the separate self and duality. Here begins the relationships with others, family members, childhood friends, and mates until we bond with the beloved partner. Through the awareness of the second chakra, the binaries of life appear: light/dark, male/female, inner/outer. A rune to match this chakra is Gebo, or initiation. In this rune, which appears as an X and means "gift," one is in partnership and relationship. It also can mean a relationship to one's own Higher Self.[104]

This chakra relates to the element of water. Water is flowing, changing, and adaptable and conforms to all containers. It can be stagnant or torrential. Here, too, is the emotional self. When ruled by emotions, this chakra is overstimulated, and one can be easily swept

---

103 Judith, *Eastern Body, Western Mind*, 106–107.
104 Blum, *The Book of Runes*, 95.

away by feelings and emotions or movements and situations that stir disturbing emotions. When the feeling center is stunted or blocked, one can feel numb and disassociated from the body and have difficulty identifying their feelings.[105]

From this center comes creativity—once again, a flowing, liquid force. A blocked sacral chakra will result in a lack of creativity and an inability to make decisions or express oneself.[106] Healthy growth and development of the sacral chakra is through fully experiencing feelings and loving and safe touch. Wounds to the second chakra can relate to suppression of the sexual nature, intuition, creativity, and shame around experiencing feelings and emotions.

A strong and balanced second chakra experiences the healthy flow of energy in life's affairs. Communication and interaction with others flow easily, as do understanding and interpretation of the unspoken rules of social bonding. Feeling supported and safe helps unleash the power of creativity so we can become cocreators of our world. At the individual level, it is essential to work toward balance and healthy flow within this chakra in order to realize creative potential, enjoy healthy relationships and sexual expression, and create loving and supportive families and communities.

At the collective level, the sacral chakra is represented well by the early cultures around the Earth that rose out of more primitive societies and developed agrarian civilization and culture. Through the development of agriculture, the ancient Mother Goddess was seen in relationship with her Divine Son, and later a father god. They mirrored the family unit, the basic pattern of society to this day. Humanity also created a more interactive relationship with nature, domesticating plants and wildlife. Complex civilizations developed the rules of relationship to one another that govern societies.

---

105 Judith, *Eastern Body, Western Mind*, 129–132.
106 Judith, *Eastern Body, Western Mind*, 144–145.

Where domination and suppressive regimes developed, this collective chakra energy became out of balance. Where partnership, cooperation, and collaboration predominated, communities enjoyed flourishing creative output of arts, crafts, and trade.[107] When a society becomes so out of balance that an oppressive ruler class dominates and controls a slave class, society breaks down.[108] The same can be true for families and the health of damaged individuals unable to negotiate safe and nurturing boundaries. Free expression is stifled and depleted.

### Practices for Strengthening the Second Chakra

One of the ways to strengthen the sacral chakra is to practice listening to our bodies, naming feelings and emotions as they arise, and allowing free expression. Another tool that helps strengthen this chakra is finding ways to be creative without judging ourselves. Whether it is gardening, cooking, painting, music, or dance, just allowing oneself to freely flow without the filter of self-criticism or the expectation that our efforts need to lead to some kind of end product or financial venture can be the thing that helps us find what creative expression our soul's purpose wishes to express.

Deep self-inquiry is another second chakra practice. We can ask ourselves, how am I feeling? What am I feeling? How does this person make me feel? And then listen with real honesty. Take time to find, name, and establish personal moral, ethical guidelines and boundaries. What do we believe in? What do we think constitutes healthy community and relationships? If we want to be in a romantic relationship, what are essential qualities for this? How do we resolve family entanglements, enmeshment, and negative patterns? Finally, one can use deep inquiry to work with the sacral chakra to help make decisions. Practice listening to the body when feelings are either too activated or too numb.

---

107  Eisler, *The Real Wealth of Nations*, 117.
108  Eisler, *The Real Wealth of Nations*, 118–121.

## Third Chakra—Yellow Chakra

The third chakra is located in our solar plexus, what many people call the belly. Here is the chakra of the will. As the first two chakras represent first our union with the Matrix (earth) and with ancestors, then the flow through the birth into family and relationships (water), this chakra represents the burning of the fire of individuality. The emergence of the ego self and the will to be.[109] A rune to match this chakra is Sowelu, or wholeness and life force. It is represented by the sun and represents our "impulse toward self-realization, and indicates the path to follow."[110] Through this chakra, our consciousness is concerned with personal power, the individual will, and the direction for how we manifest these through the choices we make in life.

In the larger concepts of civilization, it is in this power center where solar gods emerged: Ra, Lugh, Helios, and Belonus—gods whose fire brought warmth, light, growth, life, and the joys of creation. The positive energy of the color yellow for this chakra and for these deities includes warmth, joy, sunshine, happiness, and well-being.[111] Another deity who suits this chakra well is the Green Man archetype. While he is often seen as a leaf and foliate mask of greenery, his energy is that of growth and expansion, the very essence and energy of this chakra. This chakra in humanity's evolution is a positive force represented by the will to explore, invent, develop technology, and, finally, to conquer. Negatively, this chakra can lead to the binary repression of power and domination, the subjugation of the feminine, the enslavement of others, the rise of master-slave mentality, and the belief that humans must subdue the Earth. With a healthy balance, this chakra represents life with infinite choices, honoring the

---

109  Judith, *Eastern Body, Western Mind*, 176–180.
110  Blum, *The Book of Runes*, 139.
111  Jo Dixon and James Dixon, *The Color Book* (Denver, CO: Castle Rising, 1978), 22.

dignity and rights of the individual, and constructive and cooperative energy for all.

The energy of the solar plexus chakra is the energy of a healthy will and ego, the idea of the true self. A healthy ego develops from the foundation of heritage, family, and culture, but then creates a strong self-concept.

An unbalanced third chakra can make one feel helpless, controlled, confused, and accusatory of others for personal shortcomings. By reclaiming one's value and sense of self, the balance is righted. It is vital to take time to recharge oneself and to listen to the still, small voice of our true self, our Higher Self, guiding us on toward our next steps.[112]

### Practices for Strengthening the Third Chakra

A basic exercise to activate a healthy third chakra is connecting with the sun. While keeping in mind the need for protection from dangerous UV rays, getting direct sunshine helps the body absorb the crucial vitamin D, which is essential to a strong, healthy immune system. Direct sunshine also helps lift negative moods. Meditating with bare feet on the ground and the face toward the sun can help clear the body of stuck energy and imbibe positive, recharging rays of sunlight and earth energy.

Another practice to do regularly is to use the imagination. Ask the self-critic and the self-defender in our psyches to take a break in order to use the imagination to answer the question, "Who would I be and what would I do if I was allowed to do whatever I wanted?" The true self may step forward. Be sure to journal any answer that comes. If for some reason a negative or self-destructive fantasy emerges, seek guidance from a counselor or guide to gain insight and meaning. In addition, use the unfettered imagination to draw, paint, or journal whatever fantasy has emerged.

---

112 Judith, *Eastern Body, Western Mind*, 219.

It is important to journal and keep a record of dreams and aspirations regularly, especially those that emerge spontaneously. Developing and encouraging a healthy third chakra helps us feel we are in the right place and doing the right work in the world, and then we experience passion, purpose, and the fire of joyful living.

## Fourth Chakra—Heart Chakra

The fourth chakra marks the midpoint of the rainbow bridge of consciousness. Here is the heart space. This chakra is associated with the vibrant green of nature and life force. The predominant energy of the heart chakra is compassion and balance. The heart is surrounded by the lungs, which are air, but its predominant element is fire. A rune to match this chakra is Wunjo, or joy. This rune represents completeness and fulfillment. Here, knowledge merges with compassion, and understanding is suffused with the light of heart-centered expansion. When this rune is in its positive aspect, the flow of consciousness is fluid, and we can breathe into higher states of being.[113]

Joy is our natural state of being when we live a heart-centered life. It is the natural way of being for children. Yet, being joyful and heart-centered is much easier said than done. This may relate to the fact that our understanding of love itself is often limited, jealous, and fearful; it may be tainted with ideas of familial obligation and even abusive patterns. What we know as love may really be an immature possessiveness, attachment, and longing for security, not an adult love that is fearless, free, joyous, and open.[114]

The way toward understanding of healthy love begins when we learn to love and honor ourselves. Self-love is the ability to cherish ourselves, which, if we have a healthy fourth chakra, begins with appreciation, approval, and acceptance for who we are—our positive and

---

113 Blum, *The Book of Runes*, 115.
114 Judith, *Eastern Body, Western Mind*, 268–270.

negative sides.[115] Learning healthy love is often the work of a lifetime, and many people get stuck searching for a perfect love relationship that serves to complete them, as represents their better half, instead of realizing that only through acceptance of ourselves as a whole person can we be complete and attract and maintain a healthy loving relationship with another.

The heart chakra is a point of balance. In the World Tree, this position is the point where the roots from the ancestors have moved through the trunk of self and settled into the center and heart of the tree, before the branches that rise to the heavens. A healthy, functioning heart chakra functions through empathy and compassion—for self, for others, for concepts such as beauty, love, and causes dear to our heart. A healthy heart chakra literally moves us, our energy, our feelings, and our purpose; it is relational.

In human evolution, this is where humanity has achieved flourishing civilization. It is said that we can tell the level of civilization of a society by how it treats its poor, sick, young, and elderly. The mark of true civilization is always compassion for the weakest, respect for the individual, and justice to keep the strong in check. Deities associated with this archetype would be both male and female, universal and nongendered. They are always heart-centered. Here we find the loving heart of Jesus Christ, the Divine Son of God who gave his life in service and taught us to love our neighbors as ourselves and God with our whole hearts. A feminine deity is the eternally compassionate Kwan Yin, the Buddhist mother of compassion, who instead of moving on to Nirvana when she achieved personal enlightenment vowed to stay behind until all human beings could do the same.

Concepts of selfless love, devotion, compassion, service, mercy, and forgiveness all spring from the bosom of a healthy and flowing heart chakra. When we look deeper at the Christ archetype, we can

---

115 Judith, *Eastern Body, Western Mind*, 231–232.

recognize the archetypes of the dying gods of the agrarian mystery cults: Adonis, Tammuz—those grain gods who give completely of their essence as the sacrificial grain, which is grown, ripened, and then reaped, later to appear again, reborn. Sacrifice itself, when it comes from the heart, is an act of love.

The energy of the heart chakra is the feeling of love. Balancing this feeling is essential. When a person is working from an overactive heart chakra, they suffer from being too vulnerable, too easily hurt, and giving so much of themselves they lose themselves. When a person is working with an underactive heart chakra, they are unable to connect authentically with another.[116] A wound to the heart chakra shows up in physical ways as a heart attack and heart disease or problems with the lungs. Deep grief may manifest as chronic lung issues, such as CPD or recurrent bronchitis.[117]

### Practices for Strengthening the Fourth Chakra

Strengthening the heart chakra can begin with practicing concepts such as letting go of resentments and attachments and working with a professional therapist or counselor, if need be. Here, one can work through relationship issues, healing wounds from the second chakra, and learn to balance wants and desires. Self-care and pampering are other ways to nurture a healthy heart chakra.

Developing the capacity for compassion is a strong practice. There is a beautiful meditation to do this, known in Buddhism as the Metta. Metta is an active form of meditation where instead of focusing on the breath, one focuses on sending benevolent thoughts and wishes to oneself, others, out into the world, and to people we have difficulty with. In this meditation, one can imagine that whoever the object of the Metta may be, they may be relieved of discomfort or any pain as

---

116 Judith, *Eastern Body, Western Mind*, 260–262.
117 Louise Hay, *Heal Your Body* (Carlsbad, CA: Hay House, 1984), 183.

they are touched by the power of goodwill and thoughts of love and compassion generated by the meditator.

Strengthening the heart chakra can be achieved by living a heart-centered and authentic life. Ask yourself, what do I love about myself? What do I think others love about me? Whom do I love? What qualities attracted me to a beloved? What activities make me happy and why? What activities do I like to do to show my love and what activities do I wish to do to live in a love-based way in all my affairs? How can I be of service to others? Take some time to answer these questions and journal the answers for yourself. Be honest and authentic. If you find you do not love and appreciate and value yourself, send yourself more loving-kindness with the Metta meditation. Any act of compassionate service toward others, including animals and the planet, can help open and heal our heart chakra.

A third pathway into this heart chakra is through connecting with the fey—spiritual beings in nature who are the keepers of wonder and joy. The fey exist in a dimension of consciousness most closely linked to our own. In Celtic lands, they were known as the *sidhe*, but they have their cognates in many other cultures. These beings are linked as caregivers of nature and the natural world, and they resonate with a pure joy and freedom that comes from existing in close relationship with nature. They exist outside of this world's constrictions of space and time.

## Fifth Chakra—Throat Chakra

The color of this chakra is a turquoise blue, which resonates with the element of air. Our words represent symbols that unlock thought and can alter consciousness. This is the chakra of sound and vibration, language and creative verbal expression, and communication on all levels.

The rune that matches this chakra is Ansuz, or signals. In this rune, the emphasis is on receiving signals, messages, gifts, and even warnings. It represents connection and can direct us to new pathways. It connects us from our highest nature to our earthly world. This rune is a call, and it may represent a call to a new beginning.[118]

In this chakra, collectively, humans create poetry, proclamations, words of power, and affirmative prayers. Modern examples of divine revelation include the book *A Course in Miracles* and other channeled and revealed teachings, which are transformative to those who embrace the teachings.[119] This form of spiritual experience serves as the foundation for many religious movements throughout all cultures and time.

A healthy fifth chakra is aware, receptive, and responsive to one's surroundings, creativity, and reason, instead of to subconscious programming and destructive lower-brain reactions. Balance allows access to the higher cognitive abilities of the neocortex, rather than staying stuck in the primitive brain, the amygdala, which does not rise above our throats and exists at the consciousness of fight, flight, or freeze.

As this chakra represents a bridge to higher realms, it is essential to complete the work of the lower chakras and, through this chakra, to live and speak from personal truth. We have to speak the truth to ourselves and others without fear.[120] Some people never achieve this and live lives without a rooted sense of personal values, lost in an inability to speak from their own heart, mind, and experience. They may not know their true self, controlled by how they believe others view them. This represents a blocked fifth chakra, restricted by fears of what others think or a need for others to approve of who we are. This chakra blocked can result in dishonesty, or flattery, or constantly trying to please others at the expense of our own truths.[121] Physically, a

---

118  Blum, *The Book of Runes*, 96–97.

119  Helen Schucman, *A Course in Miracles* (Mill Valley, CA: The Foundation for Inner Peace, 2008).

120  Judith, *Eastern Body, Western Mind*, 305–312.

121  Judith, *Eastern Body, Western Mind*, 296–301.

fifth chakra blockage may show up as laryngitis, throat problems, thyroid problems, cancer of the tongue or throat, or sudden muteness.[122]

### Practices for Strengthening the Fifth Chakra

The power of this chakra can be accessed through sound healing work: drumming, chanting, singing bowls, and sound healing meditation, which help bring us into altered states of consciousness and alignment. The occult understanding that words have power is tied to the energy of the fifth chakra. The magick of the bards, poetry, lives here.[123] Gifted wordsmiths create worlds of their own using rhyme, poetry, prose, storytelling, and fiction. These expressions then help others access new realms of possibility and depths of feeling.

Knowing when to be silent is also a practice of a healthy fifth chakra. Not to create shame for one's ideas and thoughts, but to be discerning in whom we share our innermost selves with. An effective way to cultivate silence is to attend a silent retreat. This is particularly useful if we are tired of hearing ourselves complain or frustrated by speaking and not being heard. The silent retreat allows us to get quiet inside and out so that we may hear our inner wisdom.

An essential practice for this chakra is the practice of speaking truth, letting go of fear that others may not approve of the truth of who we are. By speaking our truth and being our authentic selves, we change our vibration and move toward others who share our resonance.

Our words create. By speaking our hopes, dreams, visions, and wishes affirmatively and in the now, we become cocreators of reality.

Learning a new language is a way of strengthening the energy of this chakra. One of our first tasks as humans is to learn the language of our birth. When we do, we became part of our community. Through language, we download our cultural heritage through the concepts, symbols, and expressions encoded within language and

---

122  Hay, *Heal Your Body*, 182.
123  Kristoffer Hughes, *Cerridwen* (Woodbury, MN: Llewellyn Publications, 2021), 34–40.

song. When we learn new languages, this same process is repeated and can lead to opening and insight.

Another practice we can use to open this chakra is enjoying music. Whether we create music; use singing bowls, bells, drums, rattles, or chanting; or listen to music that inspires and uplifts us, the music itself can help us access wordless dimensions that profoundly move us and move energy. Music creates vibrations that allow us to enter into experiences beyond what words alone are able to express. Music helps put the logical mind to rest long enough for our bodies, spirits, and other aspects of self to reorient. The fifth chakra is the bridge and doorway to higher cognition and realms of consciousness.

## Sixth Chakra—Third Eye Chakra

The color of this chakra is a deep indigo blue, and its location in the body is behind the space between the eyes, connecting with the pituitary gland in the brain. This location has long been associated with the concept of the third eye in Eastern teachings and occult thought. Through this eye, one seeks conscious connection and understanding through visions, art, dreams, and shamanic journeying.

The element associated with this chakra is fire, but specifically light. This means both the physical light we experience with the gift of vision as well as the illumination of ideas in the mind and the spiritual light of awakening. One encounters the light of awareness of other realms here, including the ability to connect with spirits and entities in different dimensions.

The rune most in alignment with this chakra is Kano, or opening. This rune represents the opening of renewed clarity, of dispelling darkness and illusion.[124] With a healthy and open sixth chakra, one can receive visions and revelation of divine truth. Good intention,

---

124 Blum, *The Book of Runes*, 118.

insight, concentration, intuition, and seeing the self and the world clearly are all associated with this rune.[125]

Collectively, the function of the third eye chakra is connected to all movements related to receiving visions, messages, and inspiration. Mediumship channelings are spiritual and religious activities related to honoring the gifts of communion with alternative realms. Those who have activated the muscle of their third eye are able to receive revelations that inspire change and perception shifts in others. We have seen the power of this chakra in the emergence of revealed doctrine. From the ancient oracles at Delphi, to Moses revealing the Commandments as spoken through the burning bush, to Mohammed reciting the words of the Quran as told to him by the angel Gabriel, here is where inspired guidelines for humankind have been revealed.

Shamanic journeying connects to this chakra, as does receiving messages and symbols that come through the inner eye in dreams. Symbols always have meaning to the person they appear to, and while some are archetypal and universal, others are culturally specific.[126] Lucid dreaming is a form of shamanic journeying. In dreams, everyone has the ability to tap into these powers. Dreams are ways the psyche and the Higher Self seek to use symbolic language to get our attention, to work out struggles we are dealing with in our conscious lives, and to receive inspiration and even visitation from Spirit. In traditional Indigenous society, dream messages were honored and visitations were not questioned or dismissed.

Some people are born with their third eye chakras open and are gifted at interacting with spirits and receiving visions. However, if one is not grounded in their body and in the truth of themselves, or they are easily manipulated, they are at risk of being crippled and overwhelmed by this information and unable to function well in wak-

---

125  Blum, *The Book of Runes*, 118.
126  Judith, *Eastern Body, Western Mind*, 353–354.

ing consciousness. For those who do have strong psychic gifts, it is essential to learn to ground, and also to protect their aura and self from illusion and any spiritual entities intent on control. This holds true for tuning out negative, controlling, and intrusive messages from our culture. Advertisers know exactly how to manipulate us through this chakra.

Physically, the third eye is connected to the pituitary gland. Medically, this gland functions as an inner watchdog to various systems of our body, including their regulation through the hormones they secrete. It is no wonder that occult knowledge places this gland as the inner secret of the soul, overseeing our multidimensional realities.

A sixth chakra that is out of balance shows itself as someone who is too intellectual, too mental, who may complain of frequent headaches. Alternatively, an underperforming sixth chakra can result in difficulty with concentration and staying on tasks, lack of creative thinking, or excessive daydreaming and fantasizing. When severely activated, it can lead to illusions and delusional thinking.[127] Delusional thinking can be painfully damaging, such as being lost in the delusion of addiction, where one keeps telling themselves a behavior or substance helps when it really harms. It can result in body image problems.

### Practices for Strengthening the Sixth Chakra

A healthy third eye chakra invites rich imagination and creative thought. A third eye working in balance is a person who has strong insight and intuition and is an expert at recognizing patterns and symbols. Through balance and development, we can achieve a higher activation of consciousness and dream the big dreams and visions that change the world.

Western culture today, especially in the United States through social media and other forms of media and entertainment, has made

---

127 Judith, *Eastern Body, Western Mind*, 371.

a multibillion-dollar industry of using persuasive psychological techniques to get us to buy things we don't need, to believe things that aren't true, and to polarize the population with manipulated news and truth. A good practice, therefore, to regain our own inner sight and compass is to disconnect from our electronic devices, including television, social media, and smartphones. Think of it as clearing your mental palate.

Unblocking, clearing, and bringing this chakra into balance is incredibly important. Another everyday practice is creating arts and crafts. The ability of the artist to visualize, create, access, and share inner worlds with others is empowering. This gift allows us to convey meaning in imagery and information in symbolic form.

Working with dreams is another fruitful practice for developing your third chakra. Keep a dream journal and perhaps join a dream group to strengthen this connection. Remember that nightmares can hold powerful symbolic messages from the psyche. You could also develop a mindfulness meditation practice, focusing on the breath and the sensations in the body to allow true sight to be activated and come forth.

Practicing journeying—through the use of drums, rattles, and other ways to alter consciousness—can allow you to take inner journeys to alternate realms for guidance and divine inspiration. Here you may meet with spirit guides, ancestors, and totem animals and beings. Alternatively, you may join a group dedicated to mediumship development. While some mediums experience full manifestation in this dimension of a spirit on occasion, the vast majority make contact through the inner eye. This skill, as with most exercises, is developed by exercising the third eye muscle repeatedly in order to strengthen it. Other forms of divination, such as reading tea leaves, scrying, or reading tarot cards, can help develop the third eye.

## Seventh Chakra—Crown Chakra

The color of this chakra is violet purple, but it can also be a golden circle of light. It is called the crown chakra and is located on the top of and around the head and represents a fully awakened consciousness. The rune that best matches the energy of this chakra is Dagaz, which represents breakthrough and transformation, a major shift in consciousness, self-change, and awakening.[128] Through this portal, one is able to assimilate all the wisdom and knowledge they have learned over their life and realize they still know little about reality, thus remaining open and teachable. In this way, we become open to the mystery of the Divine.[129]

What is Spirit? Inspiration, love, Highest Self, the energy that created and infuses the whole universe. Many seekers experience the spiritual drive as a deep longing to be in relationship with the universal Spirit. Expansion through this chakra connects oneself to the greater universe and to the collective human consciousness. Carl Jung's theory of the collective unconsciousness says it is here where culture stores all the inherited beliefs and archetypes from evolution as building blocks to the human psyche. This is in keeping with the occult theory of the living cosmos.

The cosmos itself is the manifest reality of divine consciousness. The divinity is vast, mysterious, and beyond human understanding. While people have been personifying the idea of Creator since the dawn of humanity, the truth is likely that divinity itself is beyond knowing and conceptualizing—the ultimate mystery. My belief is that this mystery can be compared to a divine jewel of light with many facets. Each facet is a ray of influence, and from these rays, the concepts that developed into different pantheons of gods, angels, Orishas, natural and astral forces emerged. All these beings and energies are

---

128  Blum, *The Book of Runes*, 137.
129  Blum, *The Book of Runes*, 137.

aspects of the whole of the Creator. The mystery is approached via the opening of the crown chakra. An awakened crown chakra in Eastern tradition represents the risen life force, the immanent divinity, and is represented as the Kundalini energy, or snake energy, activated through the whole spinal column. In Lukumi, during the crowning ceremony, or Kariocha, the initiate becomes one with their guardian Orisha at the level of their head.

A person who is experiencing an imbalance in this chakra will not be grounded in reality. They may be too spacey, have no roots, and spend their life chasing peak experience after peak experience, never realizing the need or ability to bring down the information received from their experiences into their everyday life.[130] They also may experience a spiritual emergency.

A spiritual emergency is the negative aspect of spiritual emergence. Something profoundly shifts so that the old way of knowing or old belief system is shaken to the core. It can be brought on by emotional crisis or overload, overwork, or a severe trauma, or it can be spontaneous. It can happen due to spiritual seeking, brought on by concentrated and deliberate effort to force awakening. It can also come about when we have an experience that shifts our personal belief system so strongly, we enter a new paradigm. In a spiritual emergency, a person is untethered, shattered, and they may have difficulty being in the present. They may be inundated with what feels like a download of information, thoughts, images, and even music into their minds. They may experience life as if they exist in other realms completely, or beings from those realms intrude on their everyday consciousness.

A person having a spiritual emergency may shake uncontrollably or have racing thoughts, speaking in unfamiliar languages, obsessively creating art, poetry, or prose, which sometimes appears disjointed or unintelligible. They may need little food or sleep and be filled

---

130 Judith, *Eastern Body, Western Mind*, 419–420.

with energy. Psychiatry may recognize this as a manic or psychotic state, yet it's crucial to understand the experience these individuals are describing and living is very real to them. I believe the difference between psychosis, mania, madness, divine inspiration, or spiritual possession is rooted in the cultural context it is expressed in, as we have seen with the birth of new shamans, as well as in how well the individual can integrate their experience. When an individual receives support for their vision by their culture, it can help determine their fate after the experience.

To emerge intact from a spiritual emergency requires the loving arms of family and community. In traditional Native American vision quests, after receiving a vision and sharing it with wise elders, a person may integrate this new insight in a way that supports them, because it is received with respect and appreciation, a message meant for the community as a whole. This is even true within some mystical branches of traditional religion. Visionary mystics such as Theresa of Avila and St. Paul had their ecstatic visions positively received by people who shared their worldview and faith in their version of the divine mystery. In the mystical sects of Hinduism, this ecstatic state has been called the Divine Madness of the Saints. Mental health counselors can recognize a sacred role to receive this vision of clients suffering from an overwhelming experience of spiritual emergency. They would do well to take the time to honor, respect, and listen deeply to their clients' experiences without judgment.

A person with a blocked seventh chakra may be unable to accept and access alternative consciousness outside of their everyday experience. This might be through choice, by adherence to rigid scientific and materialist thinking that overemphasizes the reality of only things that can be experienced by our five senses, measured and numbered.[131] They may choose atheism and either mock or doubt any experience

---

131 Judith, *Eastern Body, Western Mind*, 418.

that causes them to lose control or makes them feel irrational. They may secretly envy those who have the ability to shift into other states of being, yet their disbelief itself may be what is holding them back from having an experience. A blocked seventh chakra may manifest itself into feelings of disgust and boredom with life, that there is nothing else out there and life is meaningless or purposeless.[132]

At the collective level, humanity's expression of this chakra may well be reflected in the positive aspects of large religious and spiritual movements. Joining an established religious practice, one connects with others in order to collectively raise hearts and minds in prayer and longing for union with the Creator. When genuine spiritual experience happens among masses of true believers, transformative and out-of-body experiences can take place, as well as the idea of Oneness. The concept of connecting to a higher power in order to overcome substance abuse, so important to 12-step recovery, is an idea born of seventh chakra conscious connection.[133]

Also connected with this chakra is the concept of entities and beings that exist outside of the physical realm and Mother Earth. The archangels as representative of higher beings closer to God are found throughout the world in many different cultures and religions. In Hindu tradition, similar forces are deified and worshipped as particular aspects of the Divine. Within the energy of this chakra also emerges our connection to these beings who exist beyond our world, those who travel through from other planets and star systems—the star ancestors.

What we are learning about quantum physics today is an understanding that there are multiple dimensions of consciousness, and what we experience in day-to-day life is only one mode of being within that greater whole. This means we ourselves may actually exist

---

132  Judith, *Eastern Body, Western Mind*, 418.
133  Judith, *Eastern Body, Western Mind*, 407–408.

on other levels as alternate versions of ourselves on alternate Earths. In fact, what on this level we may consider as reincarnations of ourselves may only be those other selves living out other lifetimes and experiences, as time is actually happening all at once and linear time is an illusion. A transcendental experience, therefore, might be when we encounter a window into this timeless level of conscious identity. When this chakra is activated and flowing smoothly, we become open channels to the Higher Self.[134]

## Practices for Strengthening the Seventh Chakra

There are healthy ways to engage the mind to achieve altered states of conscious that lift the vibration of the seventh chakra. In religious art and icons, highly evolved beings are often depicted with an aura of light around their heads, an artistic representation of an enlightened soul. Hindu teaching shares that when the Kundalini of consciousness rises through all the lower chakras and into our crown, a person awakens into their highest cognition and awareness. They become crowned in the light of consciousness. Tantric practices, chanting, prayer, as well as sound healing through tones, bells, or drums, can help move consciousness toward a sense of wholeness.

A devotion to moral development is a practice for the seventh chakra. By keeping a focus on thoughts, behaviors, and vibrations, one can stay positive, clean, and clear. While it is inadvisable to try to spiritually bypass the sorrows, injustices, and dark side of human behavior, it is important to not dwell on them indefinitely. Attention creates our reality. The Buddha expressed this path toward enlightenment so well by sharing the eightfold path of right thinking, right speech, right livelihood, right action, right intention, right view, right concentration, and right effort. He taught that true enlightenment takes conscious and diligent effort, requiring work and dedication.

---

134 Judith, *Eastern Body, Western Mind*, 439–442.

Contemplation of our Oneness with nature is another useful perspective for this chakra. A shift of perception can be had with this simple exercise: reflect on how your size shifts when you change your viewpoint. If you consider yourself standing over a patch of grass crawling with ants, bugs, small plants, and weeds, you are aware of yourself as a giant. But if you shift your consciousness to imagine yourself against a nighttime sky filled with the countless stars of the universe, you realize how small you are and how insignificant are the problems that might be currently plaguing you. Acknowledging the interdependence with all forms of life on our planet, or how each pocket of our planet is a different ecosystem unto itself, can also help you arrive at a deeper appreciation of Oneness with all that is.

## TENDING THE FLAME
### Indigenous Māori Tradition

Puáwai Ormsby is an educator and artist and a traditional elder from the Māori community of New Zealand. She is one of the designated gatekeepers of the Temple of the Four Winds of New Zealand. She shared with me the ways that her Indigenous community revitalized their culture, incorporating into the local meeting house their cosmology, which includes an understanding of chakra healing and energy and of Oneness with all that is. Puáwai is an active member of today's revival of Māori culture in New Zealand:

> When my son was birthed, he's thirty-six now, there was a renaissance. The grandmothers got together, and they realized that once a language dies, your culture dies. So, they

decided to create early childcare centers under the umbrella called *Kohanga Reo*, another word for "the language nest." I then decided to take my son to the Kohanga Reo and to start with him, learning the language. He went there from three years old to five. My parents were so against it! They still wouldn't speak or have anything to do with Māori. From there, I took him into the total immersion schools; that was the only place where he could avail himself to the language, so he went to total immersion up to high school.

Also, in that time frame in our meeting houses, our gathering places, there came a shift of consciousness within the wider members of the community. There are a lot more Māori now going to university and studying colonization, so there was a huge awareness that we needed to understand what happened to our people, to understand the treaty that was signed and was being dishonored, and we needed to go back to grassroots and try to fix this. To reclaim our heritage. So, there was a huge movement to bring action, songs, *kapa haka*, back into our schools for everyone. It was a movement in every shape and form within our culture. You saw that movement; there were schools, Wananga Aotearoa, where they set up learning for all different age groups, right up to grandmothers, grandfathers, different ethnicities, to learn our culture, customs, and traditions, freely.

And it was a huge movement and became so popular, and that, for me, was such a pivotal point of change. Within that establishment, we got to go to class, do our Karakia, do our songs, learn the haka actions, learn our way of learning, which is very kinesthetic. There was color, there was rhythm, there was song, there was dance, so it was a whole movement of learning by the teachings of our ancestors. Not so much writing—simply our way of learning. But the learning for us was embedded in our hearts, which brought us into that deep, deep, sacred connection with our ancestors. We were then suddenly learning directly; they selected us to represent them on this Earth walk. We were feeling their talents, their gifts, that were embedded in ourselves.

This country here is the Land of the First or Ever-Shining Light. There is a violet haze above Aotearoa, so we do consider ourselves the new zeal arriving. We have a lot of Indigenous nations coming to New Zealand now to find out how we held on to our culture. They come to the schools to get inspired and excited about what they can do back home, and they invest time and energy into creating, to bring back their own culture. The Temple of the Four Winds is known in the ancient prophecies of the First Nations as the place of the Stairway to Heaven. A lot of elders from Indigenous peoples come over to discover this site; they hear of this place in their prophecies.

We are the pillars of light between Heaven and Earth. Our word for Sky Father is *Ranginui*; *Ra*, the great central sun; *Ngi*, the creative spark. You put Ra-Ngi together, you get sacred songs; *nui*, then, is the greatness. There is that understanding that the universe was sung into form, so that is the word: *Ranginui*. Earth Mother is *Papatuanuku*. *Papa* is the space, *tua* is to stand, *nuku* is the rainbow—so, the space of the standing rainbow. We stand here, we hold space, and we have a chakra system. We are the space of the standing rainbow. Can you see how there is no separation? We believe we were gifted from the Heavens and birthed upon the Earth, so cosmically enhanced, nature inspired.

Ours is such a conscious community; it really is. There is a YouTube video of our official opening of our meeting house here on the island. If you watch it, you will see all the woven panels that we did, and they asked me for a theme, and I said it should be the chakra system. They are in the meeting house. All different nationalities on Waiheke Island came together, learned the ancient Māori ways and chants to support that holy being.

We chose the rainbow because we also have living on Waiheke Island all the Rainbow Warriors, the Rainbow Warrior boat. The boat was bombed in the harbor years ago, so all those families moved to Waiheke Island to bring up their families. Our community is very rainbow-based. We have many different cultures, and they all come to our island to honor the teachings. This small community, with different people from all around the world, have chosen to now be part of our Māori culture. And for them to learn those chants, and to stand proudly, was just pivotal—the heart opens!

All these elders were so moved. It was teaching the children early on, taking them into the bush, then the children wanted to take their parents. To me, you teach the children, and then the children reverberate to their parents and grandparents. So, it goes both ways, forward and backward, because they will teach their children, and they will teach their elders, and they can heal that link.

## ❊ A PRACTICE ❊
### Spiritual Home Clearing

It is important to learn how to recognize and clear negative energy. It may be associated with a place or a person, and as we develop intuitively, it may be attracted to us and attach itself. One can experience its presence as a heavy or stagnant atmosphere of place, a sudden uptick of conflict in our relationships, a bout of illness, and otherwise bad luck. We may suddenly feel confused, angry, sickly, or depressed. Sometimes it may feel as if we are having foreign thoughts that come from someone or something else. Having some ways to clean ourselves, clear our chakras, and cleanse our surroundings of negative energy is really important. Here is one way.

## Tools

You will need an incense burner, such as a large abalone shell available at occult or New Age shops, a pinch of salt, a chalice filled with water, a charcoal block, and your choice of cleansing herb. Suggestions: bay leaf, rosemary, rue, sage, or sandalwood. You may also use a ground resin of frankincense, copal, or myrrh.

*For those sensitive to smoke, you may infuse the herb in water beforehand overnight and sprinkle the energized water instead of using smoke.*

## Begin

Cast a circle, calling in each of the directions and elements one by one, beginning in the east. In the Soul Blossom Circle tradition, east is air, south is fire, west is water, north is earth. Light a charcoal burner and add to it the dried herbs or resin and begin cleaning the space in a counterclockwise manner. Wave the incense around using a fan. Envision that you are clearing energy and say words to this effect out loud: "With this herb, I clean and clear negative energy and vibrations."

Speaking our words aloud makes them real and empowers our actions.

Next, clear the energy around yourself, beginning at the top of your head, directing the smoke toward each area of your body associated with each chakra. Imagine that any stuck, blocked, or overstimulated energy in each chakra is removed, and they spin with light and grow in clarity. Repeat your clearing mantra.

When you are complete, begin to clean your home in the same way. Walking counterclockwise in a circle, wave the smoke into all the corners, high and low, and envision the energy clearing in your home. Open the windows and doors so that energy may move out from your home.

When you have completed the circle of your home, add the salt to the water and sprinkle this mixture around the house, going clockwise now, visualizing cleansing it completely, using words of power to speak that into being. "With this salt, I now bless my home and protect it from all negative influences." Complete the cleansing, thank and release the elements, and close your circle.

As nature-based people, it is important to keep our homes neat and tidy and to take care of our mental, physical, and spiritual selves. This is a form of physical and spiritual hygiene. Regularly clearing our homes in this way can be a preventative form of removing stagnant and heavy energy.

# HERBAL WAYS AND NATURAL MEDICINE

It takes time and dedication to commit oneself to nature spirituality, but it is so rewarding. It's a deep listening and sharing with the natural world around us, and a witnessing and interaction with the seasons as they unfold. Opportunities come daily, monthly, yearly, and all are little treasures—observing birds, learning flowers, herbs, weeds, animals, seeing the changing colors of the sky and temperatures over time, taking in the smells of the forest as the seasons pass; all are captivating, and all relate to the changes within ourselves over our lifetimes.

Nature-based people from all over the world see the lessons of the natural world as lessons that teach us about creation. This rang true among ancient Pagans, where the priests of the Celts and Germanic tribes watched the flight of birds and read omens through the movement of animals. It continues through modern Paganism today and with Indigenous peoples the world over who urge us to heed of the warnings coming from nature through violent storms, melting polar ice caps, and vanishing forests. Nature herself is the holy book for all Earth-based people, because the Earth Mother herself is holy.

## HERBAL MEDICINE AND THE LEGACY OF THE BURNING TIMES

Western herbal and natural medicine did not die out. Up into recent historical times, most rural villages still held the village midwife, the root worker, the dowser, and the herbalist. During the Middle Ages and into the Renaissance in Europe, these people were both sought out by their communities yet distrusted because of their occult and, at that time, dangerous knowledge. As all humans were once Indigenous to the areas they evolved in, these folkways most likely represented the remnants of early religious tradition and natural wisdom of the earlier European people. Over time and due to persecution, the origins and meaning of these beliefs and practices were buried or forgotten. However, an idea of what they may have had in common with contemporary Indigenous peoples can be found by examining closely the documented evidence presented at witch trials in Europe from the fourteenth through seventeenth century.

With the largest number of deaths and trials numbering in the tens of thousands taking place in the Holy Roman Empire, a complex emerged that contained familiar elements of some of the shamanic practices already discussed. Witches were accused of riding broomsticks to attend Black Masses on the ancient Pagan Earth-based holidays and full moons while leaving their bodies at home.[135] Anthropologists now believe these journeys may have been induced in trance

---

135 Johnson, *North Star Road*, 134–136.

states with psychotropic drugs made from ointments or flying potions, recipes carefully preserved and handed down through the ages.

Witches were also said to be skilled in the use of herb craft. If we consider that over the course of human evolution women were the primary gatherers of vegetables and plant foods, it would make sense that women knew and preserved this knowledge of edible, medicinal, and poisonous or psychotropic plants.[136] Perhaps their lost knowledge included the use of natural birth control and abortifacients, which would be a heinous crime for a patriarchal people intent on controlling women's reproduction. Even today, historical documents of more recent Indigenous and colonized cultures, such as early nineteenth-century Puerto Rico, show that the Indigenous healers and those who were brought from Africa had knowledge of herbal birth control.[137]

The written records claim the witches worshipped deities who were nature-based and sensual and related to fertility, sexuality, and the dead. The figure of the Devil had horns, much like the old male deities of the Greek Pan and Celtic Cernunnos. A female figure was also mentioned. In these accounts, she was called Diana or Habondia and described as a lunar deity. The witches had familiar spirits whom they spoke to and made offerings to in return for secret powers.[138] Their spirit helpers often appeared in the form of animal spirits, much like the totems of the medicine men and women from Indigenous cultures the world over.

## COMMONALITIES OF HERBAL LORE

Precolonial Indigenous people of Mexico enjoyed urban centers with sophisticated plumbing and had deep knowledge of the properties of

---

136  Johnson, *North Star Road*, 132–133.

137  Emaline Reyes, "The Invisible Labors and Erased History of Puerto Rican Midwives," *The Revisionist*, September 28, 2020, https://slcwhblog.com/2020/09/28/the-invisible -labors-and-erased-history-of-puerto-rican-midwives/.

138  Johnson, *North Star Road*, 97–104.

the vegetation in their lush lands. As with most Indigenous beliefs, the Aztec doctors treated illness on both the physical and spiritual levels. A healer would work with the ill person, divining the source of the illness from the spiritual realm, then treat the body with herbs. They would offer ceremony and sacrifice to the offended spirits while treating the body together, in cooperation with the patient. The combination of pharmacological and spiritual healing was part and parcel of their Indigenous ways. The conquistadors admitted that the Indigenous knowledge was superior to their own. One friar, Toribio Motolinia, wrote, "Some of the Indians are so experienced that they have cured many old and serious infirmities which the Spanish have suffered many days without finding a remedy."[139]

As in Puerto Rico, also colonized by Europeans, the remaining herbalism that survived imperial Christianity was a combination of wisdom taken from Indigenous European, Classical antiquity, and cultural forces that overlaid what came earlier.

Some of this knowledge was hidden in the arts and crafts of the common people. Defying papal decrees, sympathetic artists and masons preserved the knowledge of herb craft and medicine through folk and high art. Pagan masons continued to carve deities of vegetation and land spirits into the artwork of cathedrals and churches. These images, such as the Green Man, the personification of the active principle in nature, and the Sheila na Gig in Ireland and the British Isles—a squat female goddess figure who spreads her vulva and represents the mystery and power of female fertility—often appeared in lintels and above doorways. Within these symbols, the common people preserved their nature beliefs.[140] An analysis of the Unicorn Tapestries, which reside at the New York Metropolitan Museum of Art at the Cloisters, by John Williamson, who designed the gardens of

---

139  Joie Davidow, *Infusions of Healing* (New York: Fireside Publishers, 1999), 31.
140  Starr Goode, *Sheela na Gig* (Rochester, NY: Inner Traditions, 2016), 1–13.

the Cloisters and studied the tapestries in depth, detailed how within these masterpieces of high art, the artists wove into them the myths, symbols, and archetypes that were part of the pre-Christian psyches of medieval people. Along with the unicorn, who became a symbol of the dying and resurrection deity, Christianized into Jesus himself, a variety of medicinal and magickal herbs and flowers was represented in great detail and encoded a secret language and lore for those who knew the mysteries.[141]

Another way ancient Earth-based knowledge was preserved was through the work of Christian mystics and holy people who cloistered in monasteries. One of them was Hildegard of Bingin, an eleventh-century abbess, philosopher, poet, and composer and also an accomplished naturalist. For her time and her sex, this bordered on heresy with the Orthodox Church.

# HERBAL MEDICINE IN THE NEW WORLD

To Indigenous people like the Yanomami of the Amazon, working with herbal medicine is not mastered by memorizing and documenting the names and families of wild herbs, the hallmark of the methodology of the West. They believe those who wish to work with plants only gain the right to heal with them when they have developed a reciprocal personal relationship, when they become friends. This is an important distinction. The idea is that we should befriend the herbs, trees, plants, and fungi local to our areas if we wish to work with them for our purposes.

Within the cosmology of Indigenous natural medicine, prevention is the best course against disease. It is believed this can be achieved by living in accord with nature instead of fighting against the tides or seasons. In New Zealand, the revival of Māori culture has revived

---

141 John Williamson, *The Oak King, the Holly King, and the Unicorn* (New York: Harper and Row, 1983), 50–54.

interest in the natural medicine within existing communities themselves. Puáwai Ormsby said the following of this:

> A lot of the grandmothers are called *matakite*, the shamanic medicine women. They are the ones who look at you and will say, "So and so is with you," and the Tohumga is the grandfather who holds all that wisdom. Part of the colonization was the Tohumga Suppression Act that stopped our people from making medicine from the bush, using our forest as our pantry, our FARM-acy, and to stop healing with all our natural resources.
>
> We now have a movement where you basically make your medicines in your own home. So many practitioners are learning and are keen to learn all about what sits in our backyards, in our gardens, what we can use to heal our children, our grandchildren. Now, we have taken the extraordinary and made it ordinary. A cup of tea this morning was what I picked in the bush, the Kawa Kawa leaf. Children are then taught when I make my tea in class, and I take them into the bush; it just becomes the normal way of being now. In fact, there are lots of Māori teas now that you can find in the supermarket with our Māori medicines. It's quite normalized for teachers and homes throughout New Zealand.
>
> Many people are choosing to sample and ingest the vibration of the plants of this land, the foods. I myself am a forager. I go down to the river and get my watercress; I know to give thanks to the spirits, to the mythical dragons, to the guardians of the fruits and waterways. I sing a beautiful healing song to the water and I thank the Earth for providing to us. I go to the ocean, I do a Kaikaranga—a chant to the God of the Ocean, Tangaroa, and Hinemoana, the Goddess of the Ocean—to ask if they can provide nourishment to my temple in the form of seafood. So that becomes a very normal practice for me. Anywhere I go to gather food, before I pick anything, it's normal for me to thank the Bush, to thank Mother Earth, for providing the medicine or the nourishment.

Mother Earth herself is the prime teacher for how to go with this flow in optimal, physically energizing, and soul-enriching ways. For those who suffer disease, especially mental diseases like depression and obsession, a natural healer might prescribe cleansing, prayers, smudging, or a quest to receive a divine revelation or song, or recommend undertaking a shamanic journey in order to help the person recover an aspect of their spirit that is lost or out of balance.[142] Health and balance are only achieved by treating a person's physical, mental, and spiritual selves as a whole.

In addition to the living herbal tradition of peoples like the Māori, there is surviving herbal medicine and lore in cultures as widespread as South America, Mexican Curanderismo, Cherokee herbal medicine, and the knowledge of herbs and healing within Afro-Caribbean communities.

# HERBAL AND NATURAL MEDICINE IN THE EAST

It is not accidental that two of the largest intact systems of traditional herbal knowledge and natural medicine are preserved within two cultures that strongly resisted European colonization and influence: specifically, Chinese medicine and Ayurveda from India. As Taoist Diane Rooney states,

> Herbal medicine is huge in Taoism; it's the understanding where Mother Nature puts our antidotes for various things. If we get something poisonous that's Indigenous to an area, the antidote will be close by. So, knowing that, too, is how you survive and live long as a Taoist.

In Chinese medicine, ingesting healing foods and herbs helps replenish the Qi energies, as do movement exercises, breath work, and meridian stimulation. Chinese medicine reveals an encyclopedic

---

142 Doore, *Shaman's Path*, 11–12.

understanding of the health benefits of working with a huge variety of herbs, mushrooms, roots, and other natural medicines to prevent illness and achieve optimal health and long life.

Ayurvedic medicine is from ancient India, is at least three thousand years old, and is practiced in various forms by millions today. The word *Ayurveda* means "the knowledge of life and longevity." It is a whole-body concept and approach to healing, which preserves the understanding that life force is located at the base of our spine, the seat of Kundalini. In the Ayurvedic natural medicine system, each person is ruled by one of the doshas, or three energies of the body. *Dosha* is an ancient Sanskrit term that means "that which can cause problems." The word also means "health types," and the three types are vata, pitta, and kapha.

Vata is about free-flowing energy and is often likened to the wind, or air. Pitta is aligned with the fire element, fiery and sometimes prone to anger. Kapha energy relates to earth energy, which can be solid, but also sluggish. Keeping the energies in balance is the goal of Ayurvedic medicine and is key to maintaining mental, emotional, physical, and spiritual health. As all people are oriented to one main dosha, balancing the dosha energy in our bodies is the goal. Each person uses foods and herbal medicine, along with body practice like Yoga, to balance out too much of one dosha, or too little of another. Good health and long life are achieved through a balance of mental, physical, and spiritual practices.

## REVIVAL OF WESTERN NATURAL MEDICINE AND HEALING THROUGH SPIRITUALISM

Allopathic and scientific medicine have been the norm in Western countries since the seventeenth century. Allopathic medicine has had amazing success treating bacteria-borne and viral illnesses, advancing surgery, and identifying the causes and conditions that create diseases such as cancer and heart disease and developing vaccines for pandemics. However, one sometimes unhelpful aspect of Western medicine is that it traditionally divides the body into its parts for treatment individually. Western doctors usually specialize in one area of the body.

This compartmentalizing also goes for how we think about ourselves. In the Western model, our bodies are viewed as existing separately from our minds, which are also separate from a soul or spiritual self. Our body is subdivided into parts like the skeleton, the digestive system, the muscular system, the nervous system, and so on. If we compare that to wisdom from the East, where the stress is on seeing the human being as a whole entity, we can see how looking at symptoms without identifying root causes or understanding how all parts of ourselves connect and affect one another can become very problematic.

This is even more so for our minds; both the conscious and the unconscious mind are essential parts of a healthy system. A more holistic and balanced identity between right- and left-brained knowledge, wisdom, and understanding is maintained when we see the whole picture.

Westerners are beginning to realize the value of treating the mind and body in this holistic way. Much of this can be attributed to the renaissance of natural medicine and interest in herbal health and knowledge that came about in the early twentieth century. The timing is not accidental. We can thank the demise of laws against practicing Spiritualism for this rebirth.

In late-nineteenth-century Europe, many intellectuals and upper-class Europeans became interested in the practice of mediumship and Spiritualism, and from these early séances and circles, the practice became mainstreamed. In England, the rise of esoteric societies, such as the founding of the Golden Dawn by upper-class Victorians, became commonplace. They grew out of the religious and mystical groups and acted as a counterbalance to the materialism and scientific rationalism of their day. These movements were instrumental in the creation and formation of Wicca and other occult traditions and borrowed a great deal from Eastern teachings. Figures like Madame Blavatsky and the Theosophists accessed esoteric wisdom teachings and paved the way for Yogis such as Yogananda in the late nineteenth century, who brought the path of Yoga to the West. It should be noted that many women were involved in these secret societies.[143]

Later, the New Age embraced natural medicine as a path to mental and spiritual wellness. Twentieth-century American spiritualist Edgar Cayce, often called the dreaming prophet because he would diagnose and channel nutritional remedies to his clients, introduced vegetarianism to thousands of interested people in need of healing. Others like him—healers and mediums like Chico Xavier from Brazil through their work with spiritual entities—have revived and shared the wisdom and teaching of natural health and healing remedies for restoration and well-being.

## GREEN HEALING WAYS

Today, many people have returned to learning about natural healing and herbal medicine. One teacher I have studied with, Susyn Weed, who considers herself a Green Witch, has been teaching her version called the Wise Woman Way in New York State for over thirty years.[144] The concept, like that of Indigenous people, is based on the idea that we should work with the herbs that share our environments and that disease is best treated through prevention. Her teachings have inspired a generation of women herbalists and healers.

---

143  Mary Greer, *Women of the Golden Dawn* (Rochester, VT: Park Street Press, 1995), 46.
144  Susyn Weed, *Wise Woman Herbal* (Woodstock, NY: Ash Tree Publishing, 1999), 5–10.

Today, many are learning and teaching the knowledge of working with herbs and natural remedies to nourish and transform the body. To these, we can also add naturopathic doctors, those who work with flower essences, and a wide variety of natural approaches toward nutrition, including the wild foraging movement. All these methods seek to return the power of caring for our bodies and our health to ourselves.

# PUTTING IT ALL TOGETHER

Vitality and health are realized in an integrated and balanced body, mind, and soul that has moved beyond mere survival and toward full expression and nourishment. When illness arises, nature-based practitioners have the choice now to opt for Western allopathic medicine and/or seek consultation with their spiritual communities, consider alternative natural medicine, or utilize energy healing. While these all can be effective, the best method for keeping ourselves in balance and in balance with nature is prevention and protecting our bodies and minds from toxic substances, individuals, and thoughtforms.

Having a regular practice of connection—whether it is gardening (including keeping an indoor garden for apartment dwellers), growing food, cooking food, or tending local birds and wildlife—allows us to develop relationships with nonhuman life-forms. The same can be said for spending loving time with pets. This provides a shift in consciousness and a slowing down to the rhythms of nature that are all around us.

A holistic, nature-centered lifestyle should include an emphasis on practices like these that enhance well-being. Nature is both Creator and creation, and esoteric tradition states we also share this power. Accessing this power and taking advantage of the rich knowledge and modalities available in alternative health, medicinally and nutritionally, is a gift of modern technology that has connected us to one another and to the ancient wisdom of the past.

As we move forward and seek to relight our own vitality as well as the vitality of Mother Earth's cauldron, we can preserve the advances and knowledge we have enjoyed through science and through this natural health revival with a hope to integrate planetary and personal healing.

## TENDING THE FLAME
### The 21 Divisions, Dominican Vodou

Daniel Rodriguez is a respected Oba, or high priest of Shango, leading ceremonies in the Lukumi tradition in the Northeast region. In addition, he practices Spiritualism and Espiritismo, both from the Cuban and Puerto Rican perspectives. As a personal practice, Danny also is an initiate of the 21 Divisions, a Dominican form of Vodou. The 21 Divisions is both a religion and a practice for many people, and Danny explains how it is a meaningful nature-based tradition for those who practice, even more so for those who have ancestral or spiritual connections to its roots in Benin, Africa. He shares with us how that path opened to him:

> The 21 Divisions is a tradition from the Dominican Republic, which is a sister tradition to Haitian Vodou. It has a lot of similarities with Spiritism and Ocha as well. It came from the same area, more or less. Some of Ocha came from Benin. A lot of the Loa, or gods of the 21 Divisions, also come from the same area, so there are a lot of crossovers between the Orishas and the Loa; they are very interconnected.

I started practicing the 21 Divisions as a teenager and got baptized later on, but it wasn't something I grew up with. It wasn't like Ocha. Ocha is something I grew up with and lived every day. The 21 Divisions caught my attention as a teenager because I grew up with a lot of Dominicans; it's a cultural thing for Dominicans, and where I grew up in Massachusetts, most of the Botanicas were run by Dominicans, and they were carrying things specific to the 21 Divisions. They say in the 21 Divisions that it's something you are born with; it's not something you go get. It's something that comes with you. I guess I didn't realize that it was with me all that time, because I took an instant liking to it, and I wanted to know more. Every time I thought to myself, "Well, I have Ocha; what do I need this for, this is just something else to deal with?" You got to feed it, you got to take care of it, you have a responsibility to it like a pet! I don't mean that in a negative way! I could never understand my calling to it, but I had to realize that I had a spirit guide who worked with it, and I also had ancestry from Benin. After doing my DNA research, understanding why I was so attracted to this became clear.

I'm not saying that just because I was born with Benin DNA, that connection must be something I have, but it is interesting that some of the Orishas come from there. Olokun comes from that area, and so does Babalu Aye; these Orishas are some I have worked with a lot. Some of the Loa are Yoruba, some are spinoffs of the Orisha. For instance, you have Ellegua, and you have Papa Elegba. You have Oggun and you have Ogu in all his different paths; and in each tradition, they have different paths, but similar, in both Ocha and Vodou.

You see the connection, and in each tradition, all the paths do different things. Their energies are very similar, their colors are very similar, their offerings are very similar. Some of the Catholic Saints that they compare them with are the same ones. That's very interesting to me from a historical and an anthropological perspective, because what are the chances of two different people from two different islands figuring out the same saint is going to be Ellegua and Papa Elegba? How could that happen? But it is absolutely a direct line back to the people of Benin. You go back to that concept of Loa; even though we have other elements now involved, it goes right back there. It's an amazing similarity.

Nowadays, everything is a fad. Everyone wants to have everything, especially with these African traditions. They want to get scratched in Palo, they want to make Ocha, they want to baptize the 21 Divisions, they want to keep getting, because more is better, because that's our culture, to buy and get things! And that can be very dangerous because if it's not with you, you are taking in something that doesn't belong to you. It's like taking medicine your body doesn't want. Your body is going to reject it, and it can make you sick. I have seen that happen with people. Anyone who practices the 21 Divisions will tell you, you have to be very careful with the Loa; you shouldn't just serve them like that, you shouldn't put up altars, and I can say the same thing with Ocha—you have to be very careful with that because you may not be doing something that needs to be done.

There are initiations in the 21 Divisions; there are different levels of initiations, different rituals. It has different ceremonies that have to be done; they call them *Puntos*. Everybody has to do different things, depending on you, your persona, what the Loa ask of you. It's very individually based. But there is a process. However, you can serve the Loa without being initiated. That is fine, but you have to be careful, because you have to know what you are doing. You can have a Punto, which is where you are taken to a certain part of nature, and that Loa is honored right there by you and you take that energy and that represents the Loa you are going to be serving, which is why you have to get that Punto because that Loa is very close.

The Loa are forces of Nature just like the Orisha. It's the same idea—every Loa represents a different area, a different force of nature. *Loa* means "spirit." So just like with Orisha, these Loa were syncretized with Catholic Saints. But, in the 21 Divisions—I can't really speak to Haitian Vodou because I am not a practitioner, and I don't know very much about it—but I can tell you in the 21 Divisions, the Catholic Saint very much took a position. So that's the image you are going to see; people are going to refer to the Loa by the Catholic Saint name, too.

People are now trying to get away from syncretic practices. And I have a problem with that; I think that's a big mistake. Because you are changing the essence by what was created with that fusion, and you are trying to separate it a little bit, and it's all on the basis of, well I'm trying to clean it up, I'm trying to make it pure. Well, if you are going to do that, you are going to have to get rid of a lot of things. I tell people the same thing in Ocha.

Synchronization is something we do as humans. When you look at the 21 Divisions and look at the Loa and what you offer them in the 21 Divisions, and you go back to Africa, and to Benin, to a shrine, it's the same stuff. In Africa, everything continued to evolve, too. They evolved, they mixed with Christianity and Islam, and they learned about what they do in the Diaspora, and they added that to it. It's a living tradition.

This is absolutely a Nature-based practice, though, because in order to practice, you have to visit the points of Nature, you have to go and present to those elements. They utilize plants and flowers and different elements, stones, shells, just like in Ocha; it does have a lot of Earth-based things. They use a lot of incense, cigar smoke, oils, a lot of different perfumes—all those things are put together, trying to get that energy. Fire and water are used a lot. Almost every one of these traditions uses these, even the Catholic Church uses that—you light the candle, and the holy water. Every tradition has to have fire and water. It all goes back to Earth-based, Nature-based practice; using elements, a relationship with spirits and ancestors. I mean, if you compare all the Earth-based traditions, this is true. In Druid tradition, they had earth, air, fire, water, and every one of them had a sacrifice of some sort. Whether it's a lot, a little, or this or that, or a food offering, it's an exchange of energy.

While some people come to these traditions to collect religious certificates, per se, with Ocha and the 21 Divisions, both give a person that ingredient every human being needs: that there is a force out there, that's listening to me. There is a force out there that is going to help me through my everyday challenges, my health, my relationship, my finances, my family. And people come looking for that. It's almost like a cane; I need something to lean on because I know I am human and weak and I need something to sustain me. You are seeing more and more people connecting with these types of traditions and walking away from the traditional religions of Christianity, Islam, Judaism, because they are not finding that connection there because they have all become very mechanical.

# ❊ A PRACTICE ❊
## Connecting to the Spirit
## of a Plant for Self-Healing

Nature practitioners today have the benefit of integrating Eastern, Western, and Indigenous sensibilities when working with plant medicine and magick. The heritage of the occult and scientific tradition of the West recommends we learn to identify a plant, observing closely its location, amount of sun, soil conditions, then its flowers, stems, seeds, scent, and other factors for identification. Then it is recommended that we identify which genus or plant family the specimen belongs to, utilize its scientific name, and research its properties for use in plant medicine and identify its signature magickal properties. Thus, a Western approach can help us identify, utilize, and memorize plants for healing and magickal work.

A shamanic approach to plants takes a more experiential route. The first rule of thumb is the plant must be local to our environment for it to be considered a friend or ally. Secondly, we must befriend the plant, and communicate with it, making appropriate offerings as a form of gratitude and reciprocity, and then wait and see if the plant responds affirmatively. Only then may we earn the right to work with a plant ally. In this way, even an urban nature practitioner can work with plants local to their environment by tuning in with their intuition to what neighbors are present.

## Tools

A journal. A knife or gardening scissors, and a container or sack to hold the gathered herb. An offering of water.

## Begin

Take a walk near your home. It is best to do this during the early spring or growing season to identify what is growing nearby. Look for what is abundantly growing through sidewalk cracks, sides of buildings, or in your front lawn or nearby wooded area.

Allow your mind to clear and check in with your body. When you see a plant that resonates with an intuitive feeling in your body, approach it. If the plant feels receptive to touch and to your presence, introduce yourself and ask the plant if it would like to be your ally and friend and help you with healing and spiritual work. You may describe or draw the plant in your journal and record the response. Thank the plant and leave it alone.

Return again, perhaps the next day, and observe the reaction of the plant. You may make an offering to the plant at this time. Watering the plant is most likely welcome. Now ask the plant again. You may get the sense it is okay to take a portion of the plant to use, dried or fresh. It may also ask to wait until a later season, perhaps when the flowers or fruit are present. It may recommend you work with its roots. You may even get a message in a dream from the spirit of the plant itself, which is more personal and direct. Above all, be open to the guidance, even if it seems illogical. This type of wisdom uses non-rational methods of knowing and cognition. Always remember to thank the plant. Be sure to record your impressions and what you choose to harvest in your journal. Also record how you used the plant gift.

For those who may have difficulty with this practice, open yourself to receiving less direct messages. Look for what is growing overabundantly in your garden patch, or which branches are tapping loudly at your window. One way that may help you accept that these messages are for you, personally, is to do some research on what the plant who is trying to get your attention is used for, either medicinally or magickally. You may realize it is the perfect remedy for whatever issue you are working on. The more you connect with the natural beings and forces near you, the stronger you will connect with the land spirits of the place you call home.

# 11
# PERMACULTURE
# AND SUSTAINABILITY

As humanity continues to evolve into the Aquarian Age, the rise of the permaculture and sustainability movement, led by progressive countries such as Denmark and Sweden as well as in Eastern places like Singapore, is an increasingly important aspect of the global paradigm shift. The urgency to expand green consciousness is not exclusive to nature-based tradition; it has been trending in mainstream secular culture as well. Even within Judeo-Christian religion, there is support for this trend. Christian theologian Father John Berry wrote in his book *The Dream of the Earth* back in the 1970s,

> More and more humans are realizing that we must place value on preserving open spaces and natural places as resources in their own right, valuing them as oases of wildlife, preserves for mental and physical health benefits for all

humans, and the creatures we share our planet with. They can no longer be imagined only for their economic value of what trees become when they are chopped down.[145]

The quest for a more sustainable lifestyle for humanity is motivating scientists, activists, artists, musicians, and poets from all around the world.

# INDIGENOUS VIEW

While attending the Parliament of the World's Religions in Utah in 2014 and in Toronto in 2018, I was struck by how this message was reinforced and repeated by many Indigenous elders and speakers from all over the world. In South America, Brazilian native activists have succeeded in creating laws to speak for the defense of the land and waters as worthy in their own right for protection from exploitation by transnational corporate and government interests.

To the Indigenous Māori, connecting with the land is an essential practice and is embedded in the concept of Karakia, a daily practice of personal prayer and a way of centering oneself in relation to the land. Puáwai Ormsby explained:

> Usually I wake up, open my eyes, and do my practice, my Karakia, my prayer. You will find that in many of the households where the older people are living. All different children learn their traditional introduction, what the mountain was, what the river was. They are able to stand up and introduce themselves, in our way, even if they are from overseas, in the language of this land. Because the spirits of this land have brought them here. They were destined to be here in Aotearoa, New Zealand, the land of the Ever-Shining Light.

Tuvan shamanic practitioner Arda Itez believes a renewed commitment to the Earth and to being a caretaker for the Earth and nature

---

145  Thomas Berry, *The Dream of the Earth* (San Francisco: Sierra Club Publications, 1988), 70–88.

is something that comes naturally as one grows practicing shamanism. Tuvan Shamanism respects all religious paths as valid and, for Arda, has been a way to connect with nature in a divine way:

> It's a personal connection, a direct link to our own relationship. I wake up in the morning, I'm very fortunate to live where I live, and I look out on the river and I'm like, "Oh, my God!" Watching the sun rise, it's a sense of awe that is almost indescribable to me. I mean I get giddy when I go to the ocean. Every time I go to the ocean, it's like I am seeing it for the first time. And that is something that has developed, the appreciation that has developed over time, because of this practice. An appreciation for things I have seen my whole life! It's like seeing the world through new eyes; you see the life in everything.

Arda believes cultivating this awareness is a way of life that can be instrumental in this shifting of one's focus from the personal to the planetary:

> If we can learn to live with the type of appreciation that shamanism cultivates, we would never, never see the pollution you see now. We wouldn't do a fraction of what we do now, we would live much more sustainably, we would be much more compassionate. I'm not saying everyone would become vegetarians, but the way we consume animal products would change drastically. We would live in a much more reciprocal way. It would completely change the environment and it would completely change the way we relate to one another. We are literally interconnected with one another—that is required for us to exist. So, the idea that you and I are somehow separate beings is inconceivable in Shamanism.

In Taoism, practicing the Tao is a way of shifting toward Oneness with nature and begins when we make these internal shifts to self. Diane Rooney explained it this way:

> It's bringing us back to the profound quietude and the understanding that Mother Earth knows what she is doing. To allow her to do

it, and if we allow her to do it, we will become one with her, and then we will get everything we want! Abundance, happiness, peace, joy, serenity, all of that stuff eventually, because that's who She is. To just let her be her in all her cycles, allowing her to be, we will feel that peace. Because think about it—all this running around we do, to get money, status or prestige, or this or that or the other thing, it's really about bringing peace. We want to feel peace inside, we want to be happy, and we think these outward things are going to make us happy, but by letting that go, and unlearning that and moving with the cycles of nature instead of fighting them, we do achieve that.

## RAISING AWARENESS IN ATR TRADITIONS

Orisha and Loa represent the forces of nature in African Traditional Religions. For instance, Mother Nature herself is Orisha. Glow Okandekun explained,

> The Earth in herself, Onile, is a divinity. Onile is the concept of Earth as a whole. Within it, inside of it, live other Orishas, like Oroina, the hotness or core of the Earth, and Ogere lies in the ore of the Earth, but for the concept of the Earth as a whole, Onile is the Orisha that manifests that concept. She gives us so much! You have all these Orishas—you have Orisha Oko, Korinkoto, those who represent the fertility of the Earth, so yes, we have to take care of her.

These forces have their counterparts in natural places. Connecting to these places is something that happens during important ceremonies, like the trip to the river as part of the Kariocha ceremony in the making of new priests. The irony, however, is that today, Orisha traditions, at least in the United States, tend to be practiced by those who live in large urban areas. Ocha houses, or Iles, exist in all the major cities in the United States, so there is often some disconnect regarding how these traditions require a living commitment to Earth-based responsibility and consciousness. Oba Daniel Rodriguez believes the problem in the community is practitioners don't always connect to the deeper commitment to Earth-based responsibility:

> You have a lot of people who do not really know what they are doing. Unfortunately, and I see this more with Ocha, about 50 percent of people who practice that tradition don't understand the intensity and the profoundness that it teaches. They get it surface-like. "Oh, I was told I had to sacrifice to the Earth and appease that." Meanwhile, "I made an ebbo, and left it in a plastic bag." Hello! What are you thinking when you appease the Earth over here and you are destroying it over there?

He believes elders have the responsibility to both teach and model behavior in our own lives, especially regarding prioritizing a commitment to recycling and cleaning up litter and pollution. Glow Okandekun also takes this approach to inspire and spend valuable time with her godchildren, visiting natural places together that are sacred to the Orisha, and engaging in group cleanup:

> I tell my godchildren that they, too, have to develop this relationship with their Orisha. You have to sit down and touch them, because without that connection, they are not fully alive. I personally love to go to the places where these Orishas manifest, where they reside in Nature. Most of all, I tell my godchildren a lot of people may take offerings to the river. Instead of taking, why don't we go and clean? Whose mother does not like for her children to come and clean? So, we do a lot of that together. We will go to the ocean and clean up. We sometimes just sit near the shore and have conversation. I think Mom just wants to have her children there, visiting and talking together. If you visit the river, or the ocean, and you see some trash, just pick it up, because people love to take all kinds of stuff, unfortunately. All of it is not always biodegradable. So, we like to go clean, and while we are doing that, we are talking and laughing because I think mothers want to hear children do that! That's how we commune with Nature. I would rather go to the mountaintop and go to talk to Obatala and take him a little something, and just be there with him. Because you feel it, you feel that energy!

# PAGAN NATURE CONSCIOUSNESS AND CREATING COMMUNITY

The concepts of service to the Earth as a religious tenant is universal for nearly all modern Pagans. In Stone Circle Wicca, for example, this is central and something Wiccans choose to inspire in others. Eldritch said,

> We believe that we are in service to all of Earth's household. This is one of our dearest tenets. We are in service to all in Earth's household, including the Earth. We have responsibility for the planet, and if we don't wake up, we are going to blow it. For those people who are only going to be self-serving, even if they won't care about the Earth, they should at least care about themselves! Sometimes you have to hoodwink people with their own self-interest, saying, "You don't want the waters to rise. Surely you want clean air." We don't have to be like the world in the movie *The Lorax,* where they have to deliver air to people's homes. Use whatever message it takes to get people to stop polluting. What used to be a free gift of Gaia, the planet, becomes something we have messed up! Even when you live in the city, there's nature in the city. As urban Pagans: Do you pay attention to Nature? To the change in the climate, the chill in the air? The source where the water in your city has come from? You are still responsible to understand your space and place in Nature.

The EarthSpirit Community of Western Massachusetts has taken the concept of sustainable living close to the land even further. EarthSpirit holds that a nature-based tradition is best experienced close to the land, and a shift in internal worldview happens precisely because of this direct encounter. EarthSpirit began in the greater Boston area and utilized the area's parks for their gatherings and ceremonies, but eventually, it became clear they wanted to buy land as a community to live on together. They eventually settled in a large area of pristine forest in Western Massachusetts. Andras Corban-Arthen described how this move helped further the group's spiritual conscious connection to the Earth:

> We made that huge change because to us as Pagans—as people whose spirituality is focused on a direct communion with the natural world—it was important to be in a natural setting, experiencing Nature as wilderness, which is just Nature being Nature. We felt that we needed to be in a place where we were permanently and thoroughly enveloped by the natural world as a way to deepen our spiritual practice. So, our kids were raised here.
>
> We have lived here for twenty-five years, and it's changed our lives in so many ways, some of which are intangible. It's truly been a very profound change, because we are not in the middle of a city. We are not surrounded by hordes of other human beings who are habitually competing with each other, dealing with huge amounts of stress in the midst of constant frenzy and loudness. We are in a place where most of the sounds we hear are the sounds of Nature—the birds, the brooks, the rustle of leaves dancing with the wind.

Andras believes a sustainable lifestyle is a vital commitment, even if it requires discomfort to adjust to sometimes:

> I think we are living at a time when the way in which a lot of our more recent ancestors have related to the natural world is now coming home to roost. Human-generated activities have been creating a huge imbalance throughout the natural world; and not just human beings, but lots of other living beings are in danger, as a result. That, therefore, needs to be one of the key motivators for us beyond everything else. There are a great many ways in which change can happen, but there can be no question that it needs to happen. One of the key premises ingrained in Western society is the idea of the one true way, the one *right* way—it's a product of Christian absolute monotheism, and it's crap. There are many different ways to effect change, all at the same time, and it's up to each one of us to find the way in which we can best contribute.
>
> For us, what we are trying to do is develop other models of culture and community within Western society: models that draw

upon the ways of life—the premises, the values, the attitudes—
that our own ancient ancestors once had; that embody a much
more harmonious relationship with the natural world. I'm not
talking necessarily about living in the countryside. I'm talking
about living a life that is much more aware of our connection to
the natural world.

However, Andras feels in some ways the Pagan community as a
whole has fallen short of its potential in making the full commitment
to a change in lifestyle that can make an impactful difference. He
explained,

> In the Pagan movement, people talk a lot about nature spiritu-
> ality, but the reality is that most modern Pagans are people who
> live in cities: who have been born and raised and will live, grow,
> work, and die in cities. Their environment, their perspective, their
> very existence has taken place in a milieu that is very specifically
> intended to prioritize human affairs above and beyond all else,
> while implicitly separating us from the rest of the natural world.
>
> That is, perhaps, the main premise that needs to change,
> because it is that fundamental premise that has led to the growing
> environmental disaster as a result of overpopulation, deforesta-
> tion, air pollution, the blighting of the oceans, the melting of the
> polar caps, and the other catastrophic changes taking place all over
> the world.
>
> Indigenous peoples tend to have much saner and healthier
> perspectives about how to live in greater harmony on this Earth,
> except that they have mostly been conquered, colonized, and dis-
> missed as savages by Western culture. Pagans, however, as the
> spiritual heirs to the Indigenous peoples of pre-Christian Europe,
> have the potential to articulate ancestral visions from within that
> culture—visions that are, in general, much closer to those of
> Indigenous peoples. But the current, urban-focused Pagan move-
> ment has been far more intent in making Paganism be accepted
> and assimilated by the mainstream Christian culture, rather than
> in Paganizing mainstream culture to bring it closer to a more har-
> monious relationship with the natural world.

As far as forming the EarthSpirit collective community, which hosts multiple gatherings a year—including the Rites of Spring gathering where the community gathers annually—Andras says living in Nature this way has profoundly integrated his spirituality and lifestyle. It has helped him integrate different possibilities and perspectives simply by being removed from urban and suburban culture. Living closer to the land has afforded a new outlook:

> We tend to have a notion of this very elusive thing we call reality, that everybody knows, and yet nobody can really describe. Most of the time, people's reality tends to be limited by the culture they live in. So, when you start experiencing something that comes from outside of that culture in some significant ways, suddenly a lot of doors begin to open, even to whom you are as a person— as a being, more than a person, as a spirit being—that you may not have had a realization of before. It also helps with changing our relationships with each other, with changing our view of ourselves, our gender roles, our perspective on educating our children, our perspective on death, on healing practices, on birth, on how and where we live. And living our spirituality, as our Indigenous European ancestors did, means that we follow the paths that Spirit points out to us, even if to do so goes against the norms of our culture.

Andras believes Pagans could be more effective if they could come together around some of these causes. Some suggestions he made in our interview was for Pagans to link up with other like-minded people and create larger, intentional communities with shared resources and values. Another suggestion was for nature-based people to purchase open spaces and let the land be natural and unspoiled, returning it to wild in order to regenerate. Finally, he said that nature-based spirituality holds a responsibility to support political movements, environmental causes, and Indigenous causes, with the goal of breaking down and changing the destructive forces of the West that serve the few at the expense of most of us. Coming together in committed spiritual communities can do that.

# WORKING FOR THE WHOLE

Living a sustainable and permaculture lifestyle requires that individuals and communities focus on personal use of natural resources, sharing of food and resources, and creating a cycle of growth, use, composting, and recycling that not only maximizes benefit to humans, but also to animals and the entire ecosystem. By not only minimizing waste but creating systems where waste can be used and reused to benefit the community and environment, change for the entire ecosystem, regardless of where we live on the Earth, can happen.

Permaculture, a movement named for the idea of permanent agriculture, has the goal to work with our natural environment, where we live, to accept challenges and limitations and use these to create solutions. The idea is reminiscent of the Eastern concept of the Tao—a flowing with nature instead of constantly trying to overcome and subdue her. This shift is already manifesting through those who are creating community gardens and for those who are supporting urban measures to bring food co-ops, rooftop gardens, solar panels, wind farms, improved public transportation systems, and green walkways into urban renewal and community building efforts, which aim to put an end to suburban sprawl and the devastation of wildlife and natural resources and habitats. Permaculture as a holistic, harmonic way of life takes effort and conscious change.

To adopt a permaculture lifestyle doesn't require a large acreage or a great deal of money. People are successfully feeding their family and friends even with compact backyards and shared neighborhood gardens, as well as enjoying the spiritual benefits that come with connecting to the Earth in this experiential way. The wild food foraging movement, where people learn to identify helpful backyard herbs and edible weeds, is part of this shift in consciousness. The important thing is to begin.

Holding this philosophy central can be an aim for all those active in nature-based spiritual communities. Oba Daniel Rodriguez said this:

> I would like to see people get a better understanding of what they are doing and why they are doing it. And I believe these traditions can show them how to understand the necessity of this. Why do we honor the Earth, why do we honor the waters, why do we honor the forces of Nature? And if these forces of Nature are altered because of our negligence, so then what are we doing? I think elders are responsible to make that known, and I don't think everyone does that. Again, just because you're an elder, that doesn't mean you understand the profoundness of these traditions!

Today, there are countless nature practices and traditions—both contemporary and within alternative nature-based communities, as well as in branches within world religions like Hinduism, Taoism, Christianity, Reformed Judaism, Buddhism, and Islam—that are realizing the truth: we are all members of one Mother Planet, interdependent with all of creation. We are not lords or even stewards of this. Embracing a lifestyle that centers around sustainability and permaculture principles is an important part of building the new paradigm. It is essential for us to put these values in place if we are to heal the planet, relight Mother Earth's cauldron, and maintain our existence upon her.

# TENDING THE FLAME
## Native American Concepts and Practices

Chip Brown is a farmstead farmer and attorney who lives in a sustainable, off-grid home built with mostly recycled materials with his spouse in the Southwest United States. He has heritage that includes ancestry from the British Isles, Scottish, Irish, English, Scandinavian, Turkish, Middle East, North Africa, Micronesia; and in the Western Hemisphere, Lenapehoking, the Mid-Atlantic Delaware people, and Mi'kmaq, who hail from Southern Canada and the Northeastern United States. Brown spoke to me at length about his passion for a sustainable lifestyle practicing his blend of Native American beliefs and Neo-Pagan tradition:

> I live on the traditional home and lands of the Navajo people, the Pueblo people, the ancestral Pueblo/Navajo Anasazi people, the Hopi, and the Apache, among others. We are in, with the Baca Chapter of the Navajo people, the Dine, what is referred to as the checkerboard region; that's where we are today, that's where we live, that's where we caretake the land we are on. As far as my ancestry, it's really diverse. Both my native heritage groups and my European ancestry are derived from native Earth-based traditions. I do work within an Earth-based tradition. I look to the turning of the Wheel, the cycles of Nature, the way the Earth evolves and changes from year to year, while being consistent from year to year. I take my cues from those changes I see.
>
> I use traditional spiritual teachings of Lenape Delaware; this is what my personal practice is. I recognize with natives across the globe there are many commonalities, many techniques that are used, many plants that are used, the cycles,

the times of the year, the phases of the moon, the sun, the growing cycle, and so on. Many of those things are held in common by people who recognize a Nature-based path. I think even folks who would claim not to be on this path, such as people who may follow a Judeo-Christian or Islamic path, still recognize, perhaps implicitly, that the cycles of Nature are part of those spiritual traditions.

There are many different techniques and avenues to pursue. Deep inward journeying, much of that is connected to a particular place you may be in. I would say, yes, my practice involves working with Spirit, working with elements of the Creator. Working with that spiritual energy, the spiritual mist that infuses all things. I believe that by virtue of existence, all things are inhabited by Spirit. I think that those elements of Spirit may be brought to the floor; you may connect with those elements of Spirit depending on the kinds of journey work you do. How you visualize the world. I typically use certain techniques to journey and to connect in a deep way.

I regularly talk to and communicate with those elements and my physical ancestors. Different techniques can be used to do that, depending on what I am looking for, what I am doing. There are certain ones I am familiar with. Individual spirits of ancestors, spirits of different kinds of energies, other physical connections like minerals, birds, nature, animals—things that are different for me. There are many, many kinds of entities, spirits in Nature, one can connect with, and I do connect with those things. I have worked with them all my life, pretty much. But I am always open for new connections, too, and they happen all the time. I think that's part of allowing yourself to be open to that—almost necessarily means you will have those contacts that continue to broaden your spiritual path, spiraling outward and more deeply, so that's all part of it.

I make use of many herbs. I gather elements of the landscape from plants from the land I live on, and I incorporate those into my work. I have physical items that I use in my work related to my ancestry. This small piece I have here is actually a very ancient piece of glass and concrete I use as a small table that connects with myself and my European ancestors, and I place items on it or use it to focus my attention.

I make my own essences for scents to help infuse a room for cleaning, using different kinds of sage, different kinds of pinion oils, juniper oils, leaves, and branches. They are all used in different ways through concoctions, different essences. They grow here, and so being from this place, it deepens my connection to here. I incorporate them all the time in doing the work, particularly if I am about to embark on a ceremony or a journey or a particular element of practice. Those things to me are very important.

Fundamentally, I think foremost, the work plugs us into the Earth, and we have already recognized the planetary crisis with Mother Earth for the continued existence of us and the other species. One can argue that the Earth will persist, and I have no doubt about this; whether humanity does, or does in this form, poses tremendous challenges for us ahead. I think an Earth-based path, if nothing else, helps you focus on the necessary fruits of the Earth that we depend on and what it means to protect those things. I think that being disconnected from that energy, the knowledge of what it means to be here, is detrimental, and I think this is a huge part of the problem as I see it, in terms of the direction that humans are pushing climate. So, being rooted spiritually as well as physically is, in a sense, what we are about, and I think it's huge.

I think we have a connection that allows us to translate some of these issues that we are going to need to incorporate in order to move forward in any kind of a positive way, and I think that this is an amazing thing. It could be a challenge when you talk to people who don't share this understanding or this path—their practices suggest more like the Earth is there for the taking. And trying to say that in a generous way, but that even in the context of those spiritual or religious paths, I don't believe that that has to be the bottom-line message. I truly don't. I believe that there ought to be in every spiritual practice—and it could be found in every spiritual practice—the idea that we must nurture those elements of the Earth that are supporting us. I don't know how you reconcile a practice that says, "Take and take and take until it's gone!" I think that is anathema to what it means to be a spiritual person. So, I take heart in that; I believe that even folks who do not have a Nature-based tradition can be shown a way forward in their own practices that incorporates new ways of living to protect the planet, and that is critically important to us now.

# ❀ A PRACTICE ❀
## Honoring the Ancestors of the Land, a Welcome to Country

This practice comes from reconciliation efforts that are becoming mainstream in Australia and is based on the Aboriginal understanding of land boundaries and ownership. I give thanks to fellow One Spirit minister Pippa Jones, who brought this idea to our community at a recent reunion for One Spirit ministers.

This practice is from the Aboriginal people of Australia, who honor the ancestors and live in perpetual interrelationship with the land and all things and all beings, considering themselves custodians only. The Aboriginal people are the oldest continuous human civilization in existence, with estimates that their way of life has been in existence for at least sixty-five thousand years and exceeds eighty thousand years. Their philosophy is, we don't own the land, the land owns us.

To the Aborigines, spirituality is the connection to the land, and all is part of the dreaming, also known as dreamtime, or intuitive nature wisdom. In their culture, the only people who can welcome you to the land are those who are Indigenous and local to it, often an elder or person of significance. In Australia, this practice is known as Welcome to Country, as the word *country* denotes the territory of a particular people group. Everyone else should show respect by acknowledging the land and its ancestors.

## Begin

Before any ritual, assembly, or community gathering, and before any business, religious, or secular celebrations take place, a leader should be sure to recognize and acknowledge the spirits of the original inhabitants of the land on which they dwell or gather. For instance, in my area of the Hudson Valley, that would be the Esopus Lenape people.

The Land Acknowledgment would then be stated:

> *We acknowledge the original custodians of the land [name the people].*
> *In this place where we have gathered today [name place].*
> *We acknowledge also the ancestor spirits of the land within the trees, the rivers, the mountains, the ocean, the stones, the Earth herself, and the Sky.*
> *We acknowledge and apologize for any harm and disrespect we or those who came before us have caused.*
> *May we work toward full reconciliation and community.*
> *So be it.*

As a side note, nowadays it has become increasingly common for people in Australia, whether welcoming or acknowledging, to state that the land was unceded. Sometimes they may even use the word *stolen*, which, of course, it was. And they often finish with something like, "We recognize that this was, is, and always will be Aboriginal land."

# REBUILDING
# THE BRIDGE

This shift toward a new paradigm is being supported by many faith communities, new scientific understanding, ecological awareness, and economic and societal shifts toward sustainable green technology and energy sources. As we have seen with EarthSpirit, it is also taking the form of creating community.

Living together or creating committed organizations with shared values is a central belief for many Earth-based practitioners. It represents a shift away from the dominant culture's ideas that personal human ownership and individual rights are superior or incompatible to valuing the rights of nature and other species or that cooperation and sharing with the humans we share our lives with is somehow less important than our own self-interests.

It is of paramount importance that the past epoch has ushered in vast improvements in democracy, personal human rights, and agency. As late as the Middle Ages in Europe, and even up to the Industrial Revolution in some areas, individual peasants' human rights were constantly under attack and often disregarded by sovereigns and those in power. Developments like the *Rights of Man*, penned by Thomas Paine in 1791, codified into law rights that ideally should have been enjoyed by all. This concept has helped us evolve as a species, develop civilization, and create modern life that consists of self-actualization instead of mere survival. However, it is clear that not all humans were included in the initial ideas of men like Paine, as evidenced by the fact that it took a civil war and hundreds of years before women, non-white men, and all Americans could be considered free and earn voting rights. This is still being played out across the world, but more and more countries are striving to realize the inherent rights and dignity of all citizens.

In the West today, however, the pendulum has shifted so far that in some ways, the emphasis on individual rights now counts for more to some than to the collective good of society. We in the United States have witnessed this with the COVID-19 crisis and attempts to coordinate a unified, national response to a terrible health crisis that has claimed the lives of millions of people in two years worldwide. It also has created the conditions for alienation, distrust, disconnection, and isolation, states that are conducive to many ills of society, such as depression, substance abuse, and violence. Hence, this new paradigm shift's goal of recreating more communal-minded living and developing stronger bonds with others who share core values and beliefs is an answer that has great attraction to many.

# INTERDEPENDENCE AND INDIGENEITY

This sense of separateness extends to a false idea that we are disconnected and separate from nature and each other. Accepting our responsibility to the Earth and one another and abandoning the idea that we are separate, therefore, is a vital step in moving forward. This is the concept of interdependence, which maintains we are actually one and connected to all others, including nonhumans, the planet, and the universe as a whole.

The values of interdependence and cooperation with one another, of the collective, and of caring for the Earth as sacred are not new; they have been preserved in Indigenous cultures around the world since time immemorial. As the Indigenous elders stressed at the Parliament of the World's Religions in Toronto, it is Westerners who need to learn to listen to their wisdom and relearn this way of life. Chip Brown discussed this idea in terms of Indigenous values:

> In fairness, I think that many of the Native people who have maintained their ethnicity and cultural lineage across the planet have traditionally maintained Earth-based practices, and it is the Western world, primarily, that is reawaking its roots in that same sense. I think that acknowledging we are all connected, that we do share resources, that we share the Earth—I think that, honestly, the great challenge we have as human beings is to overcome what we recognize now as the survival instinct. We need to learn that we benefit from sharing and protecting what we have. Compassion, love, kindness—those things weren't identified as virtues in Western philosophical context for no reason. Those are the things that, as humans, we aspire to. I think that being connected to the Earth and recognizing those roots helps us realize those virtues and goals that the Earth unconditionally shares with us.

Māori elder Puáwai Ormsby also explained how Earth consciousness is embedded in the work she does with the community school she helped found:

The practice they were talking about at Talking Tree Hill was about a no-waste policy. We taught the children about recycling, upcycling, restoring, reusing, even wind farms, composting, permaculture, and sustainable lifestyle. The center in the sky of the southern cross is where the heart is. So that is also the currency: the kindness. *Aroha* means "love," and if you give it away, it will come right back to you. That was the Nature-inspired template that connects us as a whole being. So that we are one with Mother Earth, we are one with honoring her for all she's provided.

# PAGAN CONCEPTS

This idea of interdependence is something shared with modern Pagans. The concept is embedded in the name given to the Way of Anamanta, as explained by Andras Corban-Arthen:

The name itself comes from something my teachers taught me. In their tradition, there are three main levels of manifestation. The first level is Spirit, or as they called it, *anam*, which is experienced as a pure essence; it doesn't have gender, it doesn't have form, much less human attributes—there's no focus on anthropomorphic deities that look and act like us, as is generally the case in polytheistic traditions. The most accurate way to describe it would be to say it's animistic. It's an intangible force that creates and gives life to everything, and takes everything back into itself at the end of each cycle. So, their sense was that *anam* is the ultimate spiritual experience, one that transcends language, transcends understanding; it arises from and is part of a mystery, in the literal sense of the word. It cannot be understood, as we conceive the meaning of understanding; it can only be experienced. It can only be directly communed with.

Then, that Spirit creates forms within itself, and the forms it creates compose the second level of manifestation—what we call Earth, or Nature. It's the life we experience here, not just human beings, but trees, and fire, and clouds, and animals, water, stones, and everything else that exists. Everything is a form of anam taking shape. So that's Earth, that's Nature—the web of life woven by the strands of anam.

Then, within that level of Nature is the third level of manifestation for us: our own human species. What it comes down to, then, is that the mystery manifests from the most formless aspect of experience in Spirit into the natural world that has all diverse forms and shapes and kinds, one of which is our own specific kind and manifests there as community—the complex of connections that we form and guide how we relate to each other.

# COMMUNITY VALUES

In my research, creating spiritual community serves as a vehicle for instilling shared values and important guiding principles to the community as a whole. In the interviews, this theme emerged in various practices and traditions from the indigenous Māori to African Traditional Religions, to modern Pagans and Heathens. It is clear that for those who practice nature-based spirituality, teaching and caring for one another, experiencing group rituals and ceremonies, and caring for the Earth as a living sentient being are deeply connected motivations.

This sharing of values happens within the Urglaawe tradition. Founder Robert Schreiwer discussed how many people outside of his community do not understand the communal-minded sense that is embedded within Pennsylvania Deitsch culture as it differs from the dominant culture. He highlighted this:

> You might have heard about the nine noble virtues that Heathens adhere to? Among those are things like stewardship, interdependence, and things that will actually require us to go outside of ourselves. Within Urglaawe specifically, the Old German culture still lives within our Pennsylvania Deitsch culture, and it's not one that says, "This is my farm, stay away from it." It's more like, "Okay, I'm going to grow this, you grow this, and we are going to exchange crops. So that's your specialty, this is mine."
>
> There is that interdependence and that community sharing that comes on every level, from the physical level like the food, to the

spiritual level. So that means let's talk to somebody, let's see if they need help. Everything in Urglaawe Braucherei is about balance, and balance in an imbalanced world is a very complicated pursuit. Our community's goal is to be interdependent among us but to allow people to have their own viewpoints and perspectives and do what they want to do.

# INITIATION INTO SPIRITUAL COMMUNITY

Some nature-based systems require new members to undergo a formal initiation to be considered full members of the community. Anthropologically, initiation represents a liminal time in the transformation of consciousness for those seeking entry into mystery traditions. By definition, this wisdom is right-brained and non-rational. Initiation itself, in any nature-based system, means a shedding of the old self and birth into a new state of being. One must go through a period of unlearning and take the time to allow opportunity for reflection, learning, growth, and full completion.

In Pagan traditions like Wicca, while many adherents comfortably practice solitary, initiation is recommended for those who wish to practice as part of a tradition, after studying formally with a teacher or group, usually for a year and a day. One reason a commitment of initiation and time is important is due to the fact that nature must be experienced at its own pace and in its seasons. For instance, the year is divided by the Wheel of the Year.

Modern Pagan holidays are ancient holidays recognized by European-based Pagans that coincide with the four quarter days of equinoxes and solstices as well as cross-quarter days (those that fall between) and represent the coming in of the new natural energy. Beltane, for instance, is celebrated as the coming in of summer and the awakening of fertility and life, while Samhain, its opposite on the wheel, represents the coming in of winter, the honoring of death, and the remembrance of ancestors. Each season, therefore, represents a time that coincides with certain activities, rituals, and ceremonies. There is the season of fertility, a season of harvest, and a fallow time; each have their own energy and appropriate time. This is also true for the cycles of the moon, which are an essential part of knowledge and practice.

For the neophyte witch, it is believed that each season can only be experienced and known in their own time in order to fully grasp their meaning—to utilize these energies for health and wellness practices in life and community. Another benefit for allowing time before formal initiation is to address psychological defenses, fears, and internal baggage that must be met and confronted. The words *witch* and *witchcraft*, after centuries of demonization and persecution, have taken on a sinister shadow energy for many. Even those who weren't raised in or outwardly conform to organized religion may have internalized these fears. It really is not a tradition for everyone, and it is believed by those who have practiced for many years that once you initiate and send the call out to the universe, you have chosen this way and have asked to be accepted. It's not something that can easily be undone.

It is perfectly acceptable and a long-standing tradition in Wicca that people may practice solitary or self-dedicate, and many choose this route, but there are significant benefits to becoming part of a larger group. Humans have a need to belong, and becoming part of a grove, coven, or larger community can provide learning experiences and opportunities to develop gifts under the guidance of more adept practitioners. Group experience allows for the sharing of stories, crafts, songs, and personal and creative journeys. On holidays, witches and other Pagans gather and feast, which is the original sense of communion. This is an essential aspect of celebration; we become as kin.

Eldritch explained how Stone Circle Wicca develops and trains newcomers to become equal members of the community in a very inclusive way:

> In Stone Circle Wicca (SCW), we teach a foundational series of 13 Tools, which is taught monthly for a year and a day. In SCW, we do not prescribe deities. We do not say, "You have to dedicate to Cernunnos, Gaia, or Pan," for example. We respect that people determine a personal divinity system that will work for them, but we hold that you are going to find archetypes of Male, Female, All Genders, and Beyond Gender in every pantheon of the world. That is an interesting challenge for people to uncover those stories that are there but rarely told. In our modern practice of Wicca, we are not structured as a coven system of thirteen. We initiate as ritualists who function to serve a greater community in ritual for thirty or three hundred.
>
> The first tool we teach is The Cord with lessons learned from a string, yarn, a ritual cord, an umbilical cord. Basically, The Cord is your commitment, tying a knot of commitment intentionally as an individual. This [holding a long white piece of rope] is our student cord; that's where we talk about personal responsibility. In SCW, no one has spiritual authority over any other. When students have dedicated for initiation in the First Degree, they are now our colleagues. At that moment, we stop using the language of "my students" and consider each other colleagues. We talk about communal responsibility, and we emphasize individual responsibility. We are not a self-serving religion. We are a community-serving religion, but with responsibility to yourself.

## COMMUNITY IN LUKUMI TRADITION

Many of these considerations are also true in African Traditional Religions. In Lukumi, inclusion into a greater community begins with making initiation into that tradition and creating a formal relationship with a godparent or set of godparents. One is admitted into the family of an elder of the community and welcomed into their Ocha house, or Ile. It is not a commitment to be taken lightly as it is ideally lifelong and cannot easily be discarded. We become family.

In my lineage of Ocha, there are three levels of initiation. The first is receiving the sacred beads or *elekes* of the Orishas, which grant one the blessing and protection of the Orishas and initiation into a lineage under the guidance of an elder and the belonging to an Ile. After this is the receipt of the Warriors, who are the Orishas, Ellegua, Ogun, Ochosi, and Osun. These forces help the initiate fight their battles, guide their choices, and open their roads to new experiences, quality of life improvements, and wisdom. Sometimes what are known as *addimu* Orishas are then received, such as the sacred twins, or Ibeyis, or Olokun, a mysterious aspect from the depths of the sea, which grants stability. The need to receive these Orishas is indicated strictly by consultation with elders or diviners, not simply because one feels drawn to them. Finally, the ceremony of Kariocha is where a person makes a full lifetime commitment to the Orisha who guides their head and who has been revealed within the proper ceremonies.

It should be noted that not everyone called to practice Lukumi needs to become a priest; often it is sufficient to receive the first initiation and become an initiate, or *aborisha*, with a godparent to guide you. However, to take part in the inner mysteries of the tradition, one needs to commit to Kariocha. The time of initiation and training of new priests is called the *Iyaworaje*, where one loses the identity they had before they committed to this ceremony, and must follow rules and prohibitions specific to them. They become *Iyawo*, which means "bride of the Orisha," for a year and seven days. Some of the requirements include, in most cases, having one's head shaved and covered, wearing white, avoiding touching others outside of family, avoiding mirrors, and living a humble and sober life during this period. It is a time of deep transformation.

Becoming Iyawo is beginning a brand-new life, and it is important, therefore, to keep oneself clean and pure and away from controversary. One should spend time with one's elders to learn and to grow. It is sincerely believed one's life may change drastically. As I have said before, this tradition is not for everyone and requires a great deal of submission and respect for the way it has been preserved over time. It is said the goal of Kariocha is to allow the Orisha the ability to guide our ori toward our own personal destiny. That path depends greatly on how we walk through this very important time commitment.

## MAINTAINING SPIRITUAL BALANCE

Another commonality embedded in the Earth-based traditions I examined is the importance of maintaining personal balance not only in the way we live on the Earth, but within ourselves for health and well-being. It's necessary to balance our spiritual commitments with our everyday life. Glow Okandekun gave a great example of how dangerous it can be when balance isn't maintained:

> Balance is life; we have to keep balance in life. And I know that the Orishas understand the human condition and they know we have responsibility as servants of the Orisha. As priests of the Orisha, we always have to be priestly, to be priestly in our character and how we present ourselves. We are Olorishas, but not Olorishas 24-7. There are times when we need to step aside from ourselves and just enjoy life, be human, do what we have to do. We should not obsess; we should not be fanatics. Not everything has to be Orisha. We can appreciate the beauty of Nature and how the Orishas manifest in life, but not everything has to involve Orisha. We take care of ourselves, we take care of our bodies, there are times when it is good for us to party even, but that doesn't mean I have to get drunk and make a fool of myself! Because again, we are priests, and our character, our attitude, always has to be ready to represent. But we can also represent their joy with a good time!

I think if we obsess too much with Orisha, it could take us to the point of an obsession, and we start acting crazy. I have seen people start acting like that; I'm a little wary with them. I think, they are becoming obsessed. For example, I had a godchild I crowned Ellegua, and one day he became very obsessed with Ellegua and with the *muerto* (discarnate spirit) he identified with. I warned him he should stop. His partner would tell me, "Miguel is acting a certain way!" Pretty soon, he came to my house, and he was covered in cascarilla (powdered eggshell used in ceremonies), and he was doing a prayer in front of the water heater. Then he would go outside to murmur at the trunk of a tree, and I said, "We have to do serious stuff to get that obsessing spirit away from him."

That can happen to anyone who can't find a balance in everyday life. He lost his job because he didn't show up, he lost like twenty pounds in a week, he lost his relationship. Lost all kinds of stuff because he was too obsessed with his Orisha. I told him his passion was nice, but he needs real life, too. I think we need to make sure to do that, have fun, keep it safe, and then come back and work the religion.

# CREATING CONNECTION

Dr. Gabor Maté, author of *In the Realm of Hungry Ghosts: Close Encounters with Addiction*, is a pioneer and fierce advocate for understanding the roots of addiction and substance abuse in Western culture. He believes the roots are profound trauma and alienation, which are part and parcel of living in a disconnected world. In his books and lectures, he often discusses his perspective that addiction and substance use disorder aren't necessarily rooted in genetic predisposition alone, but are created by a profound sense of isolation, which is the result of a radically individualist society that emphasizes pleasures and escape found in consumerism and consumption. He believes addiction is influenced heavily by negative environments, early adverse childhood experiences (ACEs), and trauma.[146] He sees addiction itself as a continuum of behaviors that may begin with something socially acceptable, like shopping or workaholism, and end with the destructive chemical addictions that lead to incarceration, severe mental illness, homelessness, overdose, and death.[147]

Notably, he also believes that Western colonialism, whether it was imposed on the First Nations people of his native Toronto or the ancestors of the Scots in England, leads to a profound intergenerational loss of culture—language, custom, religion—in the conquered society, which creates conditions ripe for the predisposition for addiction and depression, which we see so prevalent in Western societies now:

> If you traumatize people, if you disempower them, if you take away their spiritual place in the world, deprive them of meaning and dignity, take away their livelihood, destroy their communities, and keep this going for generations, the need for self-soothing becomes entrenched in these communities, and the trauma is passed on from one generation to the next.[148]

Those who practice nature spirituality—who are creating holistic, spiritual communities and connecting people based on shared values and interests that run counterculture to this dominant paradigm—are doing their part to heal the separation wound.

As Dr. Maté says, the antidote for addiction is connection. Vital to these connections is the input of elders willing to teach, guide, share, and listen, and to be guided themselves by principles such as living in cooperative interdependence with the Earth and one another and keeping ourselves in healthy balance. Through reconnection in life-affirming ways, nature-based communities are striving to provide meaning and connection to one another in ways that also uplift Mother Earth.

---

146  Gabor Maté, "How Intergenerational Trauma and Addiction Works," YouTube, September 15, 2018, https://www.youtube.com/watch?v=rG71S_YjTro.

147  Maté, "How Intergenerational Trauma and Addiction Works."

148  Maté, "How Intergenerational Trauma and Addiction Works."

# TENDING THE FLAME
## Lukumi Tradition

Gloria "Glow" Okandekun is a Lukumi priestess and elder who has a large Ocha family in the Los Angeles region. She is also an Espiritista. She is a priestess of Obatala, the father of the Orishas and the Orisha of peace, wisdom, and the mountain. Glow spoke to me about her extended Ocha family and the importance of community for her Ile in Los Angeles:

> That was my name that was given to me many years ago, and I feel like I am finally starting to live up to its expectations. I feel like that is true for everyone who is given one; we have to strive to meet those expectations, because they are all so strong! We aren't usually there at the beginning, but with time and experience and dealing with Orisha in our life, we start to live up to those expectations and that big, old strong name they give us.
>
> Orisha tradition is and has always been my life. Every Sunday was a drumming, every Saturday we were doing Ocha stuff, so I grew up in that cosmology of Obatala and the Orishas. If we aren't doing anything, let's go to the river and pay tribute to Oshun. Let's go to the ocean and do an offering to Yemaya! Leave six apples at a palm tree because we are rendering homage to Chango. That's how I grew up, and that's how I teach my godchildren. Obatala has always been the father of all fathers; he's the one I give *elekes* (sacred consecrated bead necklaces) through to everyone, regardless that he is my Orisha, because I was taught that before your head belongs to any Orisha, it belongs to Obatala. For the most part, I just seem to have godchildren who start with elekes then receive their Guerreros, the Warriors, then start

looking into getting crowned with Orisha. After that comes an Orisha *alagbatori*, which is the ceremony where the head Orisha is divined for the neophyte, or they can get to know who this will be as they are in preparation for Orisha.

I am planning to do ceremony for two children this weekend to welcome them as godchildren. I tend to do a lot of doubles, Ibeyis (twins), all the time. These children are siblings, and I've crowned their parents, and their big brother, and these two are ten years old and three and a half years old, being made to Chango and Yemaya, respectively. This is going to be a very emotional ceremony for me because one of the *yubonnas* (assistant godparent in the Kariocha ceremony), I crowned him when he was five years old to Ellegua. I have watched children being born and I have cared for them. The Ellegua, he lived in my house for a while, he and his parents, due to some hard times they were going through. And now he is going to be yubonna. My godchildren are my family, for sure. Unfortunately, and it shows in *ordun* (divination), sometimes our blood families are not our biggest supporters, and Oche (letter of Diloggun) will tell us that.

For whatever reason, Orisha knows that sometimes rock family (the family of Ocha connected through the sacred and blessed stones) is a lot stronger than blood family! And you respect them for it. I've performed a lot of crowning ceremonies and I have been yubonna at many. I have a lot of grandchildren in Ocha; because of this, my godchildren are very active in Ocha as well. I've done over eighty-five ceremonies.

Here in Los Angeles, we have big Ocha houses, and we have a lot going on. But as I have gotten older, I have gotten a little pickier, because while I am sure everybody loves Ocha in their own way, I have realized I just want to work with people who have a lot of heart for Orisha. It doesn't have to be rich, an Ocha where there is a lot of money involved, because it is a fact that this is the way the religion has changed. Everybody is into aesthetics and all, and it's all beautiful. But I am fine if the aesthetics are not that great but there is a lot of genuineness and love.

It's just very fulfilling when you watch the godchildren you raised in this tradition, lead. They've got it. You don't have to worry. I give them encouragement; I can walk out of the room and know that they will know what to do. My brother, who serves as Oriate (high priest), is an example. They know, and I can relax now. I don't have children of my own, for personal choices, but I can imagine that must be how it feels, that pride in your children. My godchildren are in my life; they come here, and we are family. When they come over, we have a cup of tea or coffee and just talk and laugh. They are my family. Sometimes our conversation gets really funny and weird; we talk about everything. We love each other!

# ❀ A PRACTICE ❀

## Crossing the Rainbow Bridge

You will need to find a comfortable and quiet location to do this meditation. It may help for you to record the journey first and then listen to it in meditation.

### Tools

A comfortable seat, a drum, your journal.

### Begin

Begin the meditation by playing your drum. As you drum, breathe deeply in and out. When you feel that the drum has brought you into rhythmic breathing and presence, close your eyes to bring you into yourself, with this time and place, and with the present moment.

You will be embarking on a journey. Take a moment to first connect with your breath. Feel the comfort of your chair and focus on your breath. Take five deep breaths in through the nose and out through your mouth.

Imagine you find yourself on a wide, open plain. Around the plain, the horizon is encircled in a ring of fire. Above you is a deep blue sky, filled with starlight. Below you is dry earth. Around you, there is the sound of the wind. Listen closely; you can hear the heartbeat of the Earth Mother.

You realize there is a glowing light before you on the horizon in the sky, much like the northern lights. You begin to walk toward this light. As you walk, you are aware of the eyes and sounds of animals in the darkness around you, but you are not afraid. Your heartbeat connects to the heartbeat of the Earth as you walk. You may continue to drum in rhythm with this heartbeat.

As you walk forward, you realize, below the bright lights glowing up from the Earth to the sky, you are approaching a deep and wide chasm. Crossing the chasm, you see a three-pronged bridge leading from three directions on your side of the chasm into one path across the divide. You pause and reflect on this view. The chasm is wide, deep, and dark, and you realize you are no longer alone. Listen carefully as you continue to drum.

As you look to the left of the chasm, you become aware of shadows becoming a multitude of souls crossing over the bridge and onto the other side. They are wearing the decorative traditional clothing of many early people from past times and from different cultures around the world. You begin to recognize them. Who are they? Do you see ancestors? They are united in a great throng as they cross over the rainbow bridge into the bright lights before you.

To your left, you realize that there is also another multitude of beings crossing over. Here you observe many animal spirits, as well as the spirits of many souls, unformed as of now. They lack focus, but you see they are crossing over their part of the rainbow bridge, into the light.

Next, as you contemplate the portion of the bridge before you, you realize there are many, many, people behind you, joining you and surrounding you. You recognize them as kindred spirits. Who shares the bridge with you? What do they look like? What marks them as nature's children for you? You bow to these souls with friendship, and together you walk forward across this span of the rainbow bridge, into the brightness before you. As you walk, continue to bang the drum.

Eventually you cross the dark chasm to the other side and descend the bridge. Before you in the distance is a great tree. It is the most massive tree you have ever seen, with a wide trunk and many branches and roots reaching down into the soil and up into the starry sky. It has many twisting branches laden with lush foliage and fruit and living beings are living in its branches. What beings do you notice here? Above this, a bright moon hangs in the starlit sky.

All those who have gathered now on this side of the rainbow bridge begin to make a circle around the tree, which you realize is the World Tree. As they do, they become effervescent balls of light themselves, sparkling and shining, moving in endless concentric circles around the tree, around and around, up and down, and in all directions. You yourself are now a glowing ball of light. Feel what this feels like to join in this circle around this tree, the sacred World Tree. Continue to bang the drum in rhythm to your breath.

With your intention, send love and healing to the others in your circle, down into the Earth Mother, into the sky, and, most of all, into the heart of the World Tree. As you do, listen carefully to hear what you can hear and see what you can see. Is there a message for you? Do you hear the call of the World Tree? What is it saying? Perhaps it's more of a wordless chant or a melody. Pay attention and breathe deeply and gather this message into your heart. Then let the image go and return your spirit back into your body.

Drum, and take a few more deep breaths. When you are ready, open your eyes. Be sure to journal the visions and messages you have received on your journey across the rainbow bridge.

# THE DARK SIDE, ACKNOWLEDGING OUR SHADOW

One of Carl Jung's contributions to the field of psychology is the concept of individuation, or self-actualization. He described this as the product of full integration of our personality—the dark and the light, the conscious and the unconsciousness, particularly parts of the psyche we suppress. As humanity and civilizations have evolved, the superconscious that can represent society's social norms and expectations, as well as our logical mind, has deemed primitive aspects of ourselves unacceptable for social cohesion and peaceful coexistence. These aspects or complexes include our tendencies toward violence, irrational aggression, and uncontrollable sexual lusts. Jung's understanding that self-realization requires us to acknowledge and integrate these aspects of self to be fully aware was a perspective shared by Eastern philosophies that stressed embracing wholeness of the various parts of ourselves as a pathway toward enlightenment.

Alternatively, the Western mindset has been characterized by a splitting of self into two, which explains the dominant culture's tendency toward dualism, projection, and black-and-white thinking, instead of realizing these aspects of humanity belong to all of us. This splitting can be seen clearly in the way God is envisioned in Abrahamic tradition; God is all good, all knowing, and all loving, which necessitated the presence of a devil who represents the shadow of God. Everything God is not has evil projected onto it, and it becomes the cause of all the evils in the world.

In this same way, over the span of Western history, Westerners have projected onto those different from themselves aspects they did not want to acknowledge. An example of this is when Europeans encountered Africans and Indigenous peoples in the lands they encountered; they projected onto them all negative aspects of what they believed to be primitive. They labeled them as savage and subhuman, in need of the civilizing control by Europeans. It was no coincidence that they had a darker skin tone. In the European mind, light was equated with good, and dark with evil. This allowed the Europeans to justify the murder and enslavement of Indigenous people around the world. From there, slavery was reinforced by cruelty, terror, and brutality, thus creating the conditions where that which was projected onto the other became the forces that maintained the system. This is the nature of evil.

Another tendency by many regarding the shadow self is to push into the subconscious aspects of personality we are afraid to release. These could even be positive traits such as assertiveness, boldness, self-confidence, the ability to set boundaries, or the desire to be a leader and be successful. When this happens, when these traits are noticed in others, we envy or resent them for being what we cannot allow to emerge in ourselves. This is how the shadow works to divide not only ourselves, but ourselves from others, and perpetuate feelings of envy, annoyance, and inadequacy.

## SCIENCE—BENEFITS AND LIMITATIONS

Despite Western advances and technological and scientific achievements, building civilization, and modern conveniences, the West has still not fully integrated the shadow side of ourselves, which often appears in unconscious projections and fears. How can we integrate both the best of Western progress with a more integrated approach that supports mental and physical wholeness for ourselves and our community?

Science in many ways has been a liberating force from the restrictive superstitious mentality of earlier centuries. When scientists like Galileo were imprisoned and targeted because they questioned orthodox beliefs. Over the last few hundred years, science has connected our world through technology, conquered diseases that used to eradicate us, helped us build roads and infrastructure for commerce and travel, taken us into the mysteries of space, developed medicines and massive food production, and created countless other positive breakthroughs for humanity. None of these were trivial advancements—they were crucial stepping-stones that brought us progress and the complex social systems that exist today. These are not at all worth abandoning because of the negative elements that have come with them. Science is a means to make life better for ourselves, and also a pursuit of truth. The challenge, however, is to preserve scientific advancement while seeing where it still falls short or doesn't acknowledge alternative understandings of realities.

Scientific rationalism and materialism, however, can be irrational. One such irrational tendency is its materialistic emphasis on only those forces that can be experienced by our five senses. Because of this, most

Western scientists dismiss any idea of spirits, entities, or forces as primitive superstitions. However, we know that both sound and light waves exist outside of what we ourselves can experience—why wouldn't it be possible that entities may dwell or exist in these unseen frequencies? Those who advocate hard science backed up by materially observable data often refuse anecdotal evidence that cannot be proven through material observation and replicable studies. With that in mind, if these entities exist outside of a materiality that is measurable with our current tools, they cannot be proven. Perhaps the tools that measure the subtle realms have yet to be invented or widely accepted.

## SHIFTING PERSPECTIVE AND SPIRITUAL FORCES

Even if what we call spirits only represent these barbaric aspects of humanity that exist in our subconscious mind and human potential, does their effect on our behavior make them any less real?

It can be helpful to shift the perspective that these are only figments of the imagination, the view that predominates in Western scientific circles, to one where negative entities represent conceptualizations of human weaknesses. For instance, pride, greed, wrath, gluttony, envy, lust, and sloth can represent personified entities that "roam about the world seeking the ruin of souls,"[149] as it says in the Catholic prayer to St. Michael. If we are able to do so, we can begin to appreciate the so-called superstitious beliefs of non-Western people in a very different light. In the East, Taoism does preserve a concept of negative entities. Diane Rooney explains:

> In Taoism, it is believed we have ghosts inside of us called worms. They are trapped inside of us and they eat grain; that's how they live, and they try to get us sick. Because every moment we get sick is

---

149  From "The Prayer to Saint Michael the Archangel," a traditional Catholic prayer.

one step closer to death, and when you die, they leave out of the orifices and then they can roam the land and haunt people. Often you will see that after someone dies, they put a cork in the mouth, in all the orifices, so these Po spirits don't get out. The Po is the corporeal soul. There are different spirits also that we embody, two that live on forever and three that die with the body. The Po is the one that has the ghosts and the worms that live inside of us. We can think of them as discarnate; not resting after they die, they hang around and cause trouble. It's said they wreak havoc because they are unhappy.

This different perspective, that evil spirits, devils, and dark energies are prevalent, is common among Indigenous and nature-based people. It is shared in Spiritism. Some believe that these entities are actual spiritual beings affecting us from other planes of reality, perhaps those who have died with their souls in troubled states due to dying with toxic emotions such as fear, hatred, or envy. Perhaps they were the victims of violence and addiction. Some may be confused spirits, who did not believe in the afterlife when they passed, so they are stuck between the worlds now, unable to move on.

## ENTITIES AS THOUGHTFORMS

Even if these concepts do not work with the logical mind, one can still view these entities as personifications of the negative and buried primitive impulses of living people, the result of human biofields of consciousness, thoughtforms, and subconscious entities that may linger after the death of the physical body or be sent to us by living people. These may be attracted to us by our own thoughts and vibrations with the occult concept of the Law of Attraction or "like attracts like."

What are thoughtforms? When someone focuses long enough on a given thought, it becomes imbued with power. With enough focus and energy, it enters an independent life in the ethers, or the astral dimensions of consciousness.[150] In terms of quantum physics, these may exist in different dimensional vibrations of consciousness.

A thoughtform is a powerful idea that carries intent and form and gathers more energy from others who are focusing on it as well, thus influencing the thoughts of many people. In anthropology, this idea is described as a meme. Thoughtforms can fade away in time when they are not given enough energy or attention. There are collective thoughtforms, which are those connected to groups of people. According to Stephen Robinson of the Holistic Studies Institute, if enough energy is given to these thoughtforms, they become elementals. As an elemental is a thoughtform that has come to life, it becomes an independent entity.[151] Related to this idea of thoughtforms, Jung developed a theory of collective cultural complexes, which are psychic patterns that can promote and unite group identity but manifest irrational destructive forces when they are unconscious and take hold in a population.

## Using the Power of Archetypes

Carl Jung brought to modern psychology the understanding of archetypes, which he called the building blocks of the unconscious mind. Within these archetypes, which can be compared to thoughtforms, lies great power. Jung recognized that archetypes like Mother, Father, King, Queen, Jester, Devil, Lover, Warrior, and so on all represent aspects of our collective human unconscious. He linked these to the way Pagan people from classical times conceptualized their deities. Most ancient pantheons of gods, from Hindu divinities to the Germanic peoples, Greeks, Romans, and so on, developed gods and goddesses who personified these archetypes. One connected and important aspect of their worship was that these deities were not all good or all powerful; they often appeared very humanlike in their emo-

---

150  Stephen Robinson, *Exploring Your Intuition* (New York: Holistic Studies Institute, 2001), 19–21.

151  Robinson, *Exploring Your Intuition*, 19–21.

tions and behaviors. To the non-Judeo-Christian mind, it was entirely appropriate to worship and acknowledge deities who had both positive and negative expressions of themselves.

The same goes true for the way the Orishas and Loas, who represent personifications of natural forces, are understood by those who practice African Traditional Religions. As in nature, these forces have both creative and destructive aspects that can be affected with prayer and the making of sacrifice, or ebbo. Even within the negative, destructive side of these forces, this doesn't always mean they should be judged as bad. For instance, the energy of the forest fire clears the old growth for new life, a bursting volcano creates new land, and even when society breaks down, it can break down structures that are corrupt and no longer serve us, allowing us to build anew.

Overall, this mentality represents a very different mindset than the later Western concept of deity, which came after the rise of the modern Western religions of Judaism, Christianity, and Islam. We can see how this newer idea has become problematic because it does not then make sense when bad things happen to good people, when disasters come to the world, and when disease and misfortune happen to the innocent. To return once again to a Pagan or nature-based concept of deity in this sense is to understand and accept that evil not only happens, it may be better viewed as the result of imbalance, which is being corrected by nature herself.

## Harmful Thoughtforms from Others

Perhaps negative spirits may also represent the thoughts directed toward us from others. Or by ourselves toward others. Harmful thoughts such as envy, jealousy, anger, gossip, slander, and lies can create negative vibrations directed toward us. A desire for revenge, for instance, can take over the one it possesses, blocking out reason and self-control and engendering a vicious cycle that can be repeated down through families and generations. It is apparent how disabling and disruptive this aspect of human relationships and conflict can be on our society. In one pataki of the Yoruba tradition, it is said that the Orisha Chango taught us that the most powerful part of the human body is the tongue. We can heal, harm, create, and destroy using our tongue. This is why the wise person will be careful with the words they use toward themselves and why *tiya-tiya*, or gossip and slander, is an *osogbo*, a personified misfortune, of great harm to community.

Next, consider how powerful is the use of fascination or mind control by people who have malignant narcissism, who through the use of a charismatic but selfish will deceive people and control them to their ends for fame, wealth, power, and other nefarious purposes. Advertising itself and now social media is built on the manipulation of needs and beliefs from our deep unconscious.

It is no accident that it is said the Devil is the father of lies. These entities may be personifications of negative vibrations, and sensitive people, especially empathic people, may be particularly susceptible to their influence. So, I argue that to completely dismiss the idea that negative spirits and entities exist and can affect humanity, with this broader perspective, is quite closed-minded. With this expanded understanding, negative entities do exist, and they continue to manipulate us to serve our lower natures and hold us back from moving forward as a societal whole.

# FULL INTEGRATION

Realizing that reality exists both in left-brain logical and rational understanding but also in right-brain non-rational states of being includes acknowledging the deeper truths of myth, poetry, art, archetypes, and divine revelation. It is within these realms that healing and fully integrating our shadow sides must take place if we are to heal on an individual and collective level.

By integrating our shadow—both the parts that are disruptive and fear-based as well as the parts of ourselves we may be reluctant to express—we can heal our psyches at the deepest level. This may call for work with a counselor, spiritual advisor, or psychologist. We may need to heal some wounds that happened when we were children or are a result of ancestral patterns. Fully integrating our shadow, welcoming all parts of ourselves, even out-of-control aspects that represent unbalanced archetypes or unrealized ambitions, can be deeply healing and help us make sense of or accept tragedy, loss, and misfortune as opportunities to change and grow.

We cannot repeat the mistakes of earlier times by continuing the dualistic trap of projecting our own internal demons onto others instead of realizing these disowned parts of ourselves. Projection is a natural mental defense developed by our psyche when confronting issues and behaviors we have been taught to suppress, but when it is employed at the collective level, it leads to great human suffering. Through this example, we can see how it can influence human behavior as a whole, hardening into destructive realities that become the lasting problems of racism, gender binaries, and division that prevent us from reconnecting with one another and the Earth. The overwhelming force that creates these defenses is always fear. The goal, therefore, is to release the fear of these parts of ourselves in ourselves and others.

The shadow is not our enemy, so to be fully realized, we can let go of harsh judgment of it. It represents the side of ourselves we have hidden from the conscious mind. The antidote to fear is love, and self-love begins the process. Empathy can be a superpower. Nature-based wisdom says that we, as divine representatives of nature, hold both creative and destructive potential, dark and light, male and female, none and all. These are all parts of our own psyche, which holds the stages of our evolution.

To heal the Earth and relight Mother Earth's cauldron, it is imperative to acknowledge that all emanations of the human mind and of nature are parts of ourselves. Integration of the shadow begins with acknowledgment of it. One way we can acknowledge what lies here is to recognize when another person's actions or words trigger us; we can ask ourselves, why? Is there something within me I am refusing to see? By doing this, we begin to heal ourselves by making the unconscious, conscious. Beginning at the individual and then the collective level, integration of the shadow can create a more harmonious and integrated society for all the beings we share our planet with.

## ❋ A PRACTICE ❋
### Journey to Meet Your Shadow

You will need to find a comfortable and quiet location to do this meditation. It may help for you to record the journey first and then listen to it in meditation.

### Tools

One candle, matches or a lighter, and a singing bowl or bell. Your journal.

### Begin

I invite you now to close your eyes and get comfortable. Allow the sound of the singing bowl to bring you into yourself, with this time and place, and with the present moment.

[Ring bell or chime bowl.]

You will be embarking on a journey. Take a moment to first connect with your breath. Feel the comfort of your chair and focus on your breath. Take five deep breaths in through the nose and out through your mouth.

Feel the solidity of your body. Connect with your body, beginning at the top of your head, relaxing down into your face, your shoulders, arms, chest, torso, and down into your seat, down through your thighs, and into your legs. Allow yourself to connect to Mother Earth, feeling her solid form below you.

Around you, envision a circle of light. Let that light be bold and bright, feel its warmth, feel its light surround you, keeping you safe.

Connect now with the water in your body. Visualize how your body is filled with water and connect with this internal flow.

You are now centered in yourself. Take three more deep breaths, knowing your body is safe. Allow your spirit to journey.

You find yourself upon a path leading through the woods. Feel the light through the trees, smell the earthy air. Your feet are solid on the ground beneath you. Beside this path, a river flows. You hear the sound of water flow.

You begin to walk down the path. As you walk, you realize it turns to the left, and you begin a descent through a deepening valley. It spins now, away from the water, and you descend.

You find yourself coming to a dark clearing at the bottom of a ravine. Steep rock walls rise to where you have come from, tall trees surround a hollow center here, and at this center, you see the roots of a large tree. As you approach this tree, you see a skull painted with circles and spirals beside a lit oil lamp. You realize you have come to a holy place. Notice what you feel here before it.

Within the roots of the tree, you notice there is a large opening that is filled with darkness. Sit before this opening with the light coming from the oil lamp. In your mind, invite your shadow self to come forward from the hollow of the tree and wait to see what appears.

Observe and bear witness to the part of yourself that may or may not be hidden from yourself to appear. This could be an aspect of yourself at a younger age, which may hold old wounds that have not been fully acknowledged or released. It could be a side of yourself that you fear or are ashamed of. Or it could be some part of yourself that you have not allowed to be expressed due to the pressures and opinions of others. Let this aspect of yourself fully emerge. This aspect of yourself may even be dark and still hidden, unclear to yourself. Invite yourself to see this shadow self clearly.

Ask the shadow self if there is anything they would like you to know, to embrace into yourself, or to release in peace. Listen carefully to what your shadow self shares with you via words, thoughts, images, feelings, or impressions.

When finished, imagine you are taking up the bowl of oil and blowing out the light. Feel the darkness around you and let go of any fear. Give thanks to honor what was shared and as an offering to your shadow self and the experience this has brought to you. Return to the path and begin to walk back the way you came.

You begin to ascend. You may be following the light through the trees. You feel the fresh air on your face, smell the earth, and hear the swaying of branches and the sound of birds and other forest creatures. Return to where you entered the path and then return to your body and open your eyes. Light the candle and say, "I light this candle to bring my shadow self fully into the light of consciousness."

Hug yourself and say, "I welcome this shadow self fully into myself, knowing this is part of me, and fully acknowledging and appreciating the wisdom I have gained meeting my shadow. I release any sense of shame, guilt, or fear related to my shadow. And so it is."

Allow a few minutes of contemplation before your candle to fully integrate the feelings and thoughts that have arisen from meeting with your shadow. After meditating for a bit with the candle, chime the bowl or ring the bell to close the ceremony.

You may wish to journal this experience for yourself to remember or repeat it when you feel there is some aspect of yourself that is hidden.

# 14
# INITIATION

Many who come to nature spirituality do so because it resonates with them at their core. It offers a pathway to connect with ancestors, ancestral knowledge, and spiritual practice, which is deeply embedded in relationship with all life-forms, the elements, and the spirit world. These are unique aspects to Earth- and nature-based traditions, and they have broad appeal.

For some of these practices, being a descendent of the tradition we are called to and aspire to can be strong motivation, but it isn't required. Many of these traditions believe in or advocate for reincarnation, so we ourselves could have experienced that culture in a past life, and we can receive guidance from spirit guides from these cultures to explore that particular practice or tradition because it is right for our spiritual evolution.

An important guideline to recognize is not everyone is entitled to self-initiate to all existing nature traditions or begin working with deities or spiritual forces because they want to. Some traditions are open, and some are closed to initiates only. This is especially true for those religions and traditions who historically have been oppressed, marginalized, demonized, and condemned by the dominant Western culture. These include the various Diasporic Orisha traditions, as well as certain practices of First Nations people of the Americas and the Aboriginal peoples of Australia and New Zealand. Seeking to learn from and become part of these traditions requires respect and invitation from those communities to utilize their ceremonies, regalia, and cultural practices.

## Indigenous Community and Ceremony

The first guideline is to avoid generalization. If you seek to work with a particular tradition of indigeneity, research it thoroughly. If possible, interview living and actual members of that group. Be ready to name concepts correctly. For instance, if they acknowledge the Divine as Great Spirit, that is appropriate, but if they have their own name, use the correct name. For instance, the Algonquin-speaking peoples' name for Great Spirit is Manitou or Munitoh.[152] The same goes for their practices; learn the correct names and customs and acknowledge the native people whom the tradition belongs to for their teaching.

Do not try to pass off anything taught to you or given to you by Indigenous people as your own, and if it is not recommended to monetize this practice, realize doing so would be highly offensive and culturally appropriative. If you do choose to teach something that has been taught to you, be sure to acknowledge where it came from, and if possible, give something back to that community. Doing this goes a long way toward healing the wounds of colonization. When discussing the tradition publicly, be sure to always have permission from your elders to do so.

---

152  Evan T. Pritchard, *Native New Yorkers* (San Francisco: Council Oak Book, 2007), 169.

# DIASPORA TRADITIONS

Orisha traditions are not only open to all people, they are world-wide. Daniel Rodriguez said in his interview,

> I can tell you with Ocha, it's completely international now. I have performed initiations for people all over the world. All kinds of people from all different backgrounds, all different languages, all different customs from different cultures. For example, Asian people who are very big into their customs come into this. They find solace in this, they find spiritual connection, which is beautiful.

Anyone seeking initiation in these traditions with a European phenotype can learn a lot by consistently holding an attitude of humility and respect and genuine curiosity about others' culture and lived experience. Some things to consider that are important: unlike modern Pagan traditions, where people are free to choose which aspect of God/Goddess or pantheon they wish to honor and worship, Afro-Caribbean and Native African traditions have established priesthoods, customs, liturgy, and rituals.

The idea is that we belong to the Orisha, they choose us, we do not get to select which Orisha is ours to serve. One should approach membership with honesty, defer to elders, and have a willingness to listen, learn, and practice the tradition as it exists, embracing traditional customs and rules of one's lineage.

In Lukumi, only fully ordained priests who have received initiation have the right to work directly with the Orishas. It is advisable for anyone wishing to work with the Orisha to connect with an Ocha community or Ile to seek guidance and recommendations. They may benefit from a reading of cowrie shells, coconut (Obi), or the counsel of the priests of Orula, Babalawos, who will guide them as to the appropriate way to seek assistance from Orisha or to inquire if they are meant to receive initiation. Again, this is not predicated on ethnicity, as Orisha tradition welcomes all and is worldwide, but it is predicated on the guidance of fully initiated members of the community.

In addition, Lukumi tradition does utilize the blood sacrifice of domesticated animals that are usually consumed as part of a ritual feast. If this is something that would be shocking and offensive to you, this is because this tradition is probably not right for you. As a living tradition, Lukumi has a strict lineage, established formal rules to follow, customs to observe, and an order to maintain in terms of how to relate to fellow Oloshas.

If you are welcomed to this community, it is considered very ill manners to then try to impose your cultural beliefs on the community that may disagree with these customs. For instance, in Lukumi, women are required to wear skirts during ceremonies. If this is a problem for you, again, this may be an indication that you may not be right for the tradition. Lukumi is a tradition of surrender to higher forces than ourselves and constant self-correction and improvement. The benefits of this are desirable because we who have made the sacrifice believe the Orisha only want what is best for us.

Finally, Orisha tradition is a community-based tradition. Anyone who purports to be able to initiate you without other priests and priestesses present and participating is selling you a fraud. Beware of those who prey on your hunger and ignorance. As mentioned, the full initiation of Lukumi is a series of initiations that require an investment of time, money, and study. Don't go into it without knowing that. Those who are marked to become priests and who initiate with the Kariocha ceremony will be required to host a ceremony that lasts seven days, has multiple priests involved, feeds the community and the Orishas, and requires many material goods, including animals, herbs, and renting a space. This can be very expensive. Then they will be guided by a reading, the *Ita*, meant only for them for their entire life witnessed by elders. After the seven days are complete, the newly consecrated Olosha, now Iyawo, will wear white clothing and follow the restrictions and guidelines received by them in the Ita Ceremony for a year and seven days before they are considered full members of the community.

The best rule of thumb for all those who seek initiation in Lukumi or other Afro-Caribbean traditions is to take your time finding an elder willing to initiate you, teach you, guide you, and introduce you to the community. They will become your godparent, and it is to them that you should direct your questions and concerns. This is a very important and supportive relationship that should be built on trust and mutual respect. If a godparent demands money and obedience but refuses to teach you anything, or does not exhibit good moral character, this is a good sign they are not reputable, and you should move on. Conversely, if a godparent is trying to teach you the correct way and you are refusing to abide by either the guidelines or the recommendations of a reading or divine guidance, that problem is not theirs, it's yours. This tradition may be too constrictive for your taste, and that's okay, but you will not benefit from it if you refuse to make changes that are meant to improve your life. Keep in mind that not everyone has to become a full priest; creating a relationship with an ordained Olosha in order to develop a relationship with Orisha in your life may be sufficiently fulfilling to you.

## NEO-PAGAN TRADITIONS

Conversely, there is benefit to being part of the revival of European Neo-Pagan traditions. Not only are these traditions more open in the sense of who can initiate or how to initiate, or if initiation is even needed, but also to the level of participation. Most communities are open to anyone who wishes to join as long as they are not disruptive.

While archaeology and the careful study of ancient texts can give us a glimpse and basic understanding of what the ancestral Europeans practiced before the destruction of their traditions, this can never be known entirely, which allows for freedom in modern reinterpretations. With that in mind, Pagans have consistently been creating rituals and ceremonies freely, utilizing magickal techniques and practices from various traditions, incorporating seasonal folk customs creatively into new ceremonies, and establishing tradition and liturgy. Personal relationships between ourselves and the deities that call to us are encouraged. While it is entirely acceptable to self-dedicate or practice in a solitary manner, because humans are social beings, many people decide to join working groups or larger organizations.

Guidelines for Pagan or Heathen practice are as follows: While research and reading books about specific traditions is encouraged and valuable, this does not substitute for direct experiential learning. Ways to meet others who practice those traditions include attending large Pagan gatherings, attending workshops, and making new friends.

Research and participate in reputable internet boards and online groups in order to locate local groups and resources. Some Pagan and New Age shops also have introductory circles and educational groups. It is important to take your time and check your motives. Do you want to be a witch to cast spells and control others? It's possible, but usually not recommended. Do you wish to be part of a community that honors the Wheel of the Year, learn directly how to practice Wicca, or celebrate the holidays discussed in the magickal books you are reading? That is a different story. Do you wish to be with others who share your passion for the Norse pantheon? That, too, is a great motivation. Beware, however, of any groups that stress membership is exclusive to only one religious way or one ethnic group or race.

I recommend to all that if you are to really benefit from a relationship with ancestors, spirit guides, and a pantheon of divine entities and Spirit, you must be willing to show a strong commitment to it. Soul Blossom Circle requires a traditional year and a day training before taking the full initiation. It is important to understand, when you make vows and pacts with entities in sacred space, the road is open now for you to continue, but you have an obligation to continue. These things cannot be easily undone. Think long and hard about any magickal nature-based tradition and/or practice you encounter, and never take any vows or do anything that creates fear in you or seeks to control you.

# NEW AGE PRACTICES

*New Age* is a term given to a group of practices that have emerged in the twentieth and twenty-first centuries that is more correctly a set of practices or philosophies rather than religious traditions. This allows them to be open. There are valid paths and fulfilling practices and I have listed some of these ideas and practices in this book.

A few points I would like to make about this, however: New Age traditions have been notorious about appropriating cultural traditions and then dismissing parts of them that are not palatable for Western tastes. An example of this is Yoga. Many Yoga practitioners don't realize that this practice is a basic and fundamental part of traditional Indian spirituality and religion. It is not specifically for physical exercise alone; it is meant to be part of an overall personal practice for holistic well-being, and a devotional path toward achieving personal enlightenment. Acknowledging and giving credit to the Indian spiritual roots of this practice is essential, and those who benefit financially from becoming Yoga instructors and leaders should really consider how to give back. It is completely inappropriate to deny the spiritual aspects of Yoga.

My guidelines for working with New Age traditions: Avoid anyone who is utilizing culturally specific practices without explaining convincingly how they are now able to offer those practices and services if it is not their own culture or ethnicity. Equally, avoid practices that claim to confer initiation or empowerment, but have been bastardized and changed from the original version (for example, sweat lodge ceremonies that take place in a large tent with electric stones, with many people present, outside of a Native American traditional context).

Avoid practices that are too expensive for your budget, that overcharge, claiming exclusive knowledge or powers only if you invest large sums for the training or to receive energetic transmissions. If the teaching or knowledge is outside of something you can afford and exorbitantly priced, do your research and listen to what others who have experienced it have to say before investing.

Be careful of following gurus or leaders who require unquestioning obedience, demand large sums of money or personal property, and encourage distancing yourself from friends or family outside of the group or keeping secrets. These people are most likely dangerous and can cause you great harm. Once again, take your time before committing to anything that doesn't feel 100 percent welcoming and positive.

## MIXING TRADITIONS

My final note of caution is against mixing traditions. As an interspiritual minister myself, I would like to be clear: it is perfectly acceptable to practice more than one faith tradition. This is a paradigm shift away from the exclusivity so prevalent in Abrahamic faiths. However, it is ill-advised to try to blend them all at once or at the same time. An example would be calling the names of gods from different cultural groups or pantheons, blending Orisha prayers with Hindu prayers in one ceremony, and so on. This is offensive and confusing both to those in attendance, but also to the deities and spiritual forces you are purporting to serve. And if they are confused, you will be confused as well. It is suggested that if you commit to working with a particular cultural pantheon and tradition, you should stick within that pantheon while practicing that form of ceremony or craft.

# ❂ A PRACTICE ❂
## Relighting Your Inner Cauldron

This is a practice inspired by the Magical Awakening Energy Healing® tradition, as taught by Brett Bevell at the Omega Institute of Rhinebeck, New York. Within this technique, there is a concept of Dragon Fire, which resides in our lower cauldron, located below our belly buttons. We can commit to relighting this spiritual fire. This is a great practice to start your day.

### Tools
Your body.

### Begin
Stand with your feet hips-width apart on the floor. Place one hand directly on your abdomen below your belly button and one hand on your solar plexus. Close your eyes. Envision a fire burning here, filled with warming flames, reaching from your third chakra and spiraling throughout your body. This is the Dragon Fire. This fire helps with our digestion and burns away anything that no longer serves us.

Begin an even breath in and out until it sounds like the ocean. Then say these words out loud and contemplate that the fire consumes what needs to be consumed to relight your own internal flame. Let it pass through your physical body, your mental body, your ethereal body. As you do, envision your breath feeding the flames:

*I now release to the inner flame all that no longer serves me!*
*I now relight the cauldron.*

Repeat three times and end with a long "om," which is the sound for universal consciousness and Oneness with all that is.

# 15

# RELIGHTING THE CAULDRON

As we come to the end of this book, I'd like to pause and revisit my original intentions. I began this study with a recognition of many of the problems that have come to a head at this momentous time in Earth's history. These problems, I believe, are rooted in the dominant Western culture's insistence on an unsustainable, patriarchal paradigm that prioritizes human technology, hoarding, consuming, and wasting resources, and the economic dominance of a privileged class of people that enriches a very few over the needs of many, including other life-forms.

I have suggested if we are to recognize this moment in time as a turning point for humanity and for the planet, our job is to envision and manifest a more sustainable paradigm that embraces interdependence, collaboration, a respect and embrace of diversity, a partnership between men, women, and nonbinary people, and an understanding that we all have a responsibility to the Earth, as it is the planet we share and depend on utterly for our existence.

The dominant paradigm is rooted in institutions, religious concepts, and beliefs that are inherently sexist, racist, homophobic, and divisive and keep us in separation from one another, from other species, and from nature. Many of these institutions are corrupt and collapsing, as is our biosphere. This paradigm enforces man's superiority over all beings and has created rigid hierarchies that have led to unprecedented destruction of the Earth's delicate life balance, chronic warfare, a tragic loss of shared natural resources, and worldwide economic disparity. By bringing awareness to how these destructive ideas were formed and how they are interconnected, my intention was to generate a united desire for each of us to commit to making this paradigm obsolete.

The solution-focus of this book is predicated on a conviction that a worldview and belief system that embrace nature spirituality hold the key to our ability to overcome these difficulties. Nature spirituality is uniquely positioned, and always has been, to be an antidote to the dominant paradigm.

A metaphor I have used to explore the application of these solutions has been to build a bridge between cultures and religious ideas from past Indigenous communities as well as ancient Pagan societies that encapsulated a more sustainable paradigm and bring these ideas forward again to be reclaimed, revalued, and revisioned for the modern world. Central to these beliefs is an idea that Mother Earth is sacred and it is our duty to protect her and recognize our complete dependence on her.

Second is the idea that the bridge is also between current nature-based traditions—many that on the surface may not seem related, yet when we dig deeper, it's apparent they share common beliefs, practices, and worldviews. This is a crucial element because in some ways, concepts borne of the domination paradigm, like colonialism, racism, and sexism, have the distinct purpose of keeping us divided, unequal, and distrustful of one another. By recognizing kinship and alliance, learning to acknowledge and respect one another, and taking responsibility for past harms and our own harmful programming, modern nature-based practitioners have an opportunity to be huge agents for change.

## THE BRIDGE

Nature spirituality, as we have seen, has certain aspects that are common to all traditions. One is a deep reverence for Mother Earth herself, an understanding of our interdependence on our environment and with the other creatures that share this planet. Another is an embrace of traditional practices that include shamanic, magickal, and/or mystical practices, which are designed to guide a person into non-ordinary states of consciousness for healing of self and others and direct experiential revelation. A third aspect of most nature-based spiritual traditions is the use of creative and artistic modalities, the raising of energy and healing work, which all utilize the forces of nature, the elements, or the energetic field of the Earth to bring about healing for oneself, one's community, and personal transformation. Added to this is the fact that nature spirituality usually consists of a knowledge base of natural medicine and herbal folkways and recognizes the importance of treating illness and imbalance primarily with prevention and holistic techniques.

A fourth, crucial part of nature tradition is the inclusion of practices that recognize and honor ancestors and the dead in order to maintain relationships with them, heal negative ancestral patterns, and invite their benevolent influence into one's life. Additionally, nature traditions focus on cultivating personal responsibility for leaving a legacy for generations to come by valuing nature for its inherent worth, not its monetary value alone, and recognizes kinship with all sentient life. Because of this responsibility, many who practice nature spirituality feel it is a sacred duty to make lifestyle changes that reflect a commitment to sustainable and holistic living, often at a community-minded level.

# THE CAULDRON

It is not a coincidence that one of the symbols in popular culture associated with the image of the witch is the cauldron. The witch is the granddaughter of the Wise Woman, an archetype of the female Divine Elder. Some examples of this goddess archetype are Hecate of the Greeks and Cerridwen of the Celts—goddesses of magick and inspiration, two goddesses who embodied her wisdom aspect and awe-inspiring powers.

The symbol of the cauldron appeared richly in Celtic myth, legend, and iconography. It is the symbol par excellence of Cerridwen's powers, which hold the sacred *awen*, or the blessed and holy breath and spirit of creativity, transformation, and divine inspiration. The awen has imbued the bardic tradition from the legendary bard Taliesen down through the ages and up through the present day for Neo-Pagan Druids.[153] Another association is with the Dagda, the good father god of the Earth, who owned a magick cauldron, where warriors fallen in battle could be cast and reborn, fully restored to fight another day. To the Pagan mind, the cauldron symbolizes the fiery belly of Mother Earth, where we all return at death. As the Earth Mother swallows our bones, our spirits are released, and from her belly all living things will reemerge, fully formed.

In European folklore, the cauldron is the tool for the Wise Woman ways of plant medicine and nutrition. If traditional anthropology is cor-

---

153  Hughes, *Cerridwen*, 3–8.

rect, a division of labor involved early humans dividing into those who hunted and those who foraged and gathered. And the gatherers were usually women. While it is becoming clear that women in some societies may have also hunted alongside men, as evidenced by recent finds of Neolithic hunters and analysis of their bones, it is equally clear that gathering and foraging—learning which plants were food, which were medicine, which were visionary aids, and which were poisons—was the foundation of modern medicine. It is not a coincidence, then, it was Eve, the feminine representation in the Bible, who became tempted by the forbidden fruit of knowledge. This myth recognizes the core truth that women in pre-Abrahamic tradition were the keepers of the knowledge of the plant kingdom.

As an important human artifact, the cast-iron cauldron was an important cooking development for prehistoric humans. As humanity learned to tame fire and keep a hearth warm with a cauldron to cook food, the Stone Age gave way to the Neolithic Age, followed by the age of metalworking. In addition, if one imagines the fires of the hearth as another symbol of the Earth's fiery core, we can view the hearth, usually presided over in mythology by feminine deities such as Vesta and Brigit, as the center of the home, the abode of women's power. Here, people shared the stories and wisdom of the elders with the next generation and preserved them for clan and tribe.

In the Diaspora, in Lukumi tradition, the cauldron is the receptacle for the Orisha Ogun and also the container for the trio of Warriors, received through initiation, Ellegua, Ogun, and Ochosi. Filled with instruments that represent tools and weapons of humanity, the cauldron is the container that holds the potential for the technologies of war, agriculture, and innovation. In the Palo Mayombe tradition, the cauldron becomes the *prenda*, the receptacle of the *palero* that holds all the mysteries of the cosmos. Within the *prenda*, the palero creates a home for the *muerto*, or spirit the palero is in partnership with, and also holds symbols of the Earth, the stars, and the elements. In Palo, these receptacles are also called *ngangas* and *enquises*; they are either clay urns or steel cauldrons and can be dedicated to powerful spirits. Through ceremony and offerings, especially blood, the cauldron is activated and transformed into a symbol of unlimited potential and power in kinship with the Earth herself as repository for the dead.[154]

In Eastern thought, the cauldron can be found as the receptacle of the Qi, represented by the lower dan tien present in our belly. Hindus locate this cauldron below the belly button; this is where the Agni or spiritual flame is kept. The cauldron as an emblem for the sentience of Mother Earth is universally represented in most forms of nature spirituality, which also present myths, tools, and concepts that have tended the flames of her consciousness and health for thousands of years.

# THE NEW PARADIGM

A shift in human consciousness is evident to many people from all over the world right now, not least of whom are nature-based practitioners. As my godfather in Ocha, Ilan Chester, explained,

> I have sensed that some kind of shift was coming. Something radical is coming. I have spoken to elders who were going through the same thing, that there would be a great shift in human consciousness where it was going to take us to the next level. Some are going to perish, but some are going to evolve. There is this shift in human consciousness that is pulling us to connect humans more with the spiritual world. It's like She's pulling us all to do that. It's like Mother Nature is saying we have to; it's the only way humankind is going to ascend to the next level. To help us be in harmony with the Earth.

---

154 Ochoa, *Society of the Dead*, 140.

One gift of practicing nature-based traditions is gaining this new perspective that exists outside of the dominant culture. This aspect has been remarked on by all the practitioners I have interviewed for this book. Andras Corban-Arthen explained it very well:

> First of all, it gives people a different perspective of who they are and who they can be. A different perspective on the world and the culture we live in. I think it opens up possibilities that most people in our culture are not aware of because they are locked into the norms of the culture. I think that it provides connection to spiritual experience, to ancestral work, that a lot of people haven't even conceived of in mainstream culture.

By opening ourselves to a direct, experiential relationship with nature, with ancestors, with the elements, with Earth energy, and with like-minded community, we cannot help but change. Eldritch described how magick works:

> There is a phrase that has been in my head these last few days: "What I create, changes me." So, when I create something, and put time and effort into a thing, I've helped make a thing. It's a Wiccan practice to "make it happen," and I can manifest a thing, but it also changes me.

The most important aspect that must be reclaimed within this new paradigm by humanity to bring about healing for the Earth is seeking a healthier balance with nature and equality among all. By embracing a return of reverence for the Divine Feminine, the Great Mother, and nature-based traditions, we may move forward, taking the best of what we have learned throughout our evolution in order to be of service to a future, more embodied and awakened humanity.

# THE SPIRAL

Nature is cyclical, and both aspects of creation work together: the male principle of life force and the female fertile form are essential for life to exist. We need to realize that evolution and time are not linear but move back and forth along a spiral path. We can circle back four to six thousand years ago and retrace our steps, collecting the wisdom found in ancient traditions while discarding the mistakes and beliefs that no longer serve us and threaten to continue to oppress millions and destroy the balance of life.

We should also embrace and retain the important advancements, especially scientific understanding, that have helped us along the way, inspired us, and continue to drive us with a desire to learn, explore, and transform. We need to remember our purpose of joining with the stars and taking our rightful place as citizens of the universe, children of this magical planet we are privileged to call home.

Monica Sjöö and Barbara Mor wrote in their seminal work *The Great Cosmic Mother* about this nonlinear aspect of evolution. If we are to evolve, we can retrace our steps backward to recapture some concepts of pre-patriarchal consciousness in order to move forward again, this time with more balance, wisdom, and sanctity for the Earth and the Divine Feminine, retaining kinship with other species, and in doing so reach a new level of human evolution. This, as they call it, is our magickal capacity, and it is built into the DNA of all of us; we can truly cocreate the universe. "The memory is in our genes, we have lived it, it is ours."[155]

We cannot go backward, only forward. My goal has been to inspire you to create a renewed relationship with nature herself, celebrating her rhythms, seasons, light and dark sides, appreciating both the abundant and the fallow times, and embracing the diversity of humanity and life on Earth. Only together as a united species can we begin to heal ourselves from some of the dysfunction of the failed paradigm and commit to defending the planet.

---

155 Sjöö and Mor, *The Great Cosmic Mother*, 422.

Salvation is when we realize the source of divinity is within us and we have the power to cocreate reality. It is time to reclaim this magick for yourself, but first we have to believe it is real—and real change is possible.

# CONTRIBUTOR BIOGRAPHIES

**Andras Corban-Arthen** is founder of the EarthSpirit Community in Western Massachusetts and president of the European Congress of Ethnic Religions based in Vilnius, Lithuania. He also served for thirteen years on the board of trustees for the Parliament of the World's Religions and represented Paganism at the 1991 United Nations Interfaith Conference on Religion and Prejudice. Originally from Galiza in Northwestern Spain, he lives with his extended family in a forest in the Berkshire Hills of Western Massachusetts.

**Chip Brown** is a retired attorney and historian and now an off-grid sustainable farmstead farmer. He is working with a Native American organization to develop Food Sovereignty programs, policies, and laws for Tribal members, on-reservation, supporting traditional foods, farming, and ranching opportunities; to improve the health of the people and the land; to bolster necessary skills to produce local and traditional food; and to create and expand access markets to distribute this food to the people. He and his spouse are building the first State-permitted, tire-bale constructed, sustainable, off-grid home in their state. They live on their land, growing food, raising chickens, collecting and hauling water for all personal and agricultural use. Their efforts are intended to be a model for folks to live a carbon-neutral lifestyle while supporting themselves and assisting their families, communities, tribes—much needed in this time of devastating climate change. Chip plans to institute a spiritual center for transformative growth on this land in the near future. In his interview, he shared how he incorporates the traditional beliefs and practices from his ancestral Middle Atlantic Lenape/Delaware and North Atlantic Mi'kmaq Algonquin people into his personal spiritual practices. Chip considers himself Pagan; since 1982, his spiritual "home" has been with the Circle Sanctuary Pagan Community of Wisconsin. He continues to work with and for Circle Sanctuary in an advisory and administrative capacity, having done so for several decades.

**Ilan Chester** is a Babalosha, an elder and priest of the Lukumi tradition, a practitioner of Palo Mayombe, and a gifted Espiritista from Philadelphia. Ilan Chester initiated me into the Lukumi tradition in 2012, becoming my godfather. He discussed the tradition known in Latin America as Espiritismo, a folk tradition that combines European Spiritism with African religious practices from Yorubaland and Indigenous practices from the Caribbean Taino and Arawak people of the Greater Antilles.

**Rev. Eric V. Eldritch** is a Third Degree Wiccan priestx in The Stone Circle Tradition of Wicca (USA) based in the mid-Atlantic region of the United States. In 2019, he was ordained by Circle Sanctuary, a nature spirituality church, based in Southwest Wisconsin. He grew up in a devout Christian family near Pittsburgh, Pennsylvania, and his spiritual journey includes coming out as both a Radical Faerie and as a Pagan priestx. He is also a member of the Stone Circle Council community that hosts festivals and regular moon services and annually raises Standing Stones. Eldritch has lived in and worked in the Washington, DC area for nearly forty years and holds a master's degree in applied sociolinguistics.

**Rev. Arda Itez** is an interspiritual and humanist minister, ordained at One Spirit Learning Alliance in New York City. As a private consultant, she works with major universities and mission-focused, values-driven institutions to cultivate conscious leadership skills and develop human potential. She has dedicated her career to inspirational healing, empowerment, and working toward sociopolitical change. Rev. Arda is of Karachay ancestry, the Indigenous Turkic people of the North Caucasus. She is trained in Tuvan Shamanism.

**Gloria "Glow" Okandekun** is an elder and Iyalosha of a large Ile, located in Los Angeles, California. She is from Los Angeles and her family hails from Mazatlan and Durango, Mexico. Glow is a long-time practitioner of La Regla de Ocha. She has officiated dozens of Kariocha ceremonies and is the godmother to many Ocha godchildren and great-godchildren. *Okandekun,* a name which means "the heart and crown of the leopard," also practices Espiritismo and Palo Mayombe. Professionally, Glow works as a nursing professional and holds a master's degree in biology.

**Puáwai Ormsby** is a Māori elder, educator, and artist from New Zealand, the land known in the Māori tongue as Aotearoa, or the Land of the Ever-Shining Light. She discusses the revival of Māori culture happening within New Zealand. She is a gatekeeper of the Temple of the Four Winds, a holy place in Aotearoa considered the Stairway to Heaven. She is also a founder of Talking Tree Hill, a school for children that implements nature-based curriculum based on the Southern Cross with concepts that include Māori values of mindfulness, hospitality, being guardians of the planet, and the connection to Oneness.

**Daniel Rodriguez** is a well-respected elder and active member of La Regla de Ocha community in the New York and New Jersey region, with over thirty-five years as a priest of Chango. He has presided over many Ocha ceremonies on the East Coast. Daniel is also a practitioner of the 21 Divisions, which he discussed in his interview. The 21 Divisions is a form of Vodou specific to the Dominican Republic. Daniel holds a master's degree in education and works as an educator in the New Jersey school system.

**Rev. Dr. Diane Rooney** is a Taoist practitioner and an interspiritual minister, ordained at One Spirit Alliance in New York, New York. She holds a doctorate in ministry in Taoism from the New York Theological Society. She is a professional Chinese medicine practitioner and a passionate teacher and advocate for Qigong. Taoism is an ancient Indigenous nature-based philosophy and practice from the Far East.

**Robert L. Schreiwer** is the president and founder of the Urglaawe tradition within Heathenry; *Urglaawe* is a Pennsylvania Deitsch term that means "primal faith." He is currently the president and CEO of the Troth, which is the oldest and largest Heathen organization in existence. He is the manager of Heathens Against Hate, a Philadelphia-based outreach organization, and he's a prison chaplain for Heathens.

# RECOMMENDED READINGS

## THE DARK CAULDRON TOPICS

Eisler, Riane. *The Real Wealth of Nations: Creating a Caring Economics*. San Francisco: Berrett-Koehler Publishers, 2008.

Gimbutas, Marija. *The Goddesses and Gods of Old Europe: Myths and Cult Images*. Los Angeles: University of California Press, 1982.

Goode, Starr. *Sheela na Gig: The Dark Goddess of Sacred Power*. Rochester, NY: Inner Traditions, 2016.

Kendi, Ibram. *How to Be an Antiracist*. New York: Penguin Books, 2019.

Menakem, Resmaa. *My Grandmother's Hands: Racialized Trauma and the Pathway to Mending Our Hearts and Bodies.* Las Vegas: Central Recovery Press, 2017.

Pinkola Estés, Clarissa. *Women Who Run with the Wolves: Myths and Stories of the Wild Woman Archetype.* New York: Ballantine Books, 1992.

Sjöö, Monica, and Barbara Mor. *The Great Cosmic Mother: Rediscovering the Religion of the Earth.* New York: Harper and Row, 1991.

# SHAPE-SHIFTING

Adams, Barbara. *Prayers of Smoke.* Berkeley, CA: Celestial Arts, 1990.

Castaneda, Carlos. *A Separate Reality: Further Conversations with Don Juan.* New York: Washington Square Press, 1971.

Doore, Gary. *Shaman's Path: Healing, Personal Growth and Empowerment.* Boston: Shambhala Books, 1988.

Johnson, Kenneth. *North Star Road: Shamanism, Witchcraft and the Otherworldly Journey.* St. Paul, MN: Llewellyn Publications, 1996.

Katz, Richard. *Indigenous Healing Psychology: Honoring the Wisdom of the First Peoples.* Rochester, VT: Healing Arts, 2017.

Manitonquat. *Medicine Story, the Original Instructions: Reflections of an Elder on the Teachings of the Elders, Adapting Ancient Wisdom to the Twenty-First Century.* Bloomington, IN: AuthorHouse, 2009.

# ANCESTOR REVERENCE

Bayles-Paton, Lewis. *Spiritism and the Cult of the Dead in Antiquity*. New York: Forgotten Books, 2016.

Ochoa, Todd R. *Society of the Dead: Quita Manaquita and Palo Praise in Cuba*. Berkeley, CA: University of California Press, 2010.

# THE ELEMENTS AND SPIRIT

Fontana, David. *The Secret Language of Symbols: A Visual Key to Symbols and Their Meanings*. London: Duncan Baird Publishers, 2003.

# DIVINATION, REVELATION, AND MEDIUMSHIP

Blum, Ralph H. *The Book of Runes*. New York: St. Martin's Press, 1993.

Greer, Mary. *Women of the Golden Dawn: Rebels and Priestesses*. Rochester, VT: Park Street Press, 1995.

Schucman, Helen. *A Course in Miracles*. Mill Valley, CA: The Foundation for Inner Peace, 2008.

# ENERGY HEALING

Bevell, Brett. *The Wizard's Guide to Energy Healing: Introducing the Divine Healing Secrets of Merlin*. Rhinebeck, NY: Monkfish Book Publishing Company, 2015.

Hay, Louise. *Heal Your Body*. Carlsbad, CA: Hay House, 1984.

Hover-Kramer, Dorotea. *Creative Energies: Integrative Energy Psychotherapy for Self-Expression and Healing*. New York: Norton and Company, 2002.

# CHAKRA HEALING

Bruyere, Rosalyn. *Wheels of Light: Chakras, Auras and the Healing Energy of the Body.* New York: Simon and Schuster, 1994.

Judith, Anodea. *Eastern Body, Western Mind: Psychology and the Chakra System as a Path to the Self.* New York: Celestial Arts, 2004.

# ESPIRITISMO AND SPIRITISM

Bragdon, Emma. *Spiritism and Mental Health.* Philadelphia, PA: Singing Dragon Press, 2012.

Canazares, Raul. *Helping Yourself with Selected Prayers, Volume 2.* New York: Original Publications, 2004.

Dos Ventos, Mario. *Sea el Santisimo: A Manual for Misa Espiritual & Mediumship Development.* Nzo Quimbanda Exu Ventania: Lulu Publishing, 2008.

Kardec, Allan. *Collection of Selected Prayers, Special Edition.* New York: New Devotion Spiritist, 2022.

———. *The Spirit's Book.* Guildford, UK: White Crow Books, 2010.

# HERBAL WISDOM AND NATURAL HEALING

Bennett, Robin Rose. *The Gift of Healing Herbs: Plant Medicines and Home Remedies for a Vibrantly Healthy Life.* Berkeley, CA: North Atlantic Books, 2014.

Davidow, Joie. *Infusions of Healing: A Treasury of Mexican-American Herbal Remedies.* New York: Fireside Publishers, 1999.

Reid, Daniel. *The Complete Book of Chinese Health and Healing: Guarding the Three Treasures*. Boston: Shambhala Publishers, 1994.

Weed, Susyn. *Wise Woman Herbal: Healing Wise*. Woodstock, NY: Ash Tree Publishing, 1999.

Williamson, John. *The Oak King, the Holly King, and the Unicorn: The Myths and Symbolism of the Unicorn Tapestries*. New York: Harper and Row, 1983.

## PERMACULTURE AND SUSTAINABILITY

Berry, Thomas. *The Dream of the Earth*. San Francisco: Sierra Club Publications, 1988.

## ASTROLOGY, WITCHCRAFT, AND MAGICK

Robbins, Heather Roan. *Moon Wisdom: Transform Your Life Using the Moon's Signs and Cycles*. New York: Cico Books, 2015.

Valiente, Doreen. *Witchcraft for Tomorrow*. London: Hale Limited, 1983.

Weinstein, Marion. *Positive Magic: Occult Self-Help*. New York: Phoenix, 1981.

# BIBLIOGRAPHY

Adams, Barbara. *Prayers of Smoke*. Berkeley, CA: Celestial Arts, 1990.

Adams, Donna, and Melinda Chichester. "Integrating Healing Touch for Advanced Illness and End-of-Life Nursing Care." *Beginnings: The Journal for Holistic Nursing* (2019): 14–26.

Bayles-Paton, Lewis. *Spiritism and the Cult of the Dead in Antiquity*. New York: Forgotten Books, 2016.

Berry, Thomas. *The Dream of the Earth*. San Francisco: Sierra Club Publications, 1988.

Bevell, Brett. *The Magical Awakening System of Healing*. Rhinebeck, NY: Monkfish Book Publishing Company, 2015.

Blum, Ralph H. *The Book of Runes*. New York: St. Martin's Press, 1993.

Bord, Janet, and Colin Bord. *The Secret Country*. London: Warner Books, 1976.

Borges, Philip. "Myths, Shamans and Seers." YouTube, 2012. https://www.youtube.com/watch?v=q2VzhyIyGkA.

Bragdon, Emma. *Spiritism and Mental Health*. Philadelphia, PA: Singing Dragon Press, 2012.

Brockovich, Erin. "Plummeting Sperm Counts, Shrinking Penises: Toxic Chemicals Threaten Humanity." *The Guardian*, March 18, 2021. https://www.theguardian.com/commentisfree/2021/mar/18/toxic-chemicals-health-humanity-erin-brokovich?CMP=oth_b-aplnews_d-1&fbclid=IwAR28mT2L5DjtgurBioSu8-0PC9vqdZEXIolq1k1mwaIvaM0TmkWnI6VDEDc.

Bruyere, Rosalyn. *Wheels of Light: Chakras, Auras and the Healing Energy of the Body*. New York: Simon and Schuster, 1994.

Castaneda, Carlos. *A Separate Reality: Further Conversations with Don Juan*. New York: Washington Square Press, 1971.

Cohen, Hadar. "Violence Done in Our Name." *Lilith*, May 13, 2021. https://lilith.org/2021/05/the-violence-being-done-in-our-name/?fbclid=IwAR3JWjNMljlrAhi-K_UPyVM64zoZmh-Wopvvrn-_Nmk8hLpzmMLmg0HTy2c.

Cohn, Norman. *Europe's Inner Demons*. New York: Basic Books Press, 1975.

Davidow, Joie. *Infusions of Healing: A Treasury of Mexican-American Herbal Remedies*. New York: Fireside Publishers, 1999.

De La Torre, Miguel. *Santeria: The Beliefs and Rituals of a Growing Religion in America*. Grand Rapids, MI: Eerdmans Publishing, 2004.

Dixon, Jo, and James Dixon. *The Color Book*. Denver, CO: Castle Rising, 1978.

Doore, Gary. *Shaman's Path: Healing, Personal Growth and Empowerment*. Boston: Shambhala Books, 1988.

Drewal, Henry John. *Mami Wata: Arts for Water Spirit in Africa and Its Diasporas*. Los Angeles: Fowler Museum, 2008.

Eisler, Riane. *Building a Partnership World*. Rhinebeck, NY: The Omega Institute, 2020.

———. *The Real Wealth of Nations: Creating a Caring Economics*. San Francisco: Berrett-Koehler Publishers, 2008.

Fontana, David. *The Secret Language of Symbols: A Visual Key to Symbols and Their Meanings*. London: Duncan Baird Publishers, 2003.

Gimbutas, Marija. *The Goddesses and Gods of Old Europe: Myths and Cult Images*. Los Angeles: University of California Press, 1982.

Goode, Starr. *Sheela na Gig: The Dark Goddess of Sacred Power*. Rochester, NY: Inner Traditions, 2016.

Graves, Robert. *The White Goddess*. New York: Noonday Press, 1948.

Greer, Mary. *Women of the Golden Dawn: Rebels and Priestesses*. Rochester, VT: Park Street Press, 1995.

Hall, Shannon. "Exxon Knew about Climate Change almost 40 Years Ago." *Scientific American*, October 26, 2015. https://www.scientificamerican.com/article/exxon-knew-about-climate-change-almost-40-years-ago/.

Hay, Louise. *Heal Your Body*. Carlsbad, CA: Hay House, 1984.

Hover-Kramer, Dorotea. *Creative Energies: Integrative Energy Psychotherapy for Self-Expression and Healing*. New York: Norton and Company, 2002.

Hughes, Kristoffer. *Cerridwen: Celtic Goddess of Inspiration*. Woodbury, MN: Llewellyn Publications, 2021.

Jackson-Cherry, L., and B. Erford. *Crisis Assessment, Intervention and Prevention*. 3rd ed. Pearson, 2018.

Johnson, Kenneth. *North Star Road: Shamanism, Witchcraft and the Otherworldly Journey*. St. Paul, MN: Llewellyn Publications, 1996.

Judith, Anodea. *Eastern Body, Western Mind: Psychology and the Chakra System as a Path to the Self*. New York: Celestial Arts, 2004.

Karade, Baba Ifa. *The Handbook of Yoruba Religious Concepts*. Newburyport, MA: Red Wheel Weiser, 2020.

Kardec, Allan. *Collection of Selected Prayers, Special Edition*. New York: New Devotion Spiritist, 2022.

———. *The Spirit's Book*. Guildford, UK: White Crow Books, 2010.

Katz, Richard. *Indigenous Healing Psychology: Honoring the Wisdom of the First Peoples*. Rochester, VT: Healing Arts, 2017.

Kendi, Ibram. *How to Be an Antiracist*. New York: Penguin Books, 2019.

Leland, Charles. *Algonquin Legends*. New York: Dover Publications, 1982.

Manitonquat. *Medicine Story, the Original Instructions: Reflections of an Elder on the Teachings of the Elders, Adapting Ancient Wisdom to the Twenty-First Century.* Bloomington, IN: AuthorHouse, 2009.

Markale, Jean. *The Druids, Celtic Priests of Nature.* Rochester, VT: Inner Traditions Publishers, 1999.

Maté, Gabor. "How Intergenerational Trauma and Addiction Works." YouTube, September 15, 2018. https://www.youtube.com/watch?v=rG71S_YjTro.

————. *In the Realm of Hungry Ghosts: Close Encounters with Addiction.* Berkeley, CA. North Atlantic Books, 2008 (reprinted in 2020).

Menakem, Resmaa. *My Grandmother's Hands: Racialized Trauma and the Pathway to Mending Our Hearts and Bodies.* Las Vegas: Central Recovery Press, 2017.

Montaigne, Fen. "How Humans Came to the Americas." *Smithsonian Magazine,* January—February 2020. https://www.smithsonianmag.com/science-nature/how-humans-came-to-americas-180973739/.

Ochoa, Todd R. *Society of the Dead: Quita Manaquita and Palo Praise in Cuba.* Berkeley, CA: University of California Press, 2010.

Pinkola Estés, Clarissa. *Women Who Run with the Wolves: Myths and Stories of the Wild Woman Archetype.* New York: Ballantine Books, 1992.

Pritchard, Evan T. *Native New Yorkers: The Legacy of the Algonquin People of New York.* San Francisco: Council Oak Book, 2007.

Reeve, K., P. Black, and J. Huang. "Examining the Impact of Healing Touch Intervention to Reduce Post-Traumatic Stress Disorder Symptoms in Combat Veterans." *Psychology Trauma: Theory,
Research, Practice and Policy* (2020). http://dx.doi.org/10.1037
/tra0000591.

Reid, Daniel. *The Complete Book of Chinese Health and Healing: Guarding
the Three Treasures*. Boston: Shambhala Publishers, 1994.

Reyes, Emaline. "The Invisible Labors and Erased History of Puerto
Rican Midwives." *The Revisionist*, September 28, 2020. https://
slcwhblog.com/2020/09/28/the-invisible-labors-and
-erased-history-of-puerto-rican-midwives/.

Robinson, Stephen. *Exploring Your Intuition*. New York: Holistic Studies
Institute, 2001.

Rooney, Diane. "Internal Alchemy." Workshop presented at One Spirit
Learning Alliance, New York, January 2021.

Schafer, Edward. *The Divine Woman: Dragon Ladies and Rain Maidens*.
Berkeley, CA: University of California Press, 1976.

Sjöö, Monica, and Barbara Mor. *The Great Cosmic Mother: Rediscovering
the Religion of the Earth*. New York: Harper and Row, 1991.

Tattersall, Ian. *The Monkey in the Mirror: Essays on the Science of What
Makes Us Human*. Orlando, FL: Harcourt Press, 2002.

Thunberg, Greta. "Climate Strike in New York City: September 20,
2019." YouTube, September 21, 2019. https://www.youtube.com
/watch?v=GqEhLK7YWgI.

Valiente, Doreen. *Witchcraft for Tomorrow*. London: Hale Limited, 1983.

Weed, Susyn. *Wise Woman Herbal: Healing Wise.* Woodstock, NY: Ash Tree Publishing, 1999.

Weinstein, Marion. *Positive Magic: Occult Self-Help.* New York: Phoenix, 1981.

Whitley, David. "How Mental Illness Changed Humanity for the Better." YouTube, 2013. https://www.youtube.com/watch?v=yVwfJzZdkQ0.

Williamson, John. *The Oak King, the Holly King, and the Unicorn: The Myths and Symbolism of the Unicorn Tapestries.* New York: Harper and Row, 1983.

# █NDEX